Sshhhh!

FANTAGRAPHICS BOOKS • 7563 Lake City Way NE • Seattle WA 98115

Edited by Kim Thompson • Designed by Jason • Production by Jacob Covey and Paul Baresh
Promotion by Eric Reynolds • Published by Gary Groth and Kim Thompson

Special thanks to Erik Falk of Jippi.

Distributed in the U.S. by W.W. Norton and Company, Inc. (1-212-354-5500) • Distributed in Canada by the
Canadian Manda Group (1-416-516-0911) • Distributed in the UK by Turnaround Distribution (1-208-829-3009)
Distributed to comics stores by Diamond Comics Distributors (1-800-452-6642)

First printing: July 2002
Second printing: September 2008

ISBN: 978-1-56097-497-0
Printed in China.

Sshhhh!

by Jason

FANTAGRAPHICS BOOKS

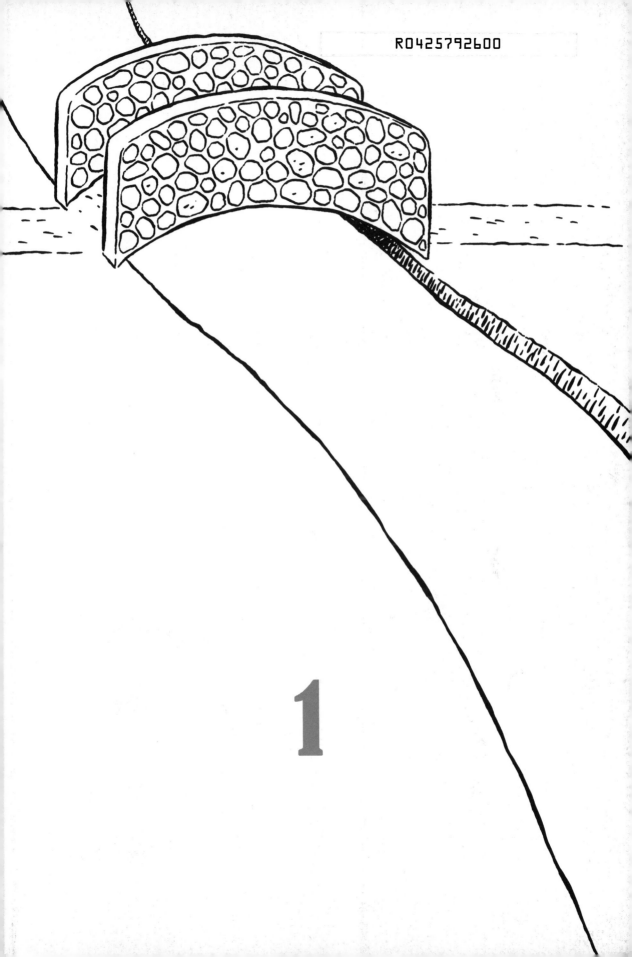

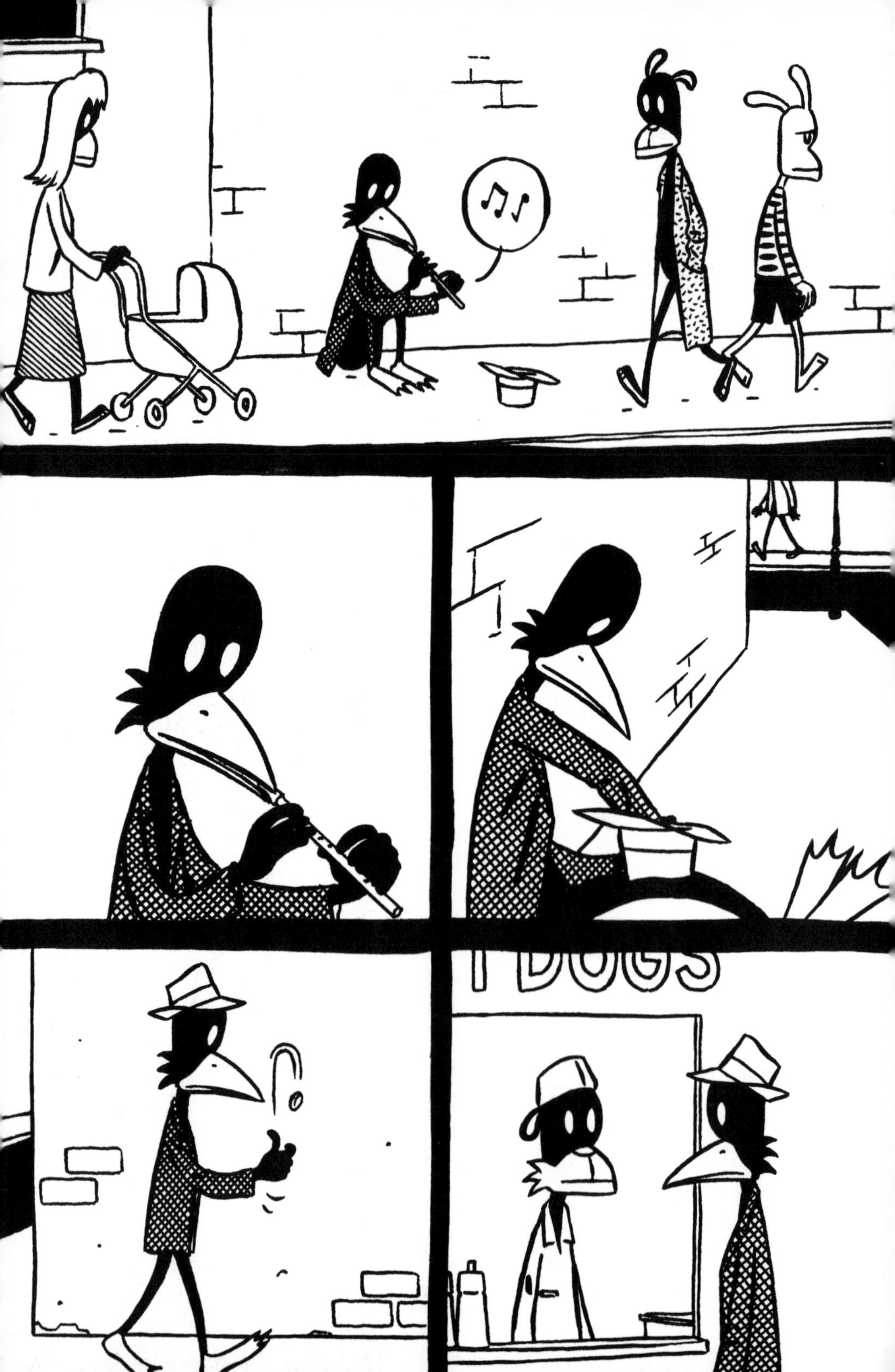
DOGS

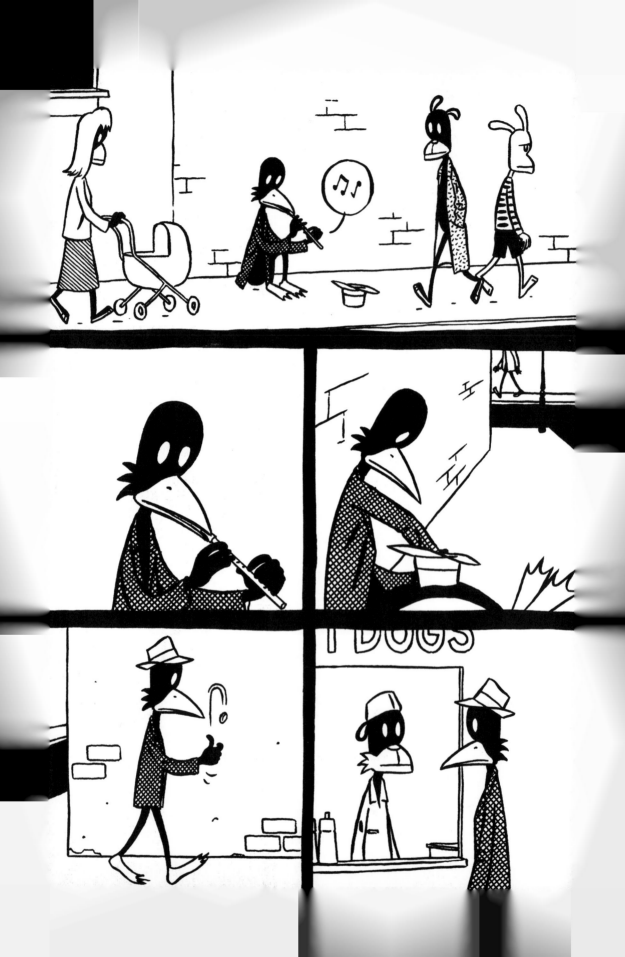

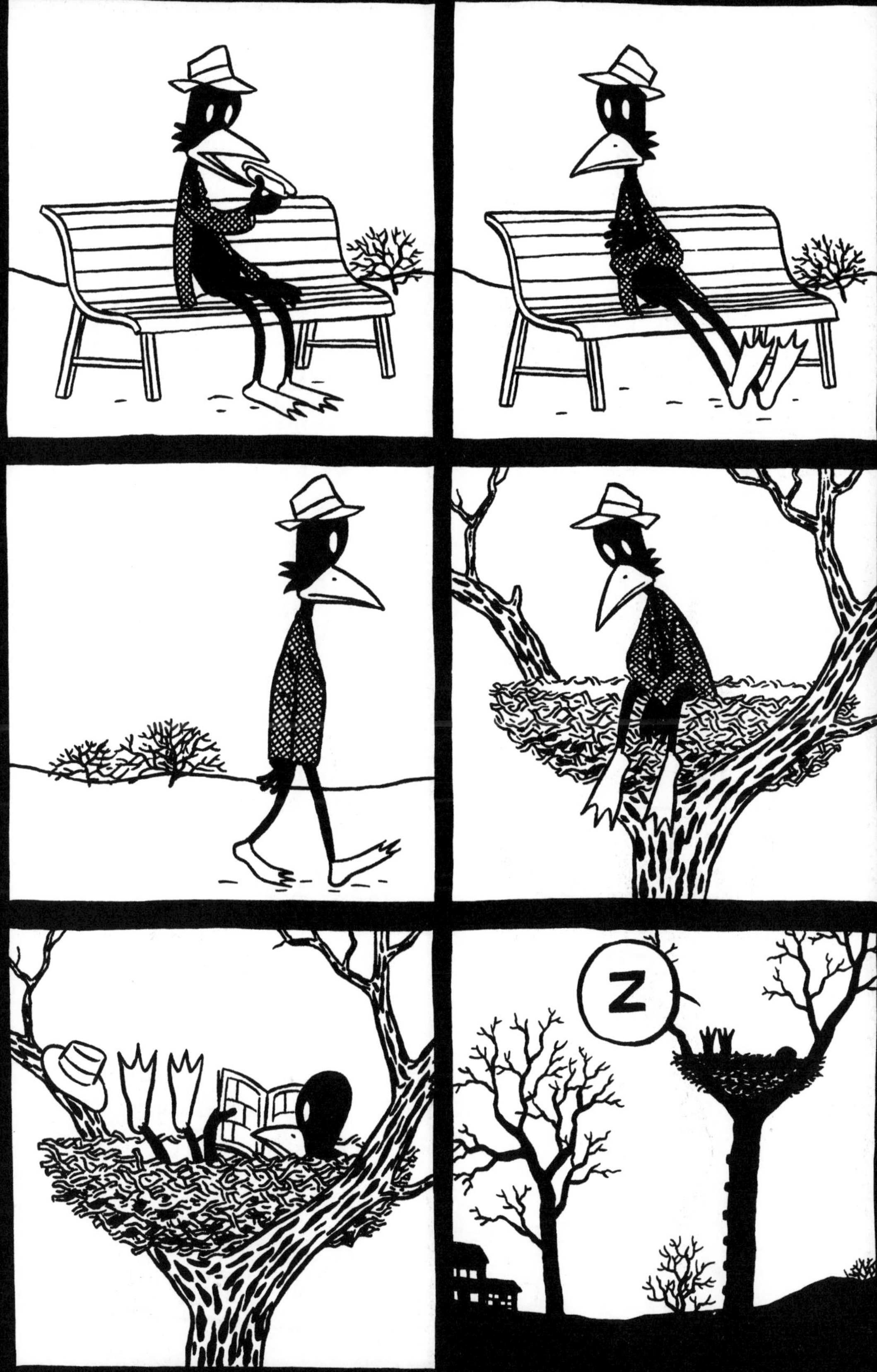
Z

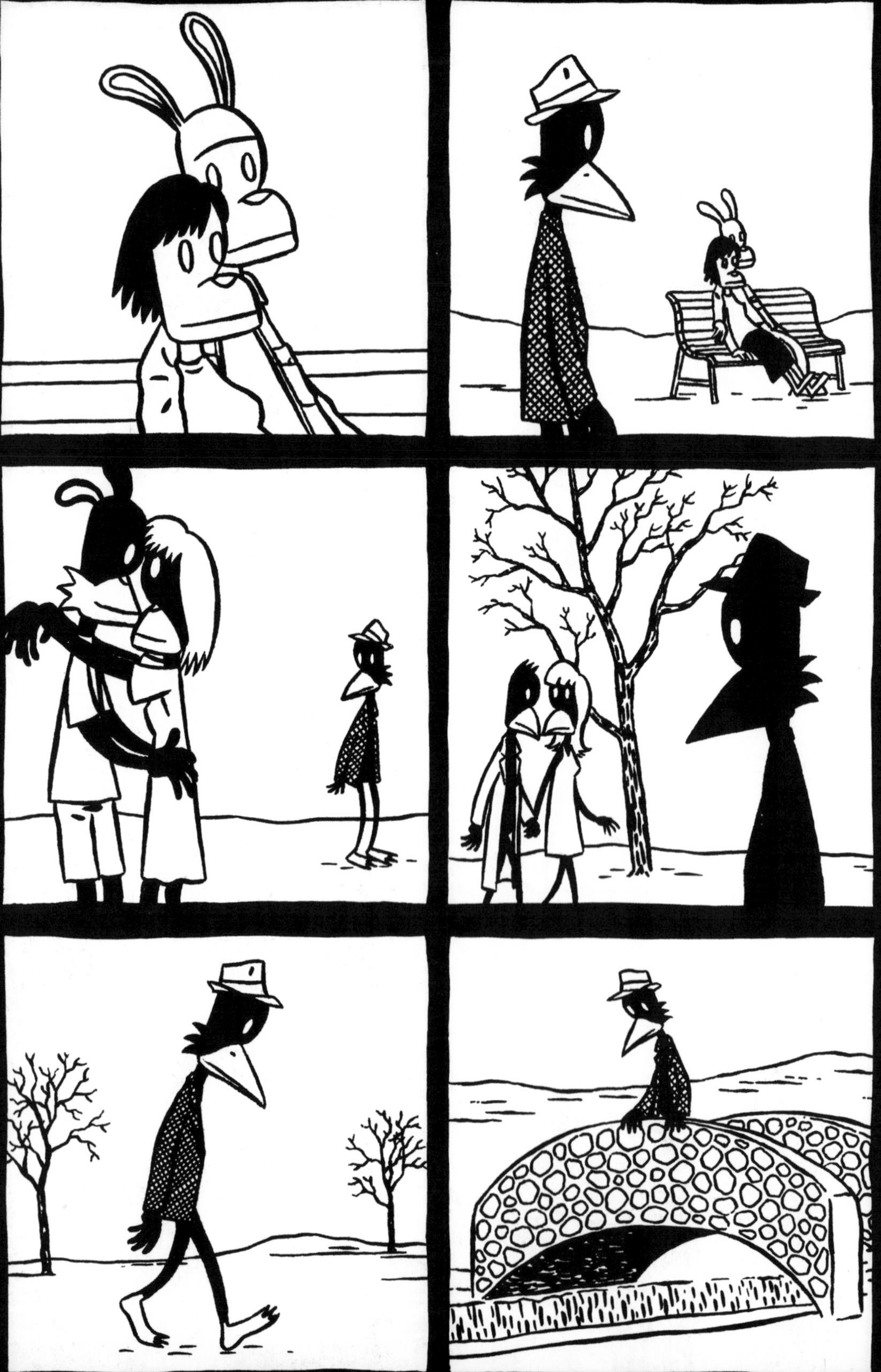

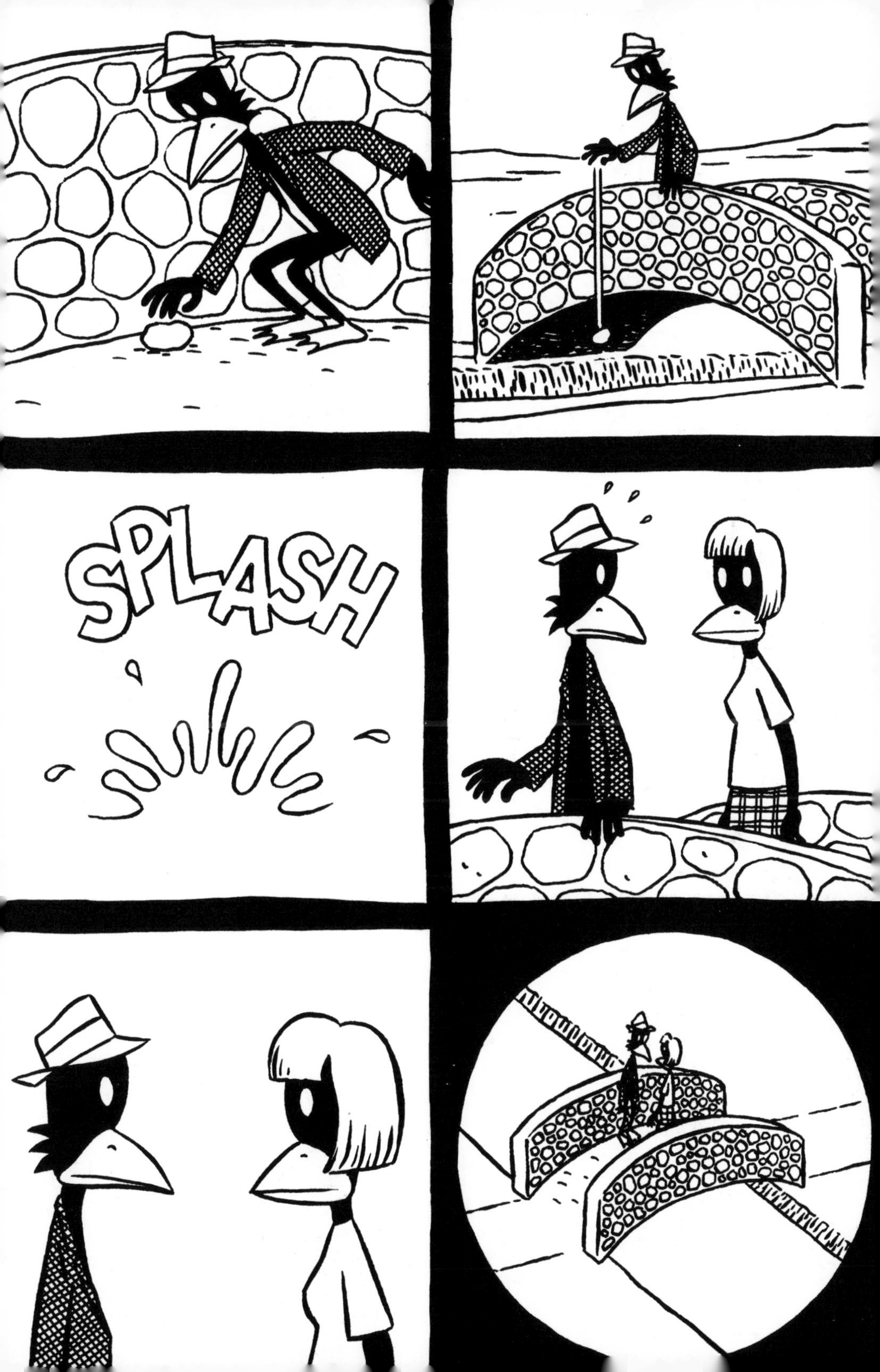
SPLASH

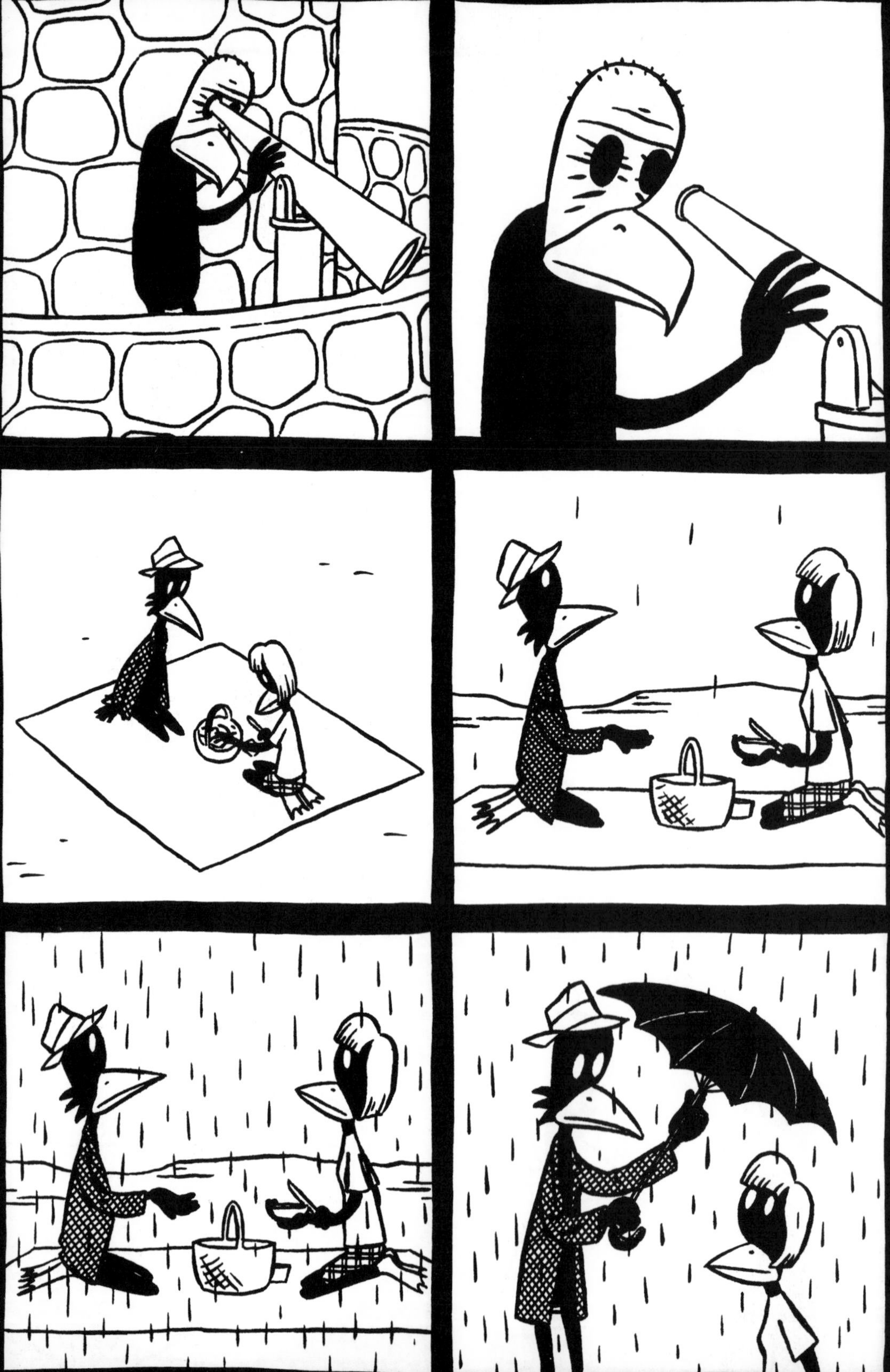

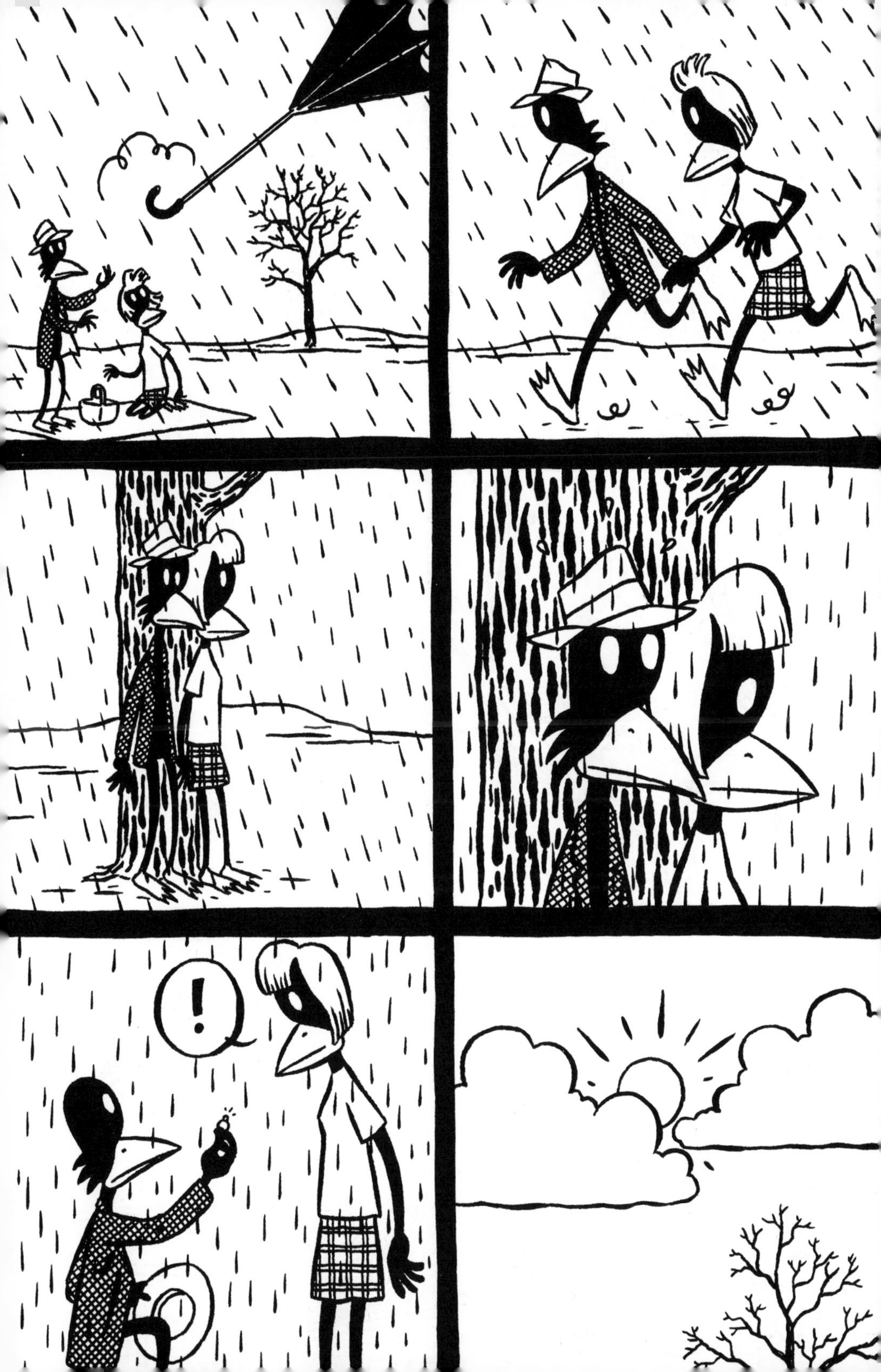
!

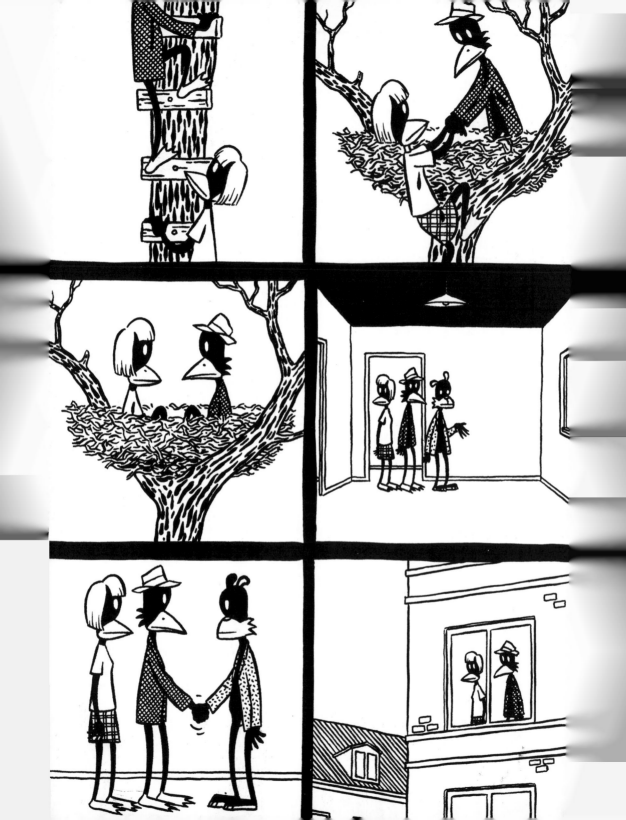

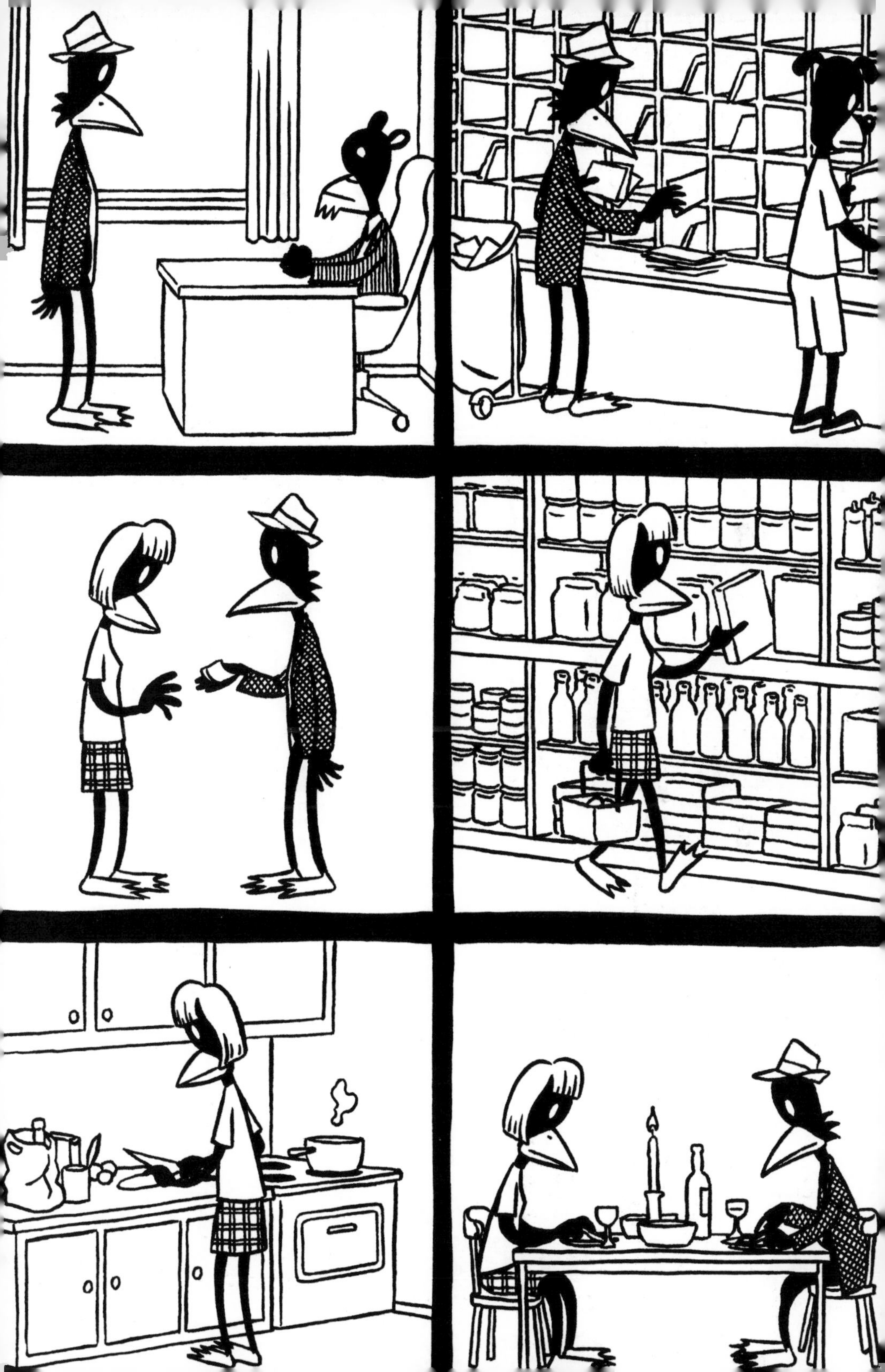

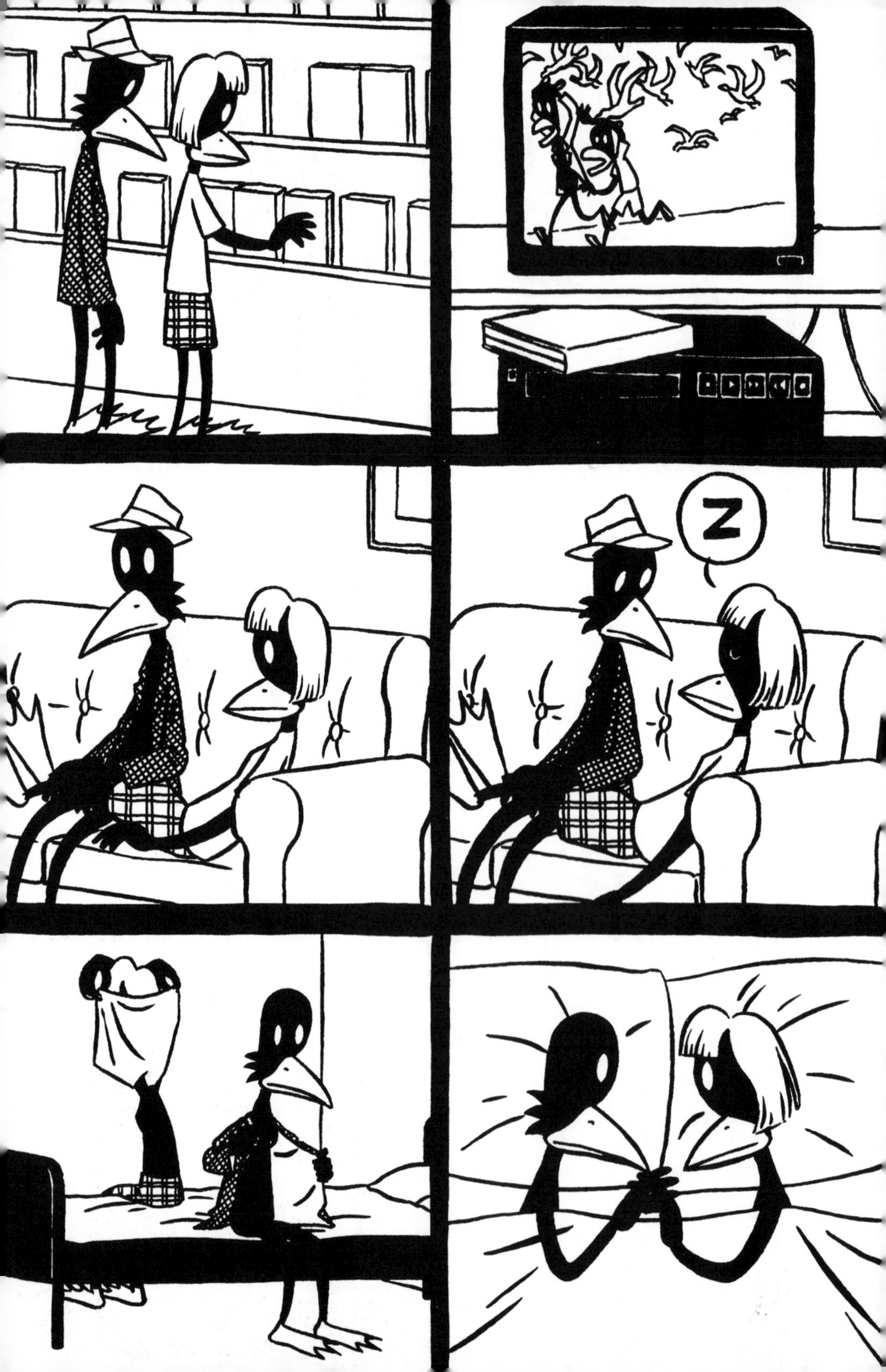
Z

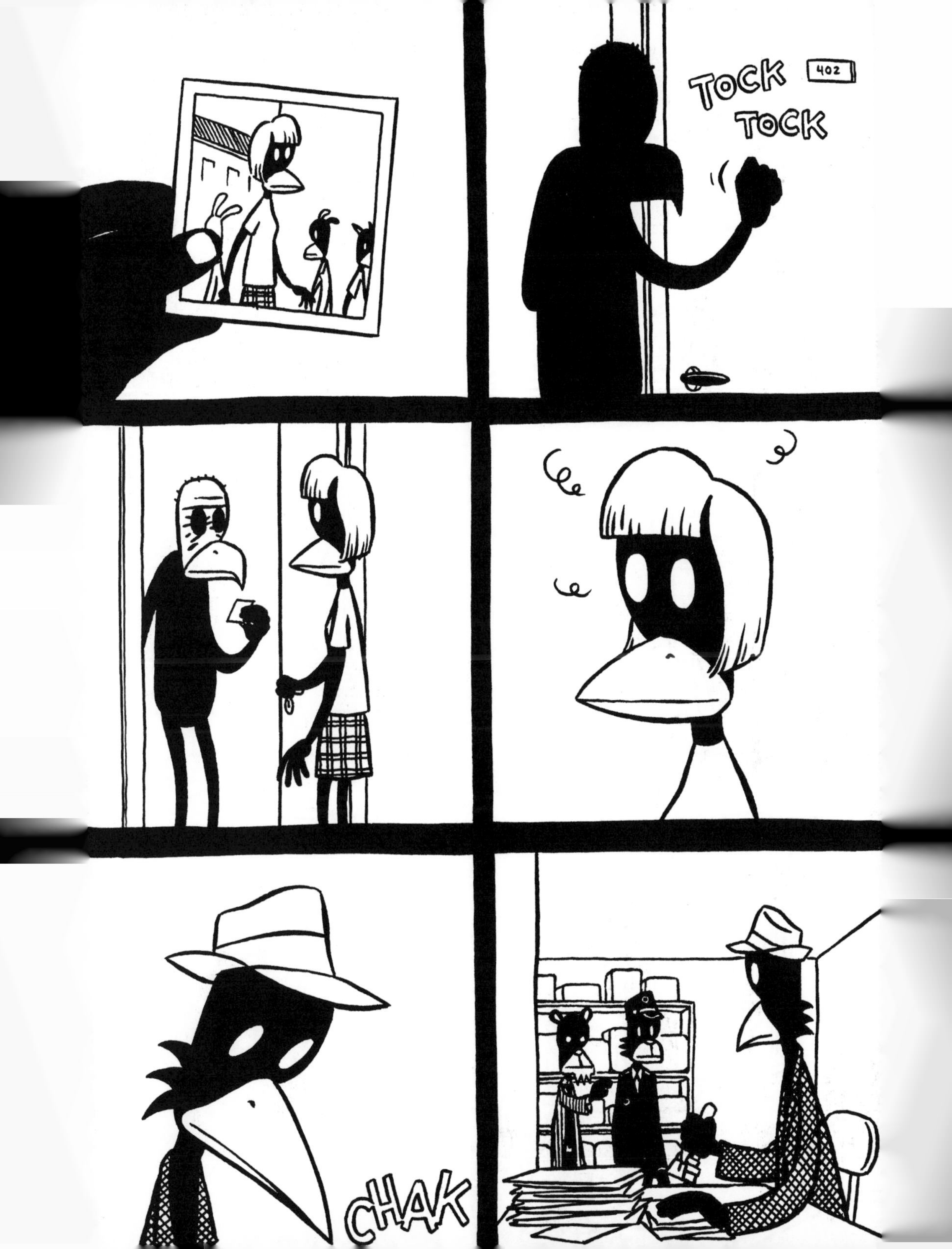
TOCK
TOCK
402
CHAK

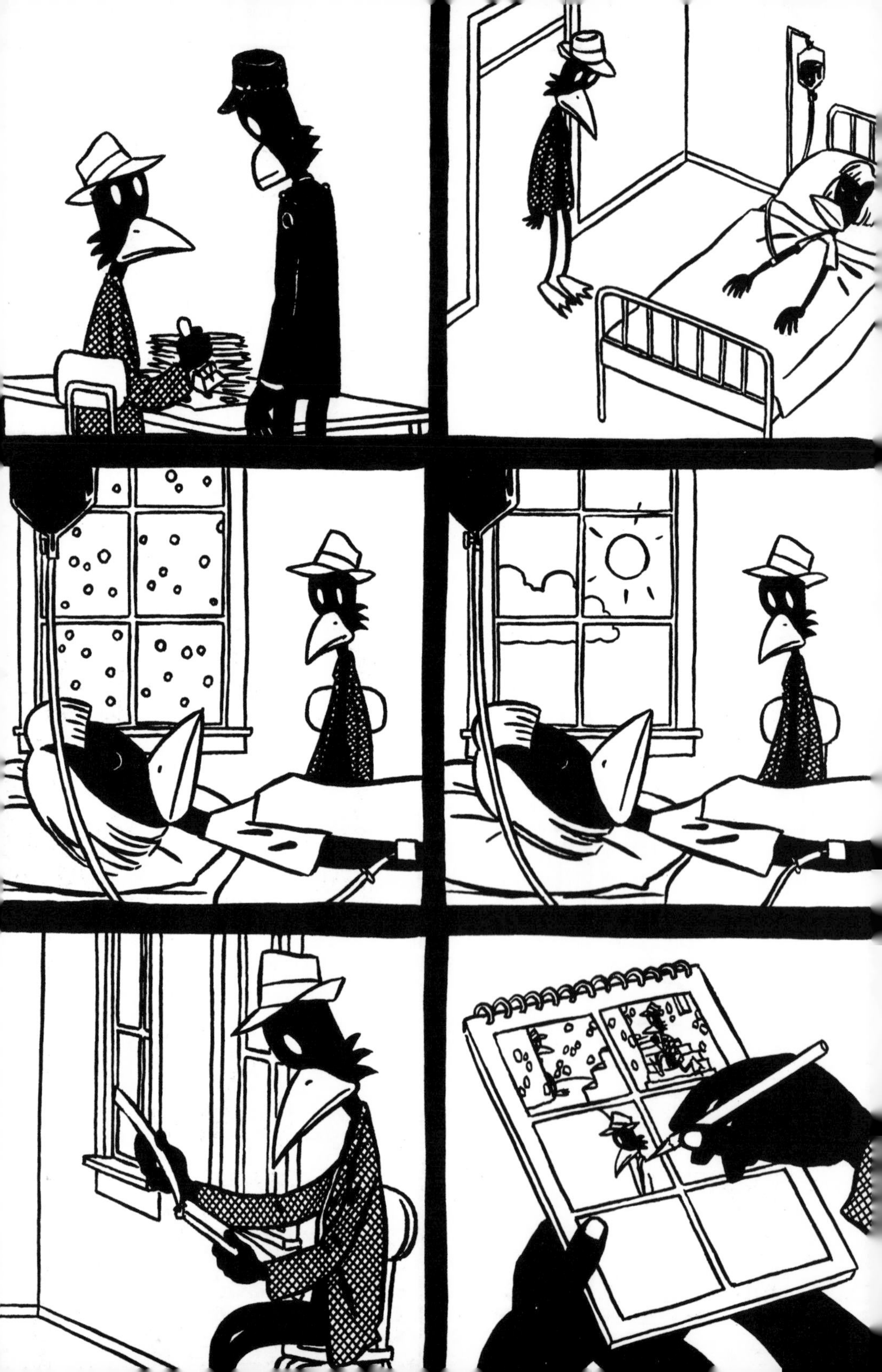

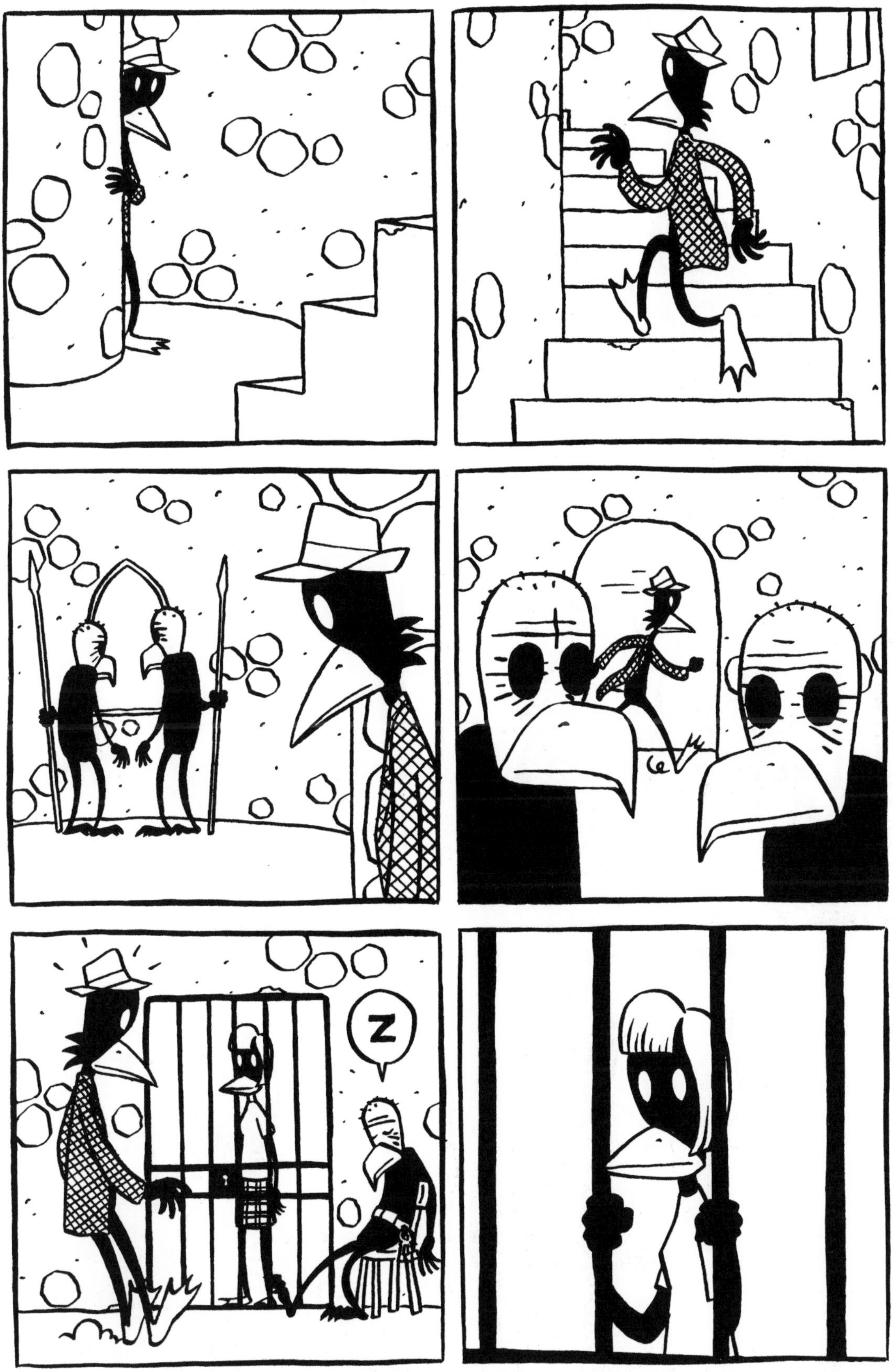
Z

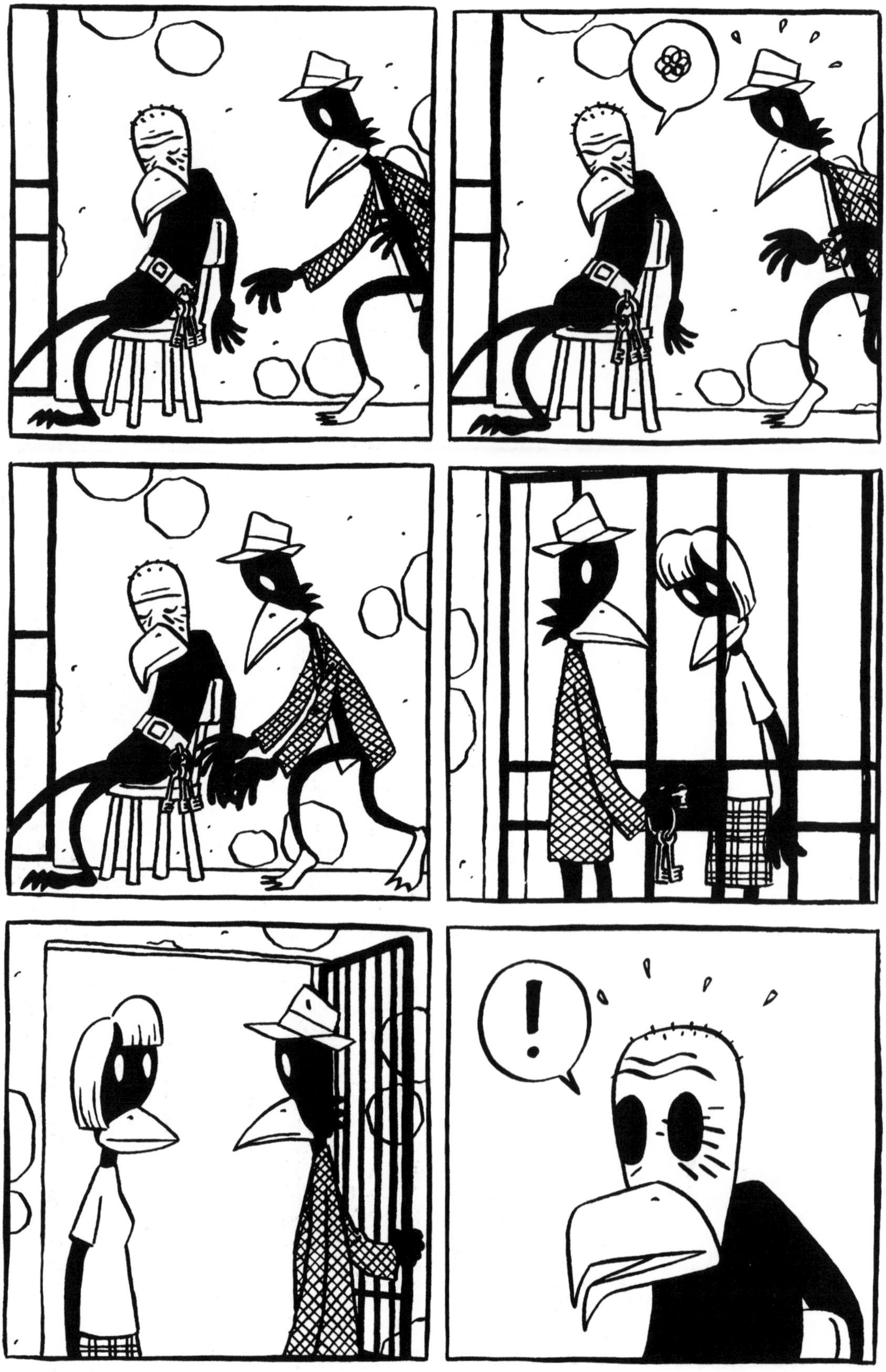
!

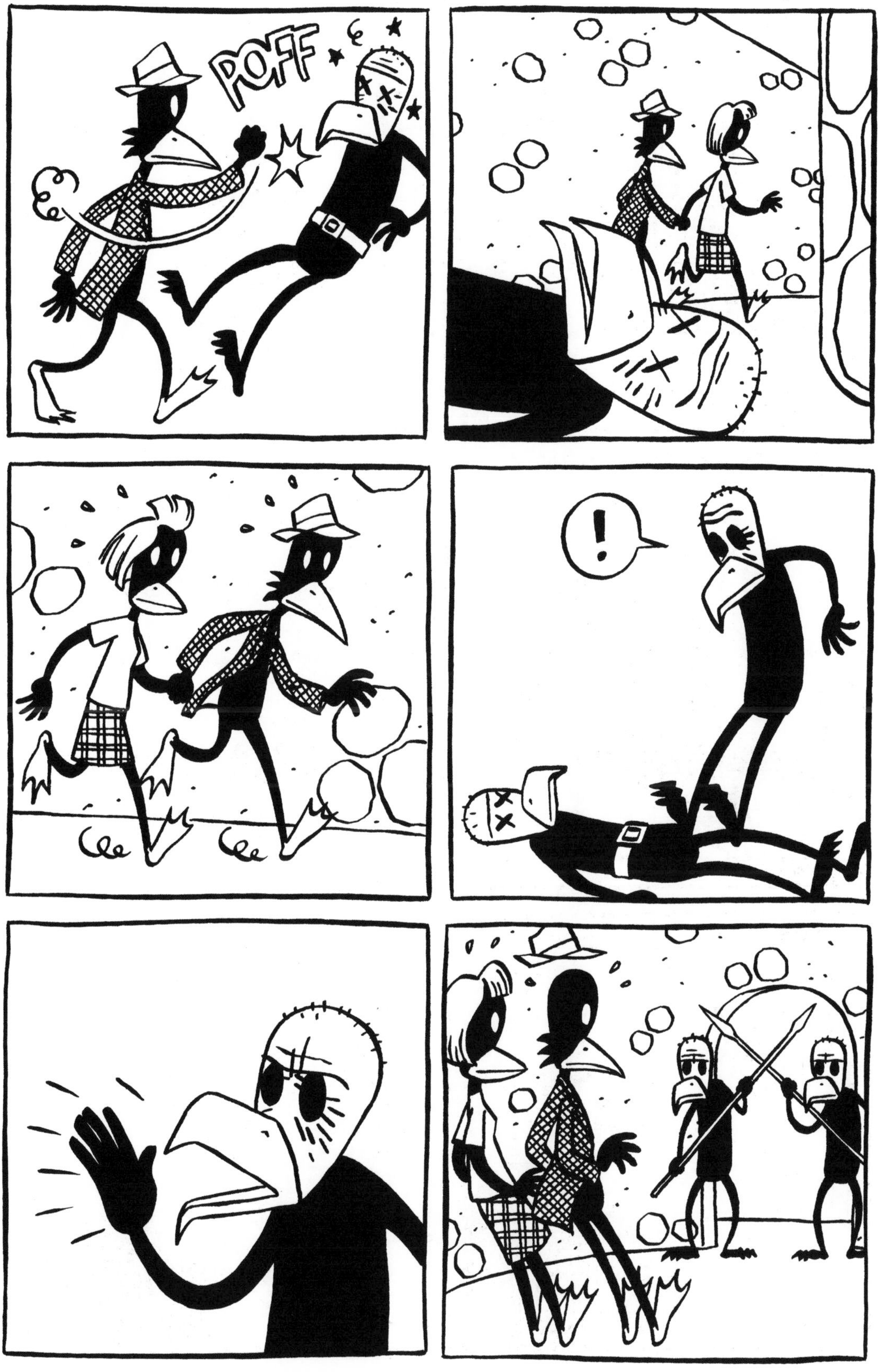
POFF
!

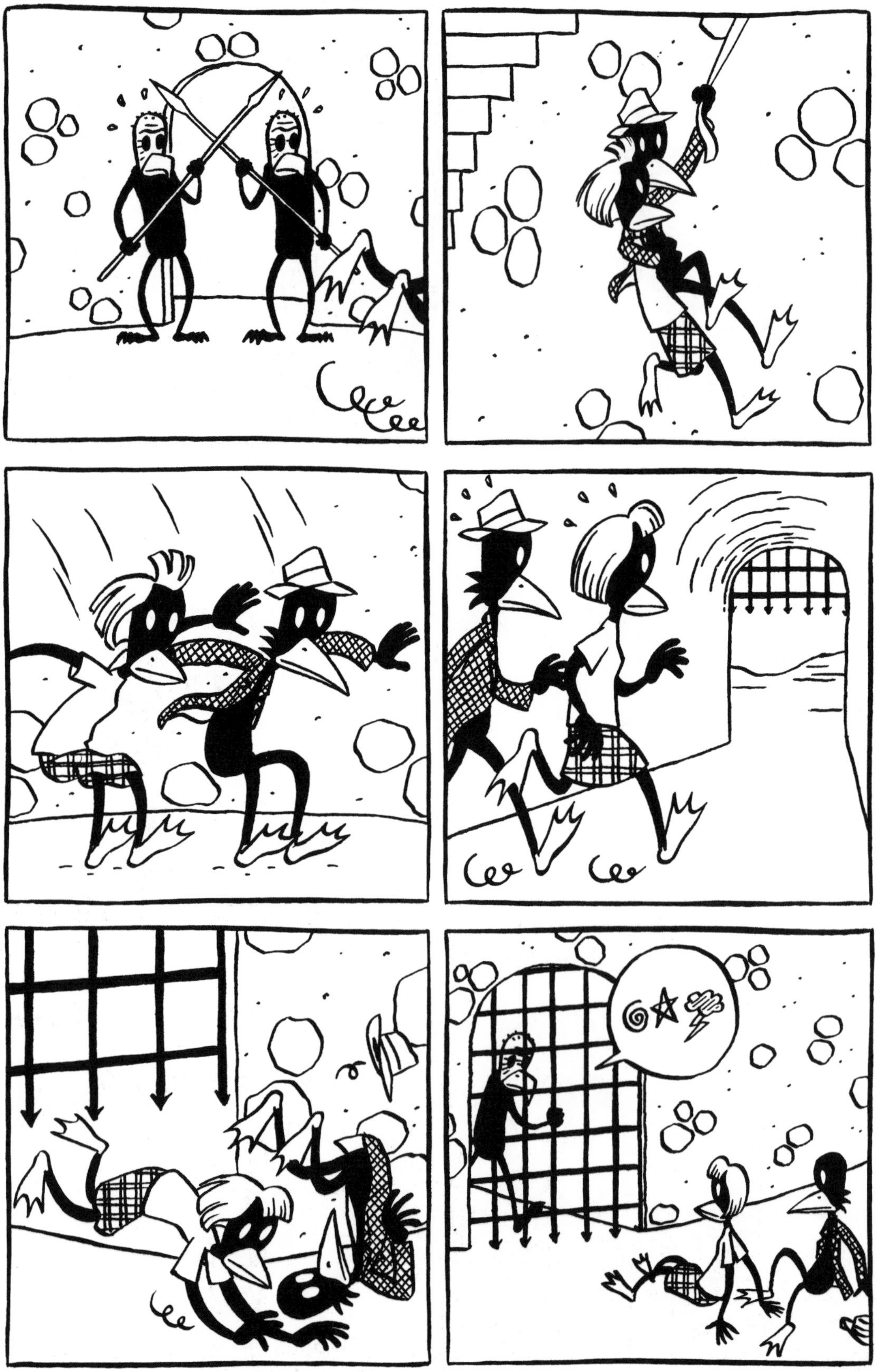

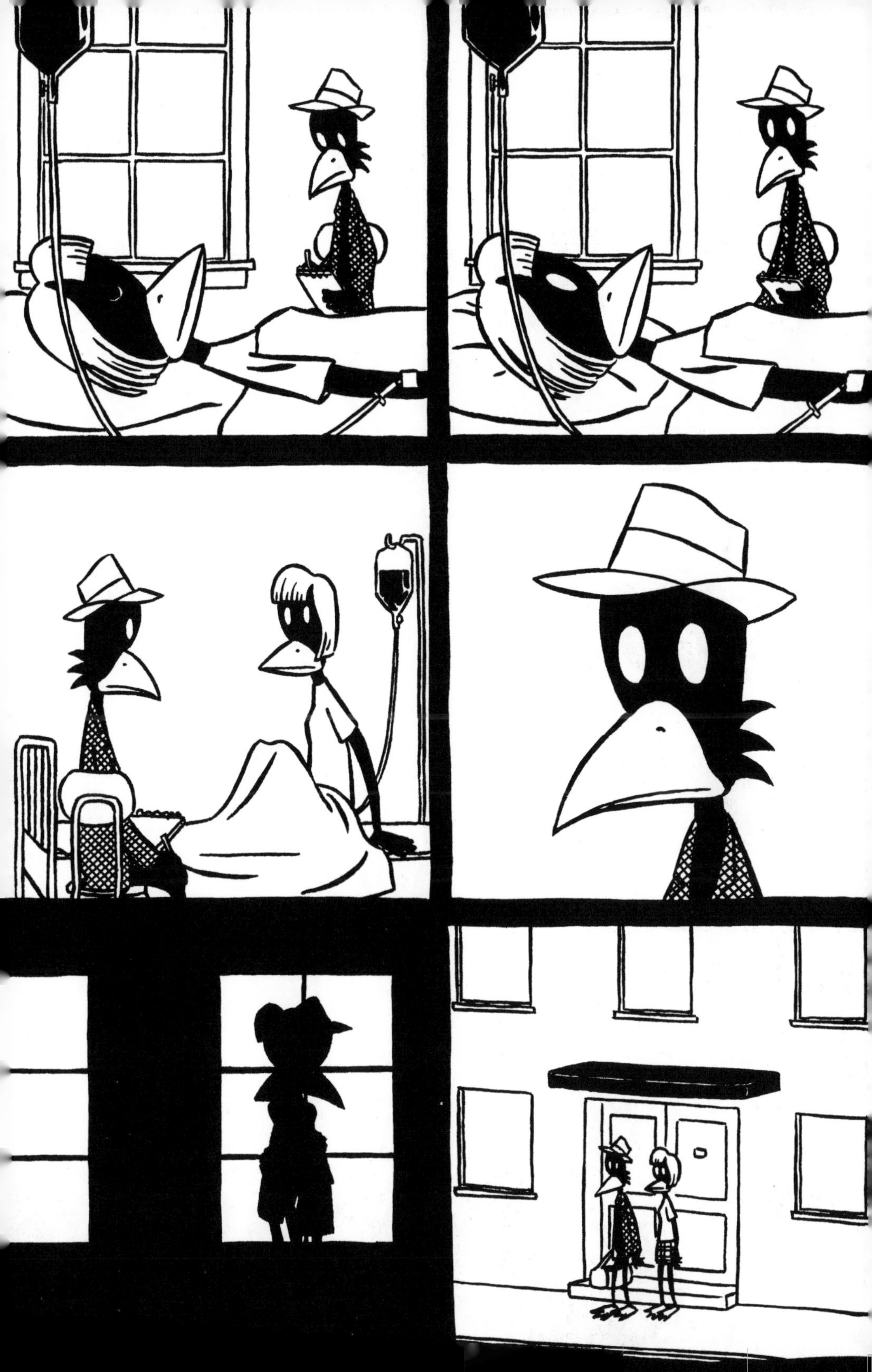

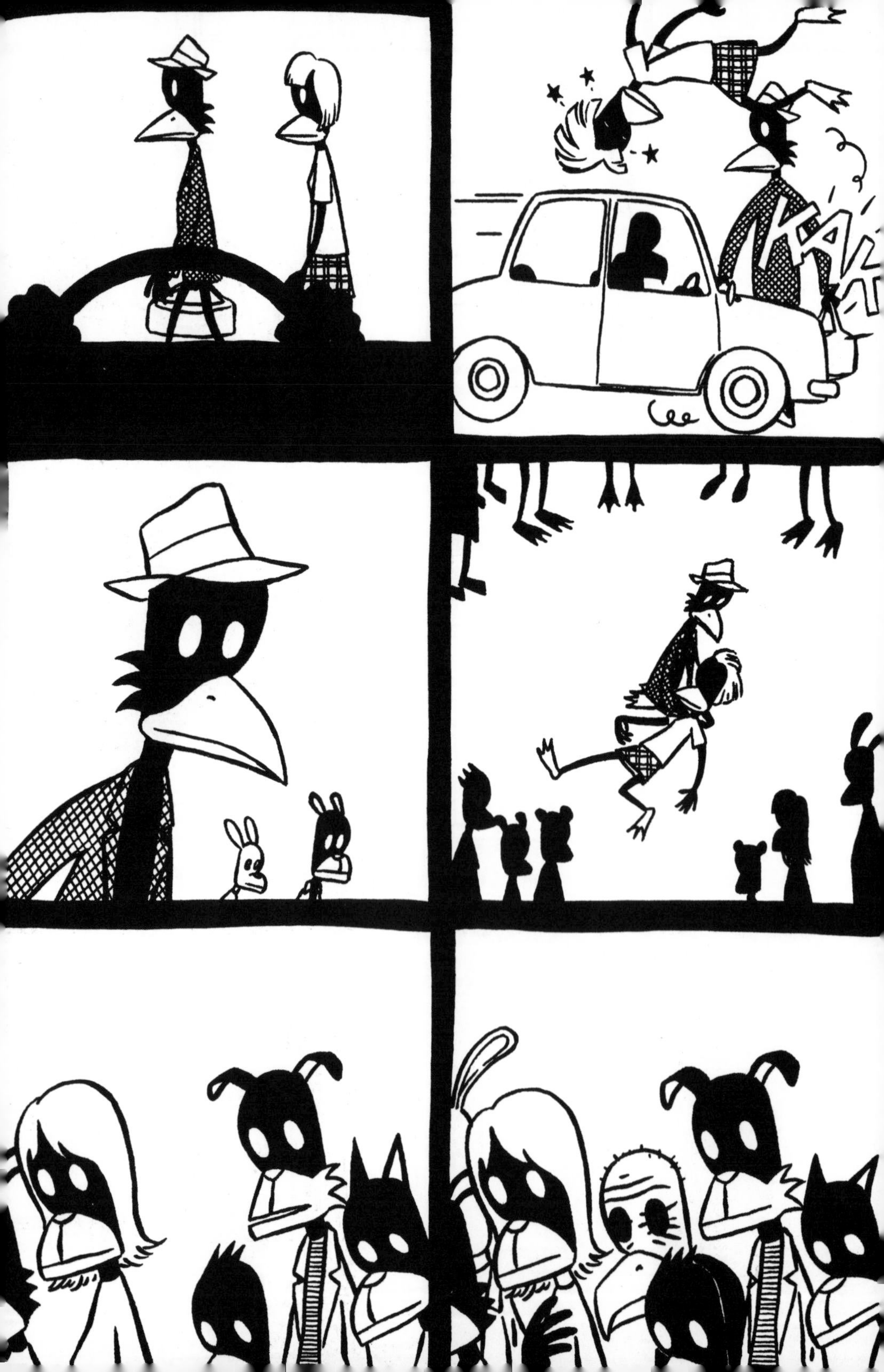
KA

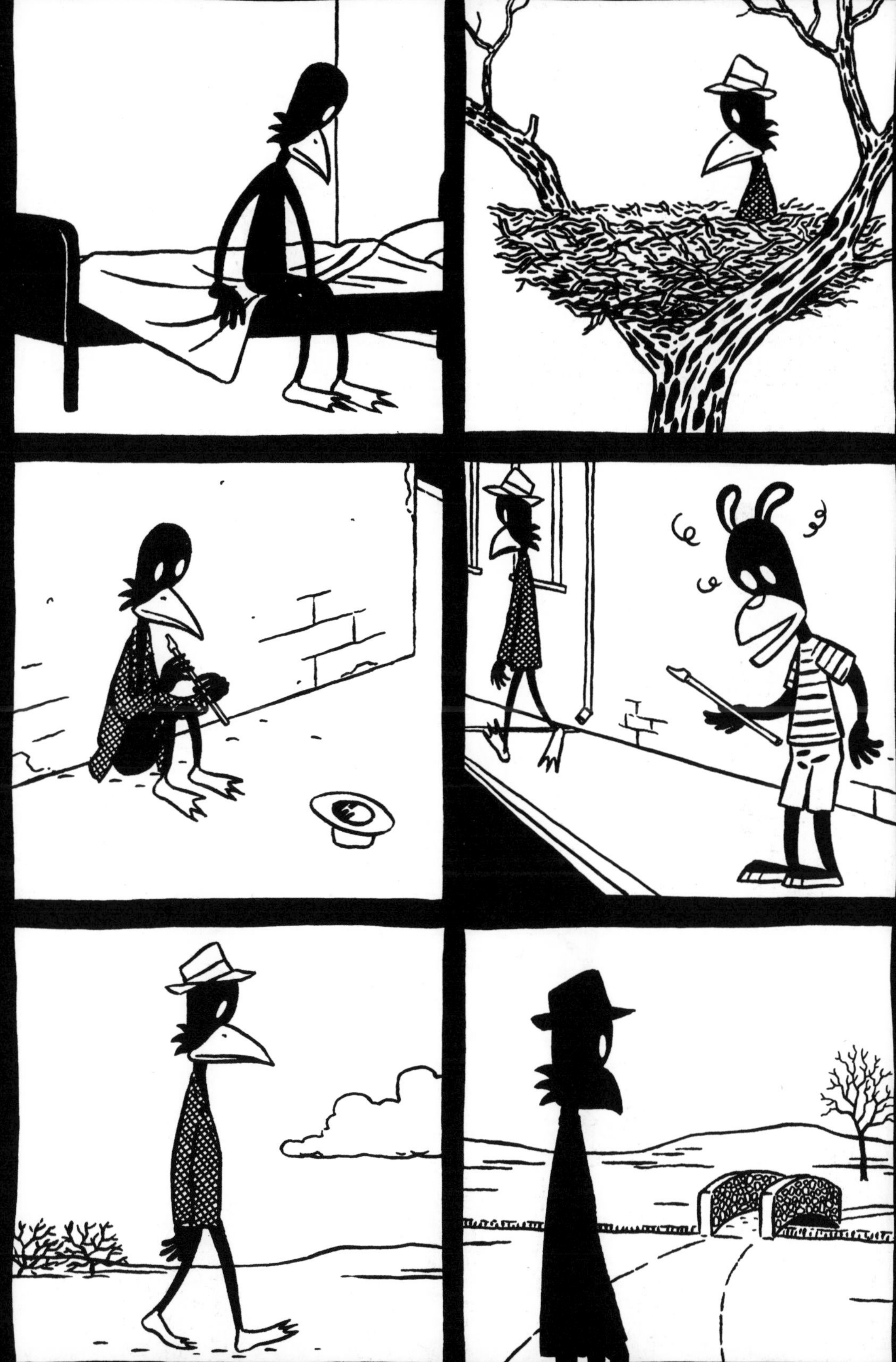

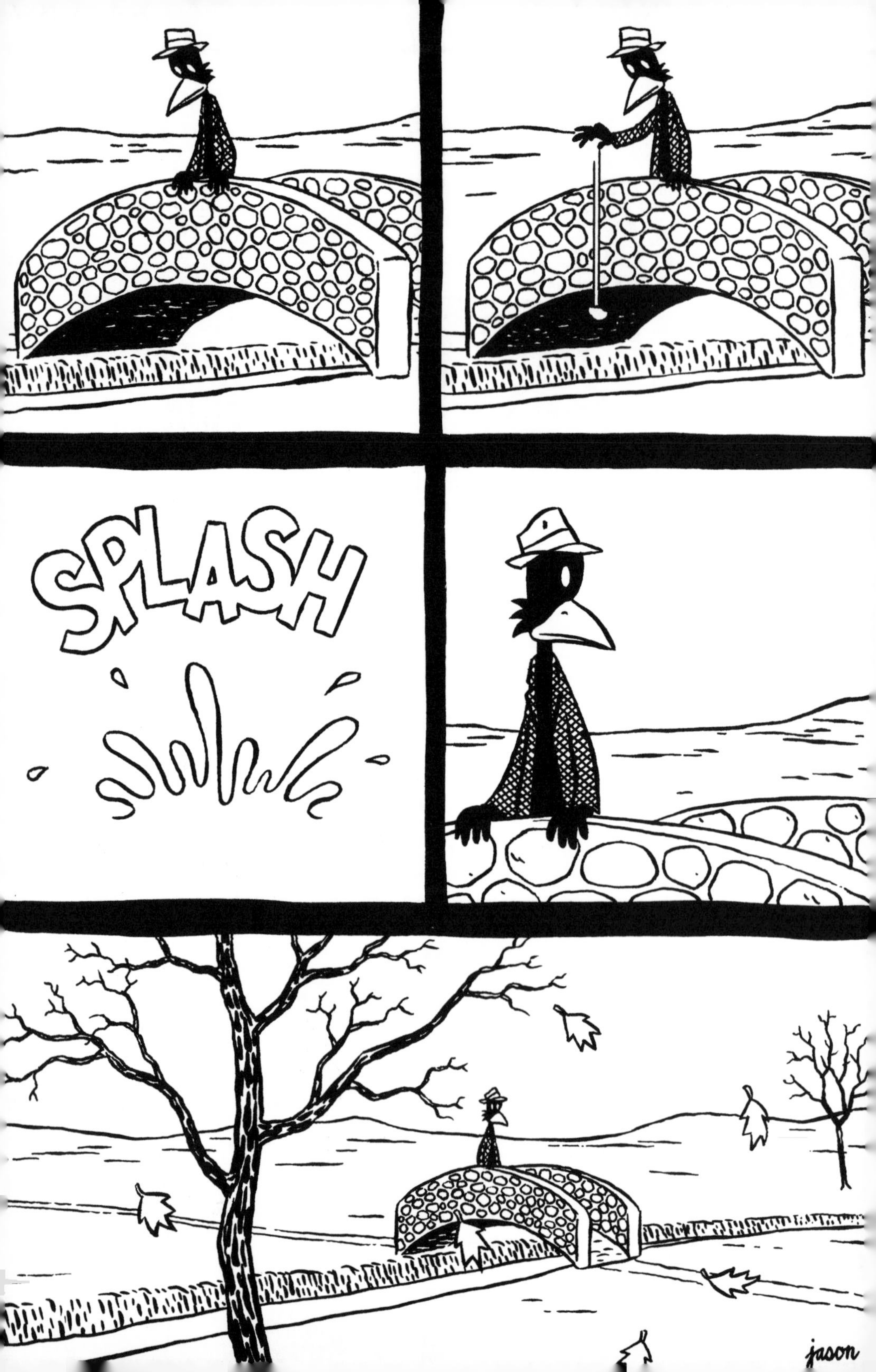
SPLASH
jason

2

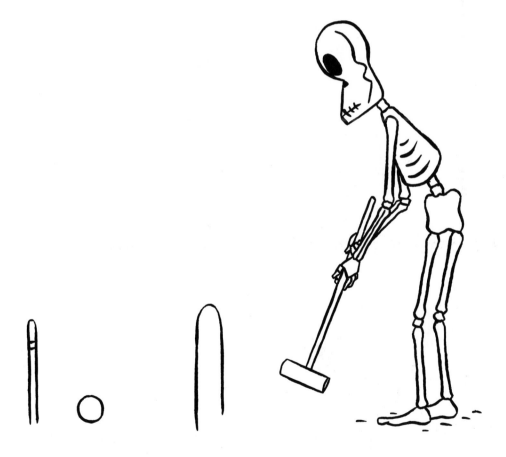

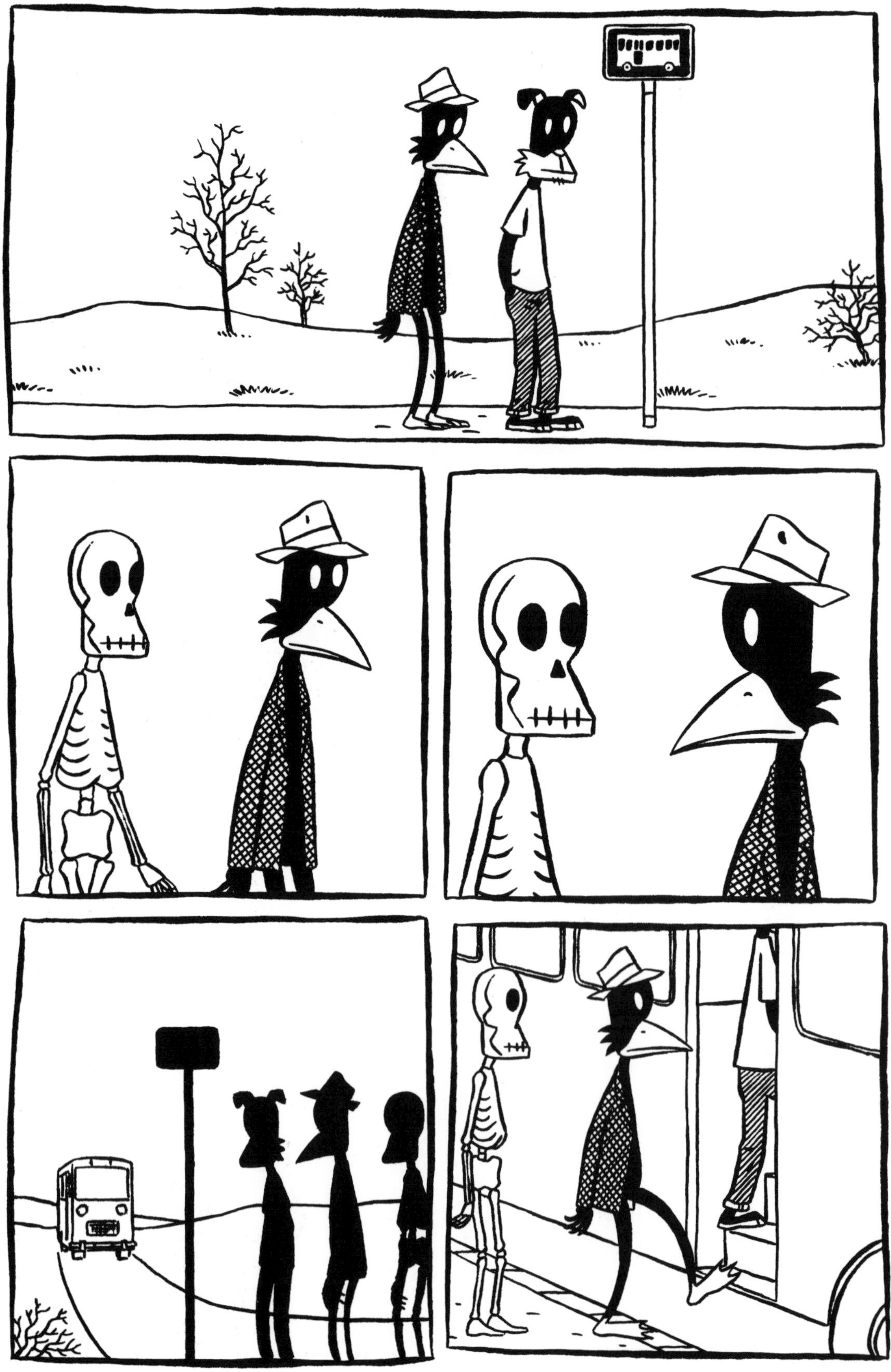

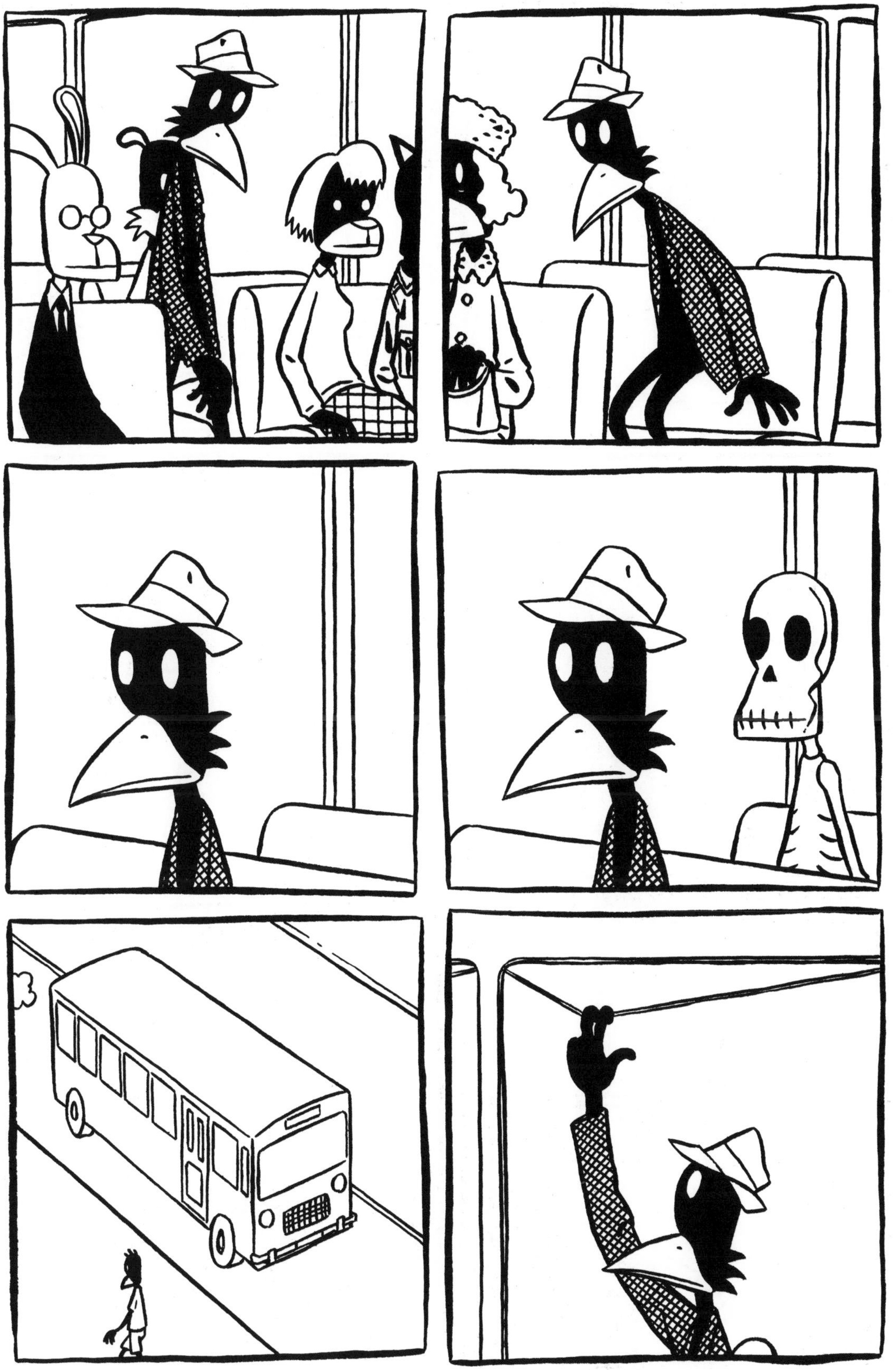

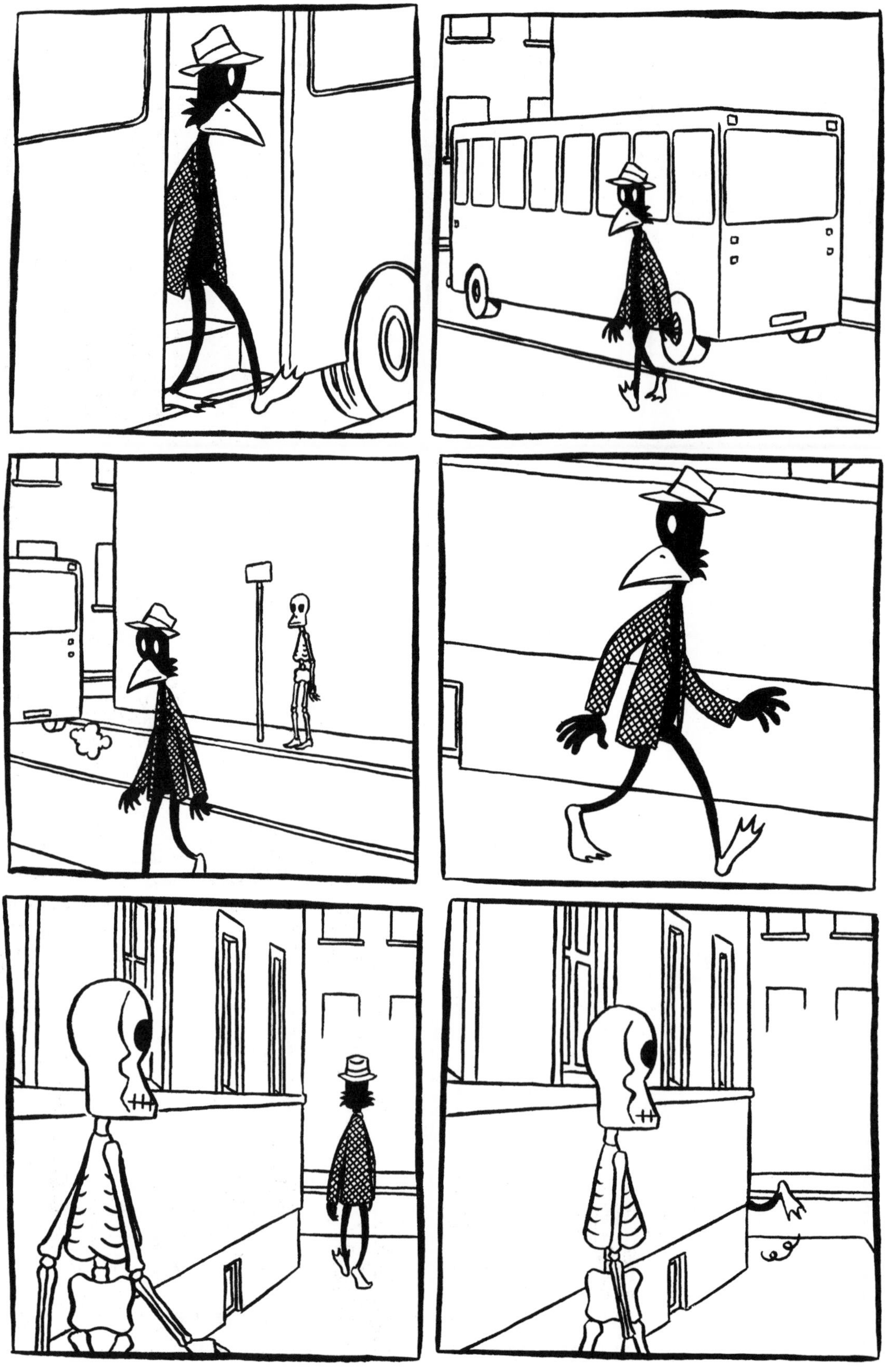

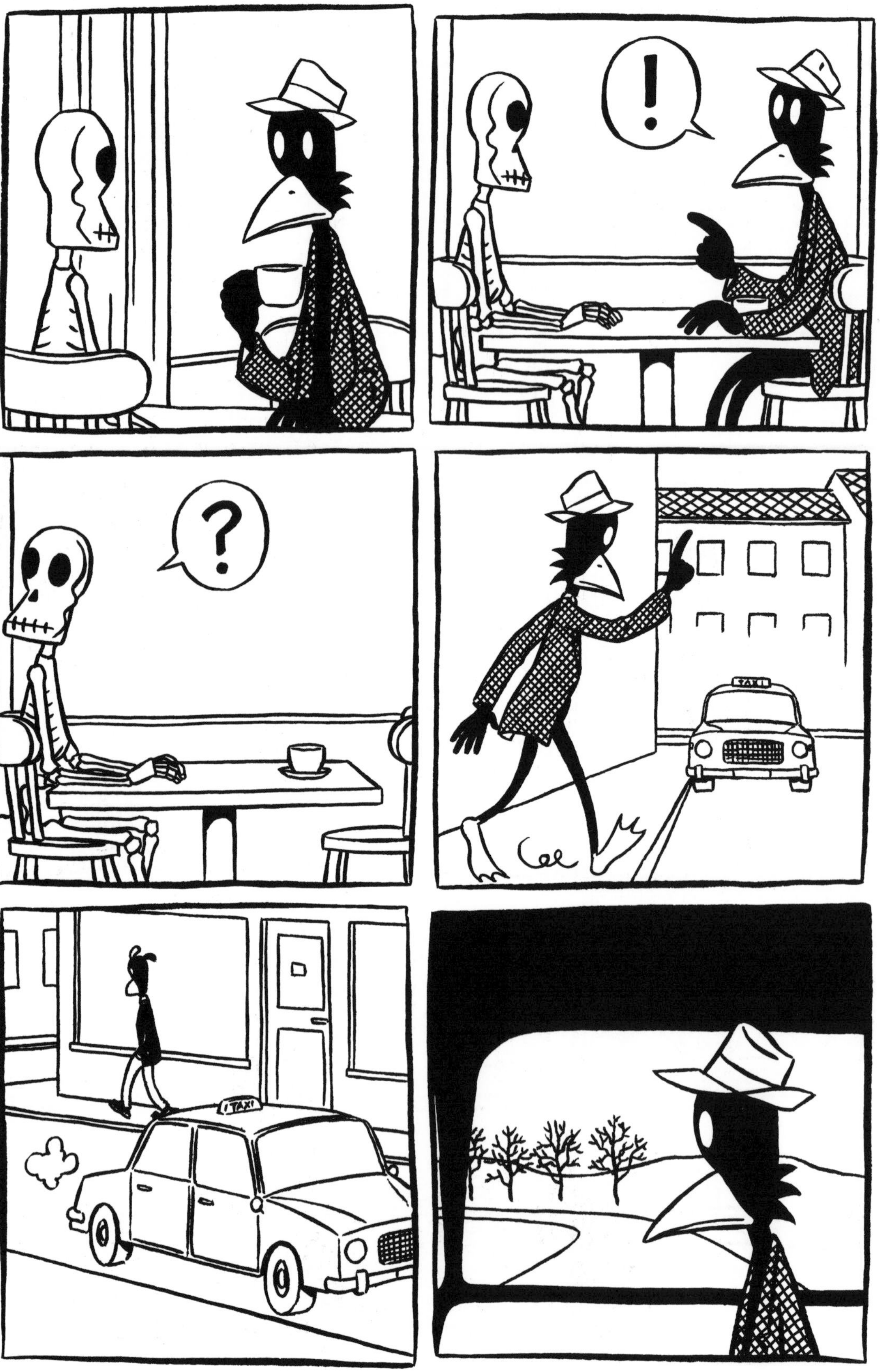
!
?

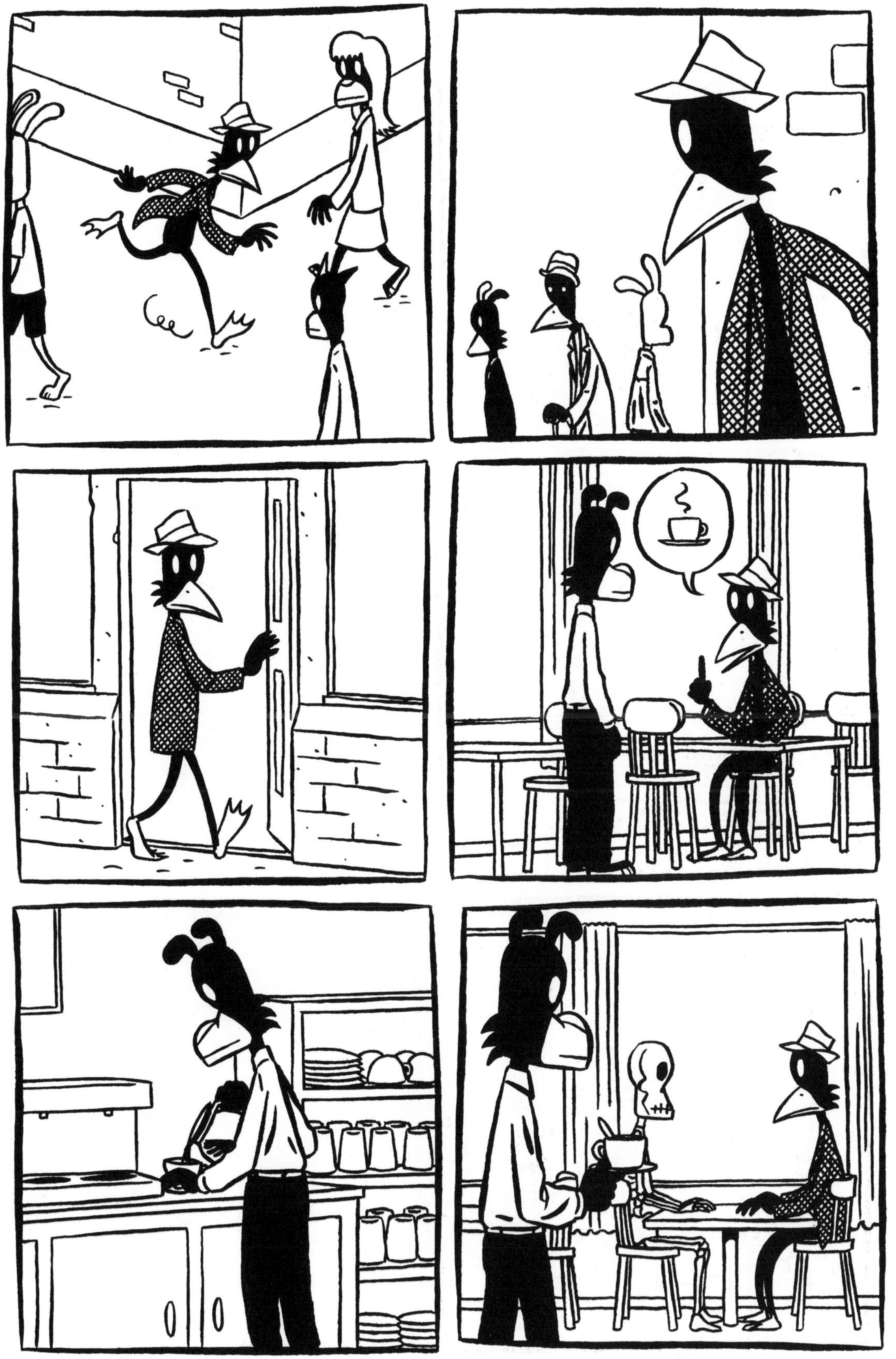

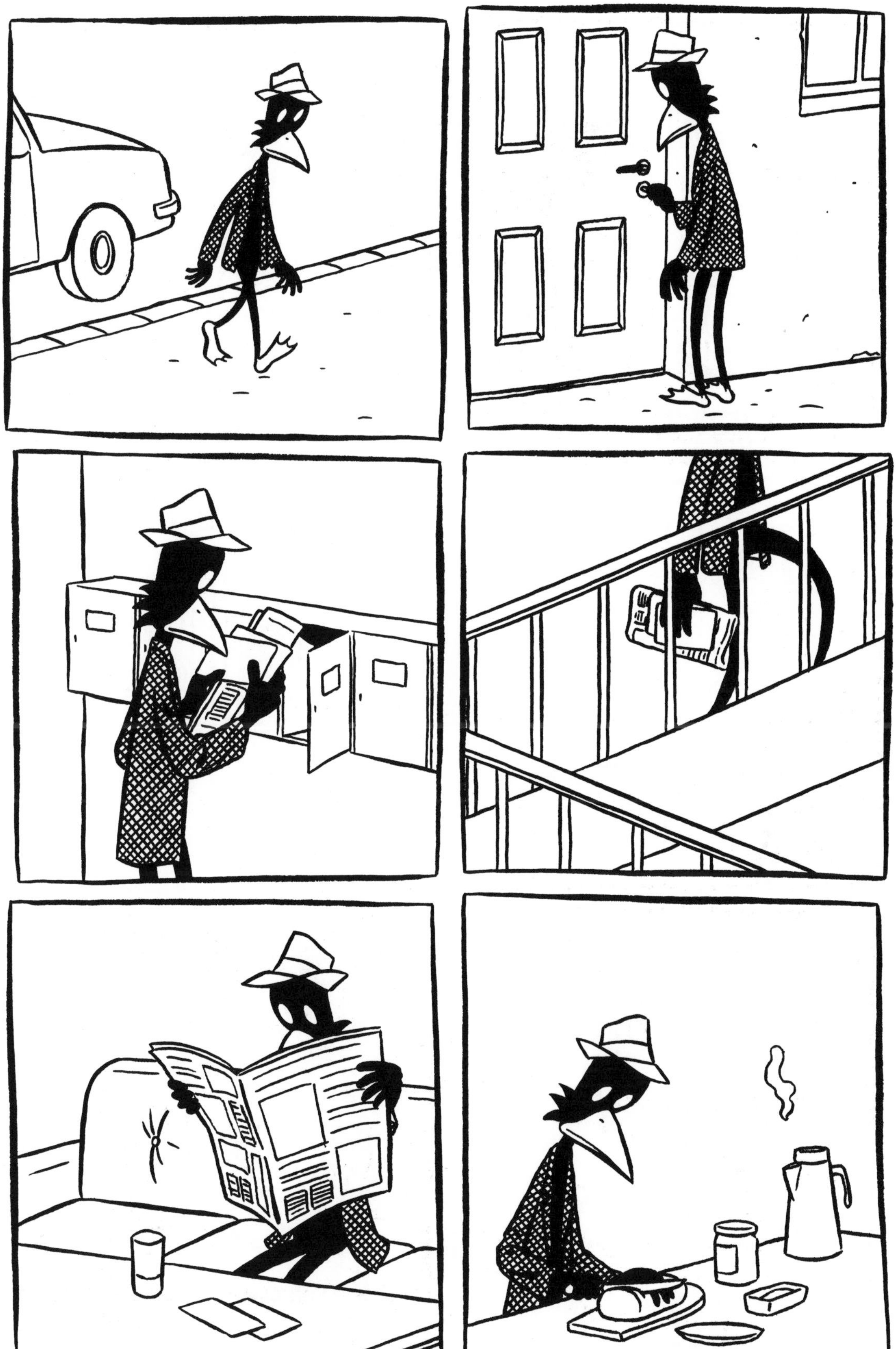

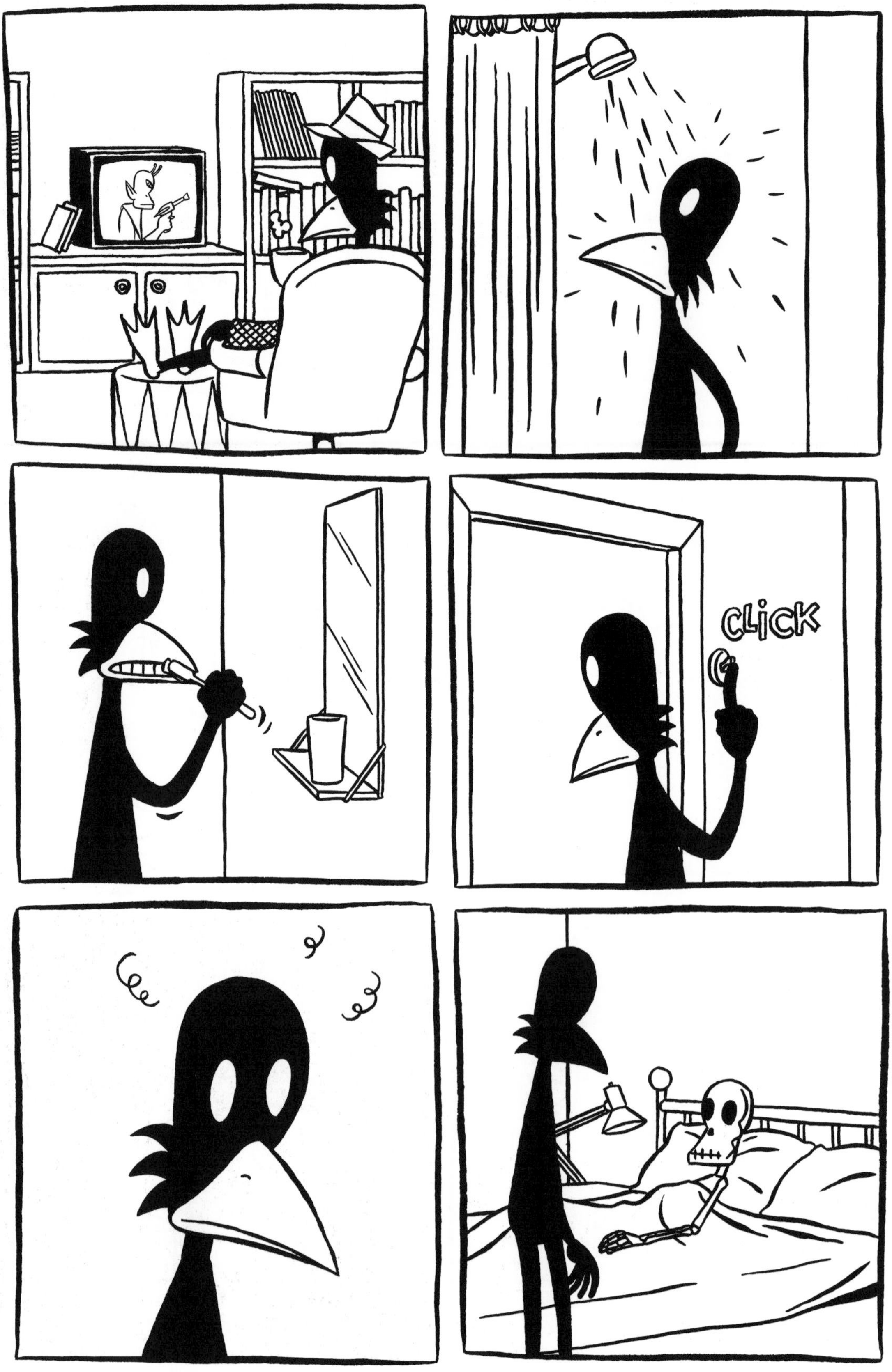
CLICK

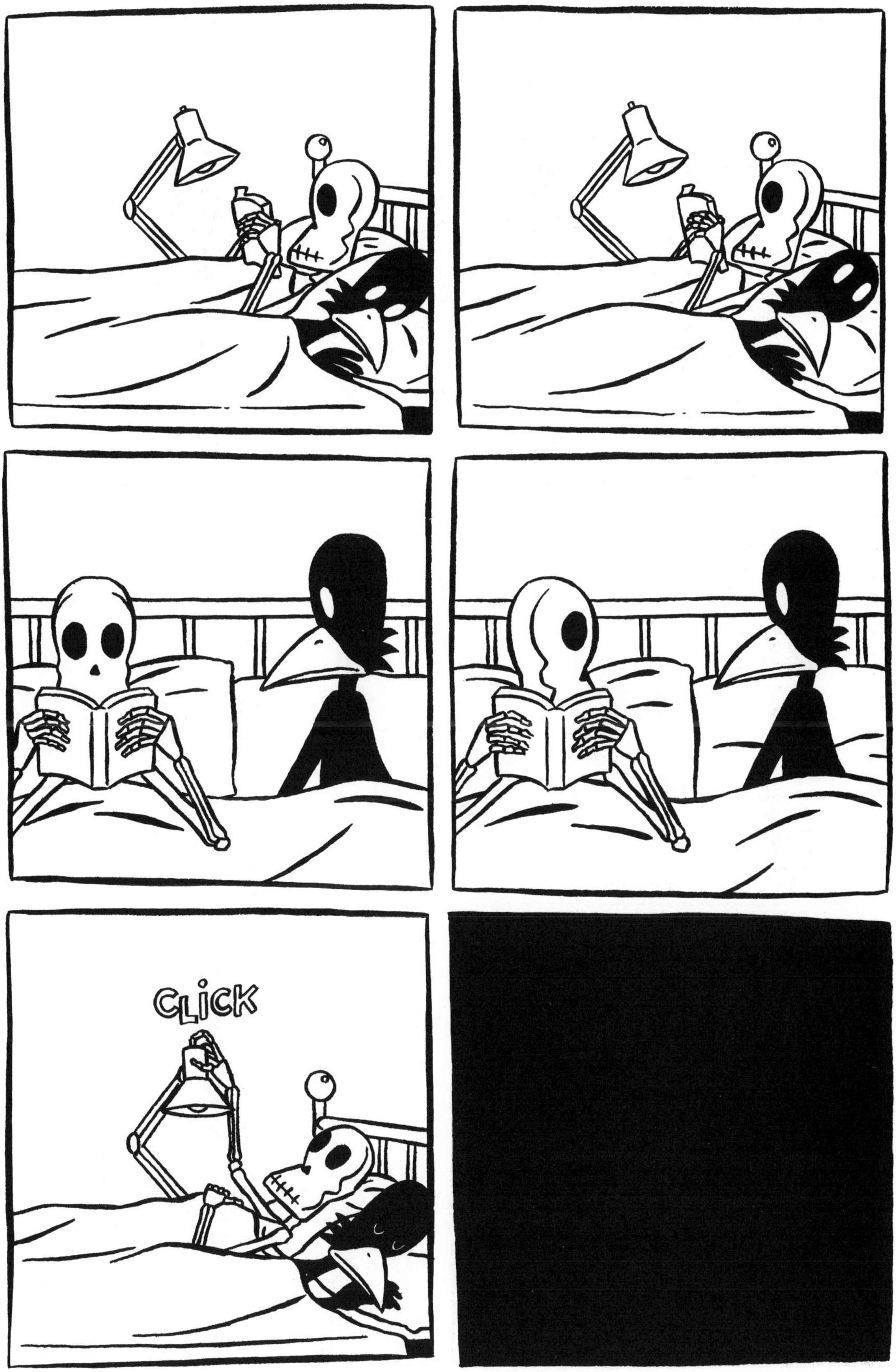
CLICK

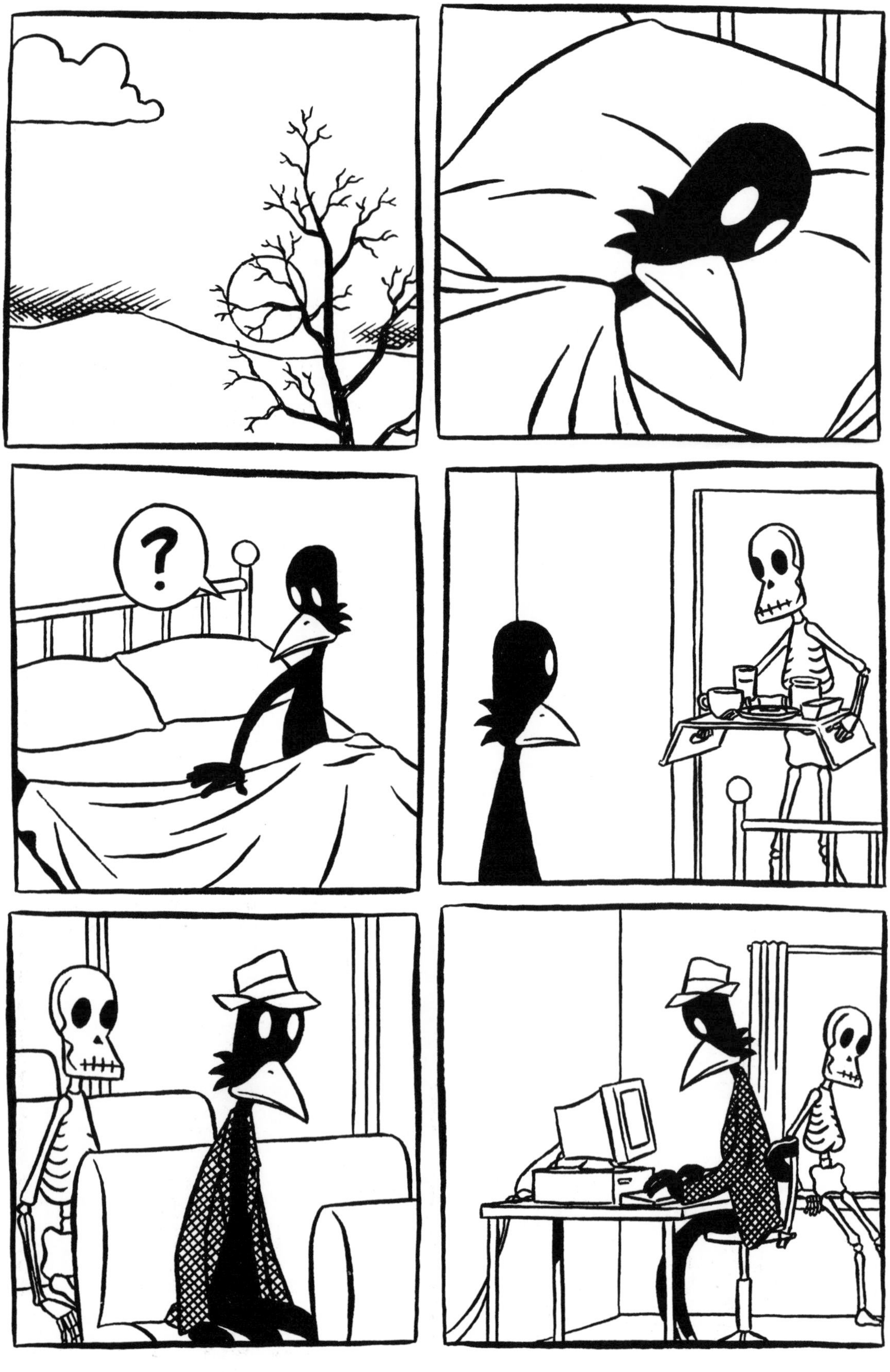
?

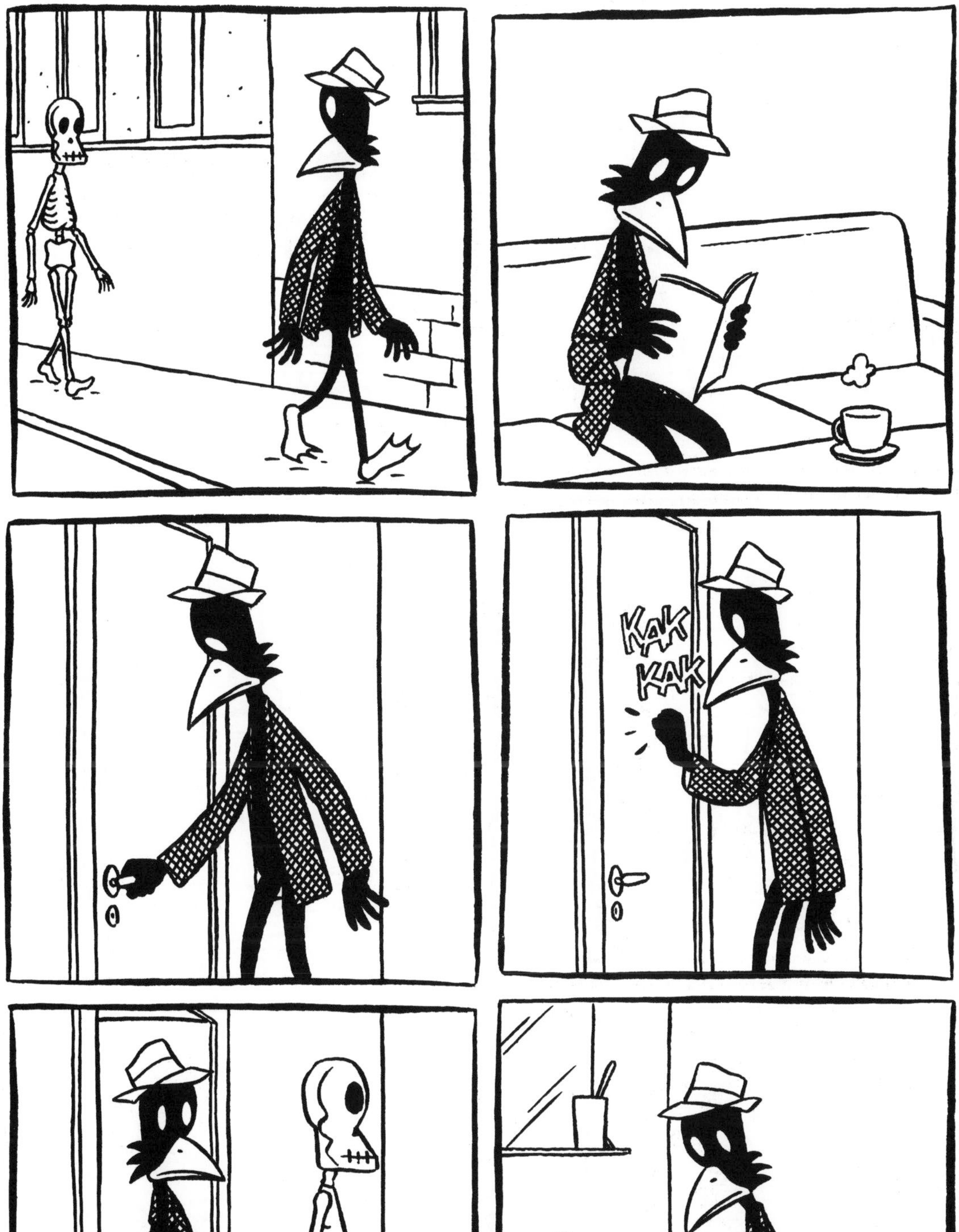
KAK
KAK

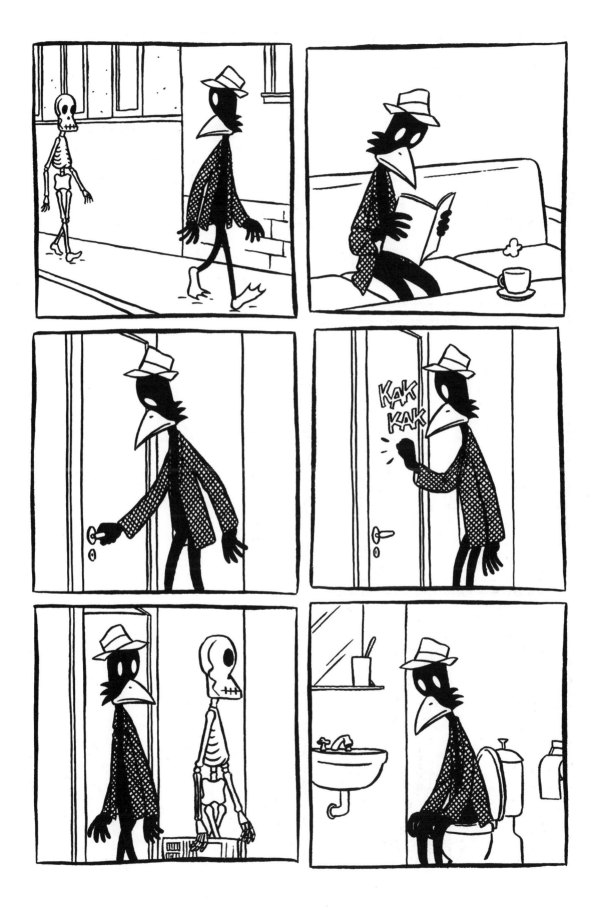

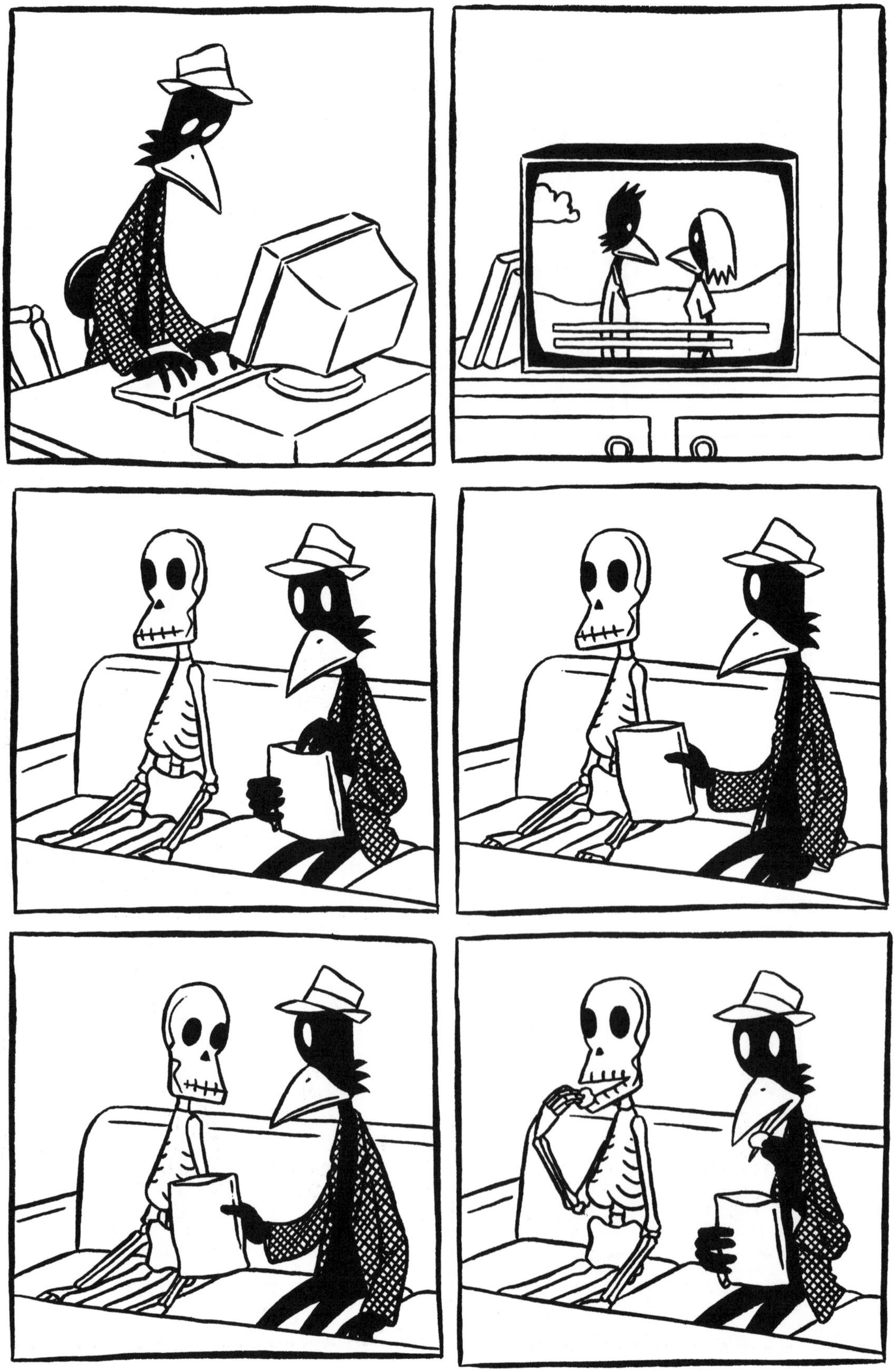

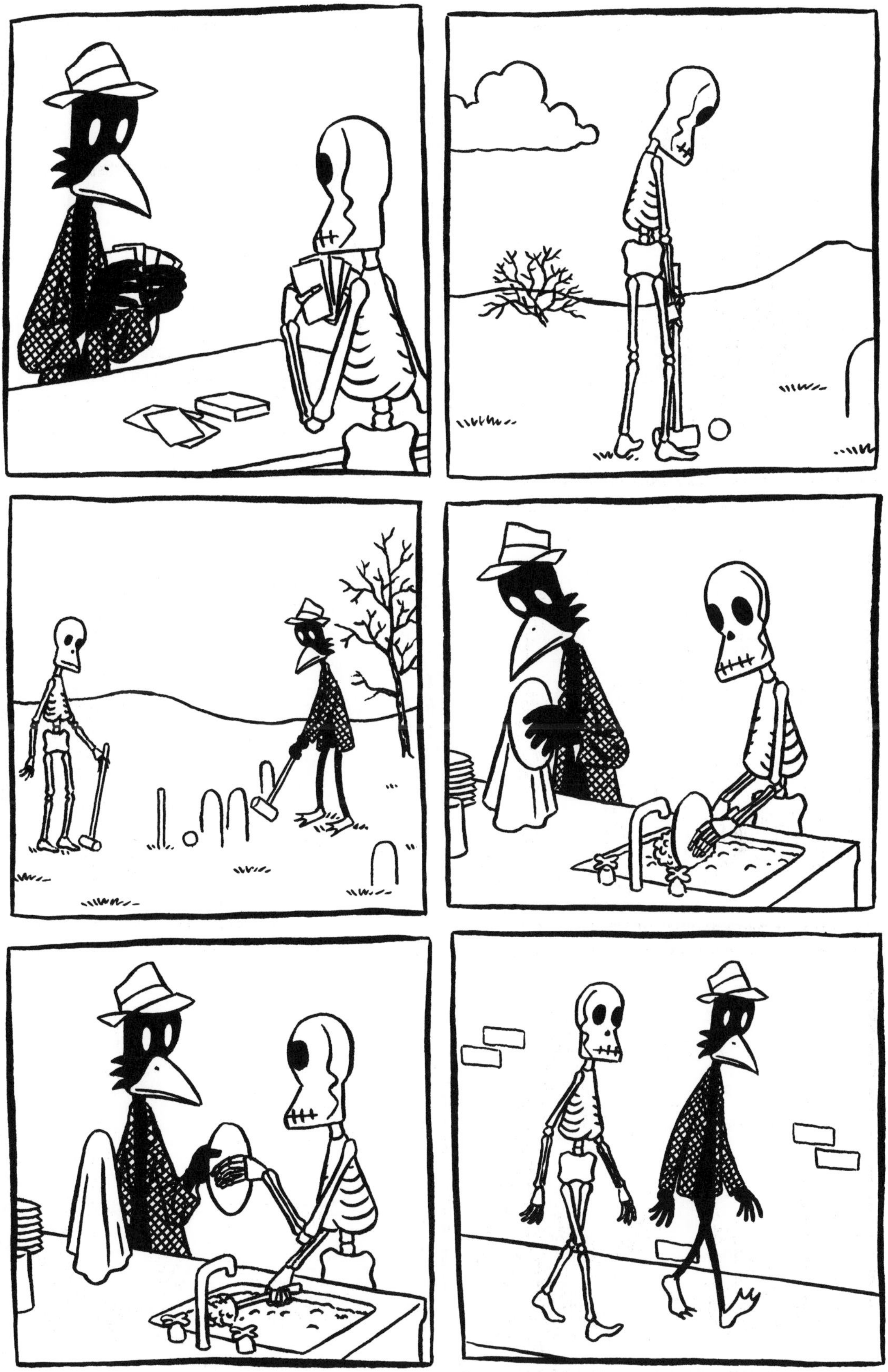

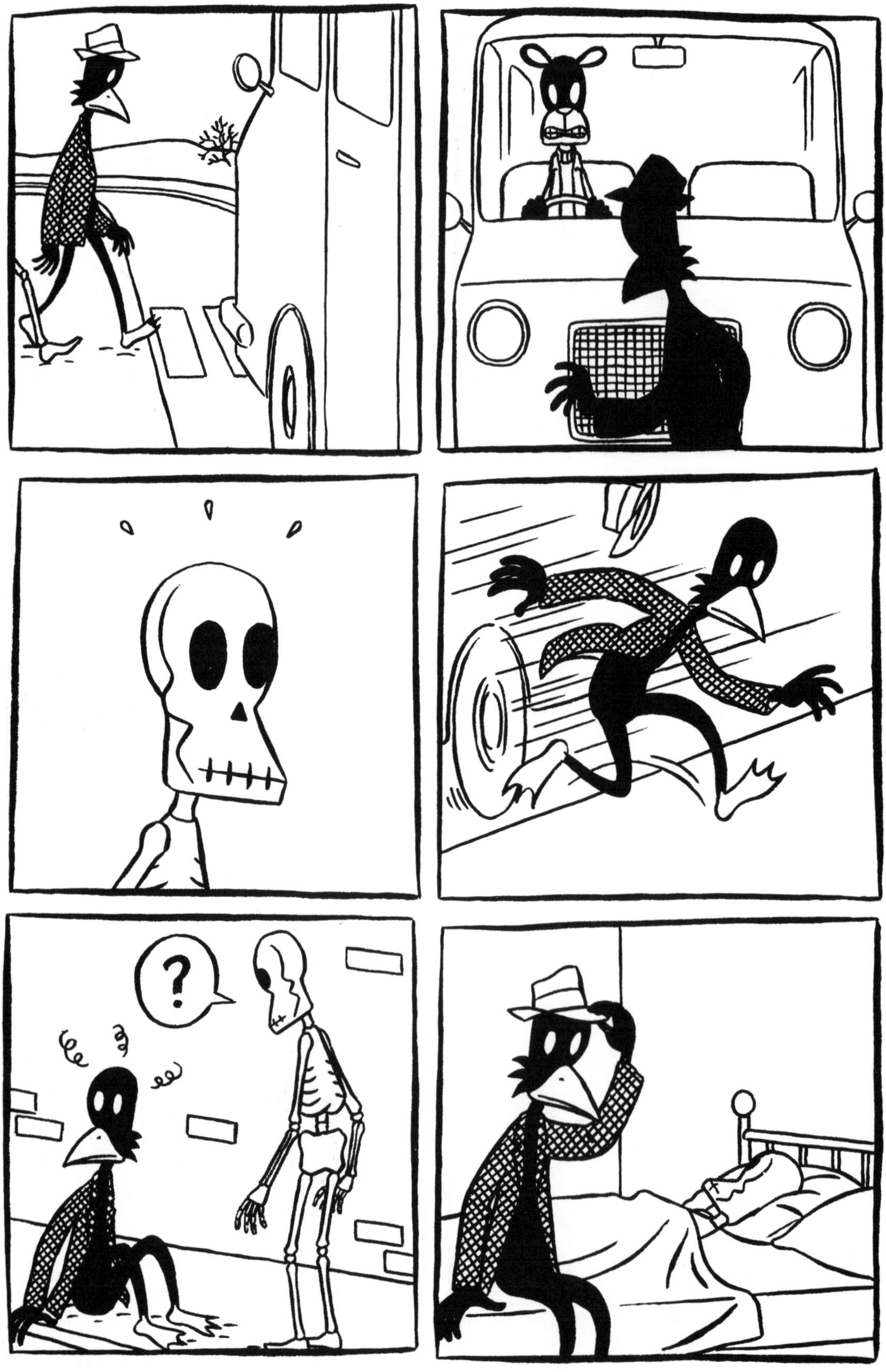
?

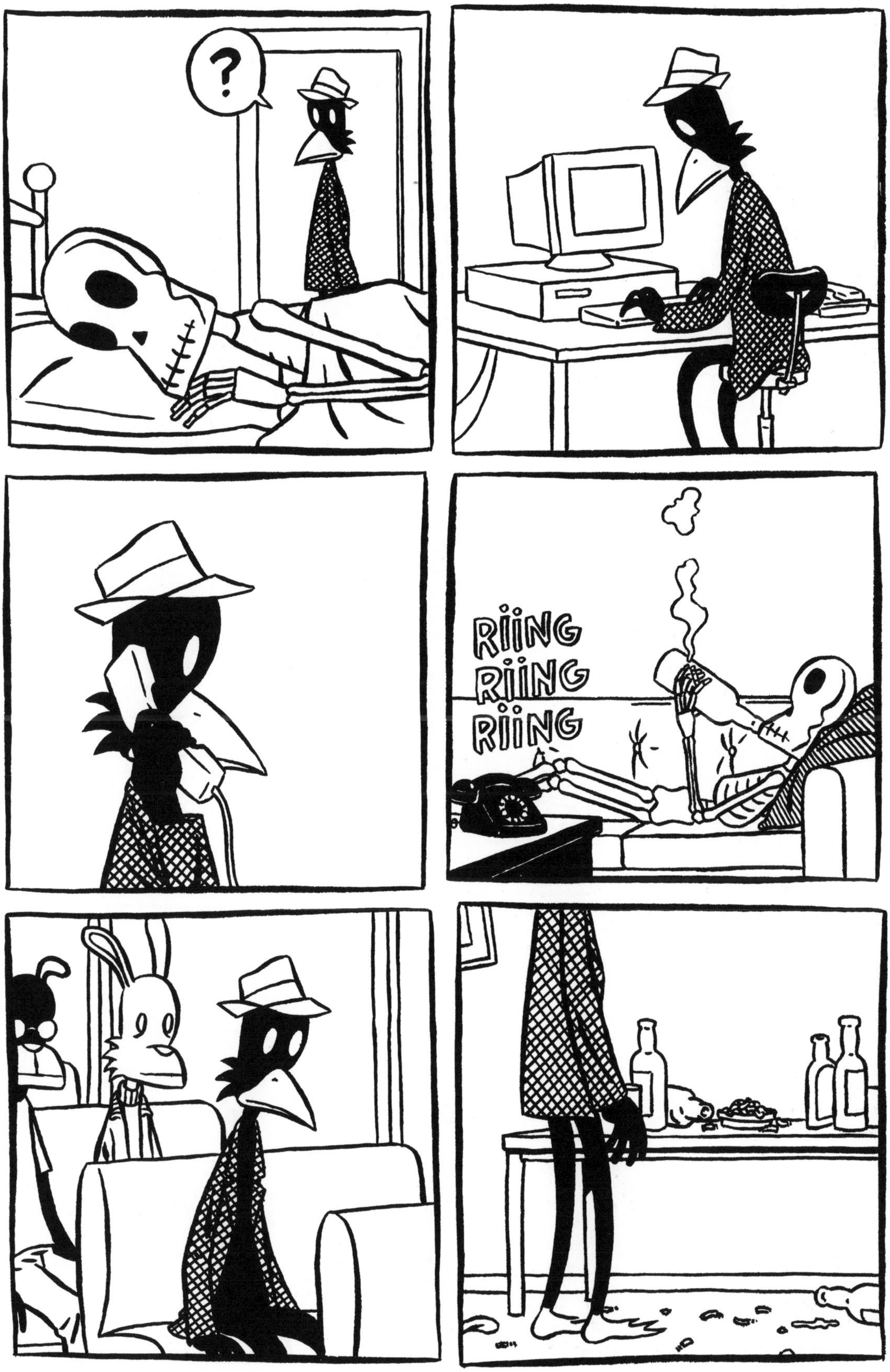
?
RIING
RIING
RIING

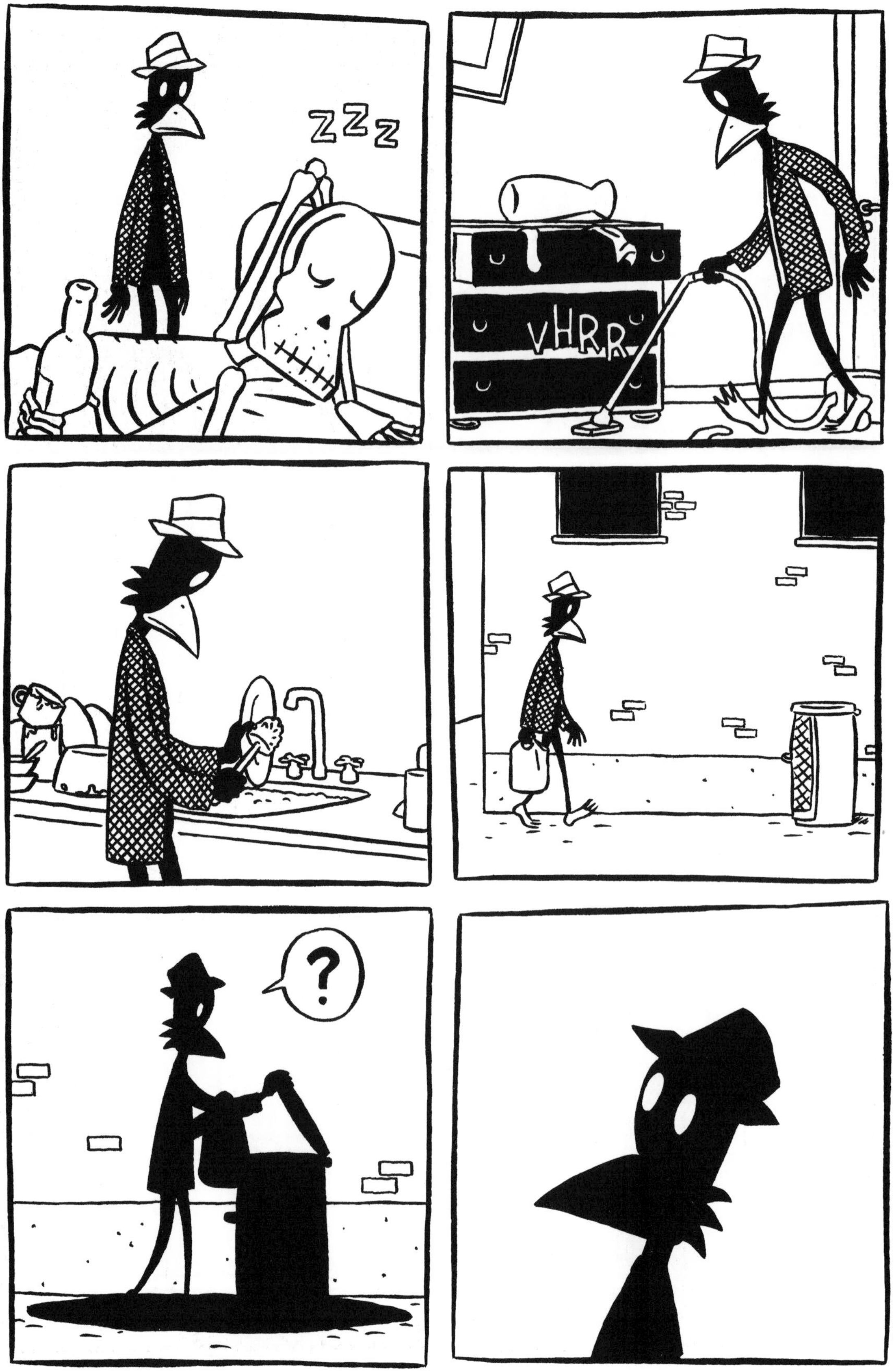
ZZZ
VHRR
?

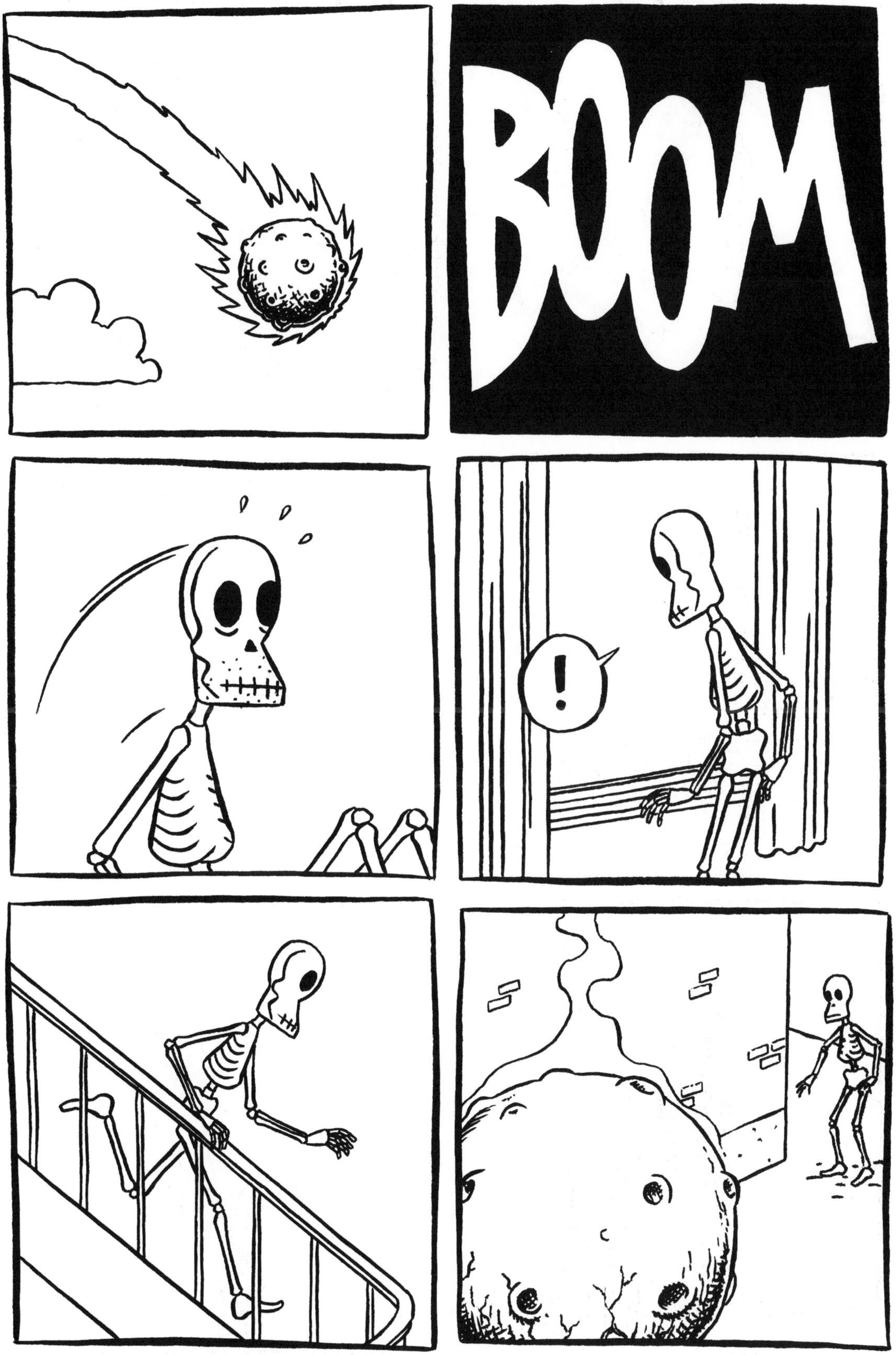
BOOM
!

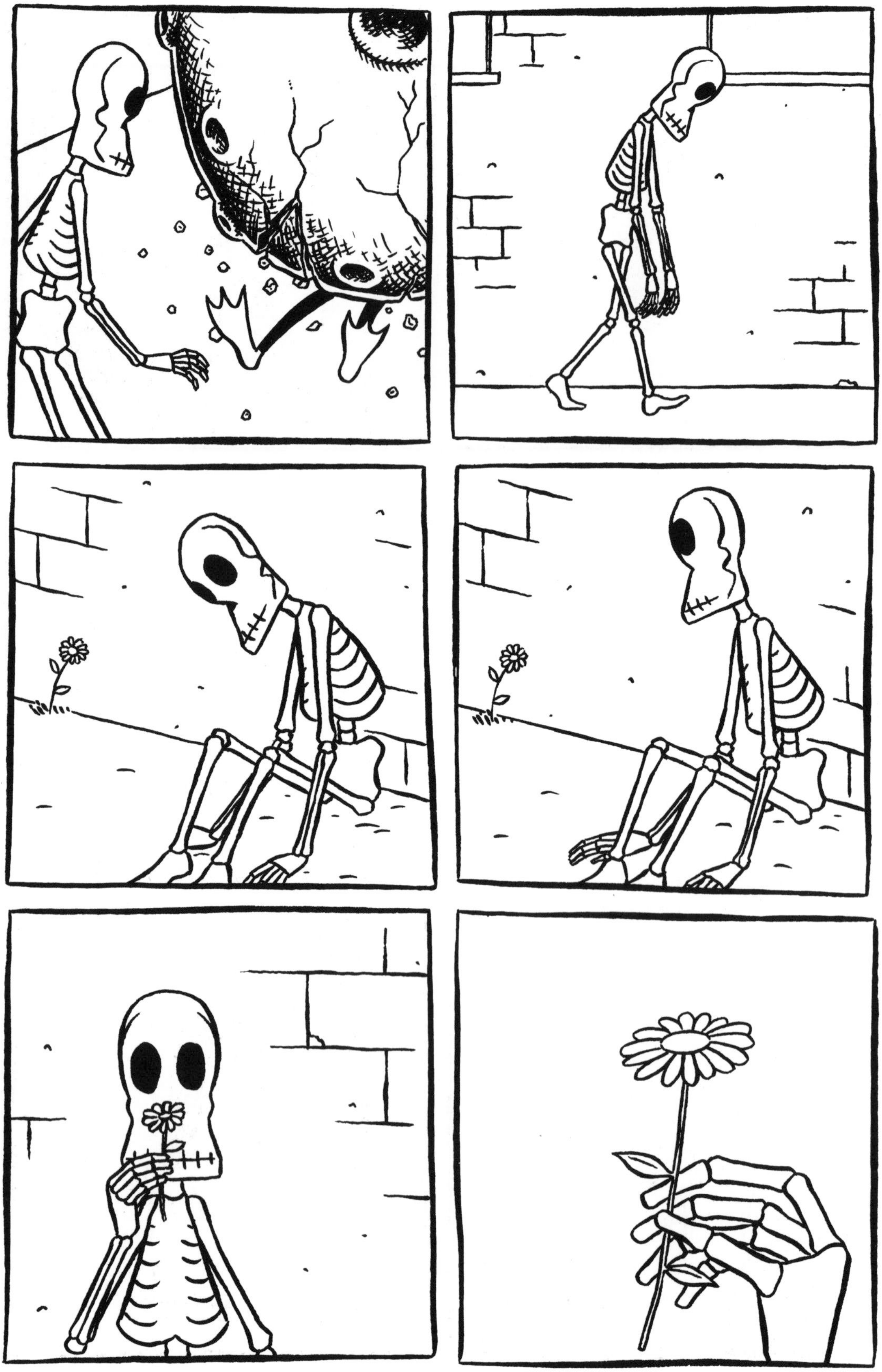

DRRRRR

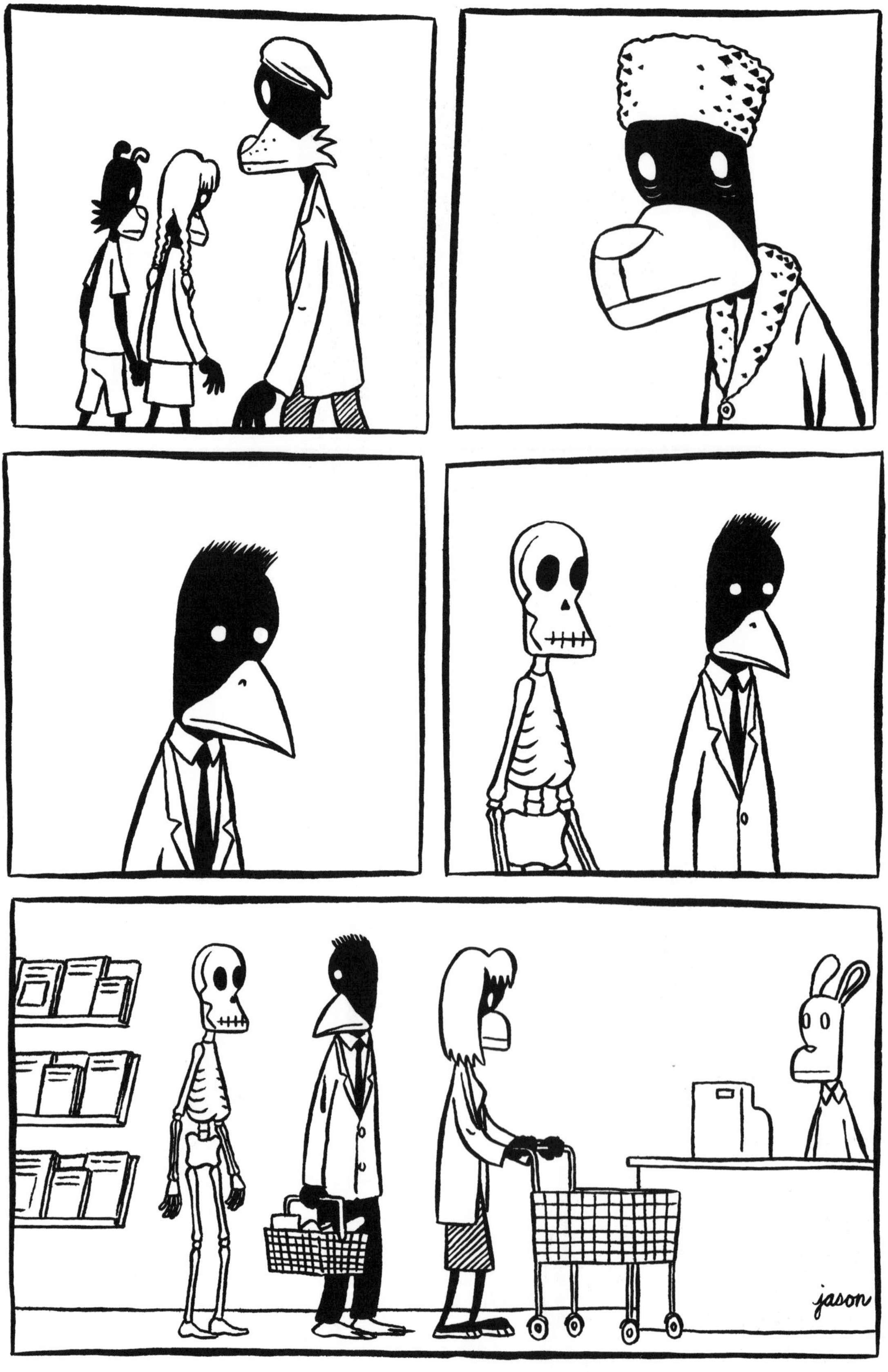
jason

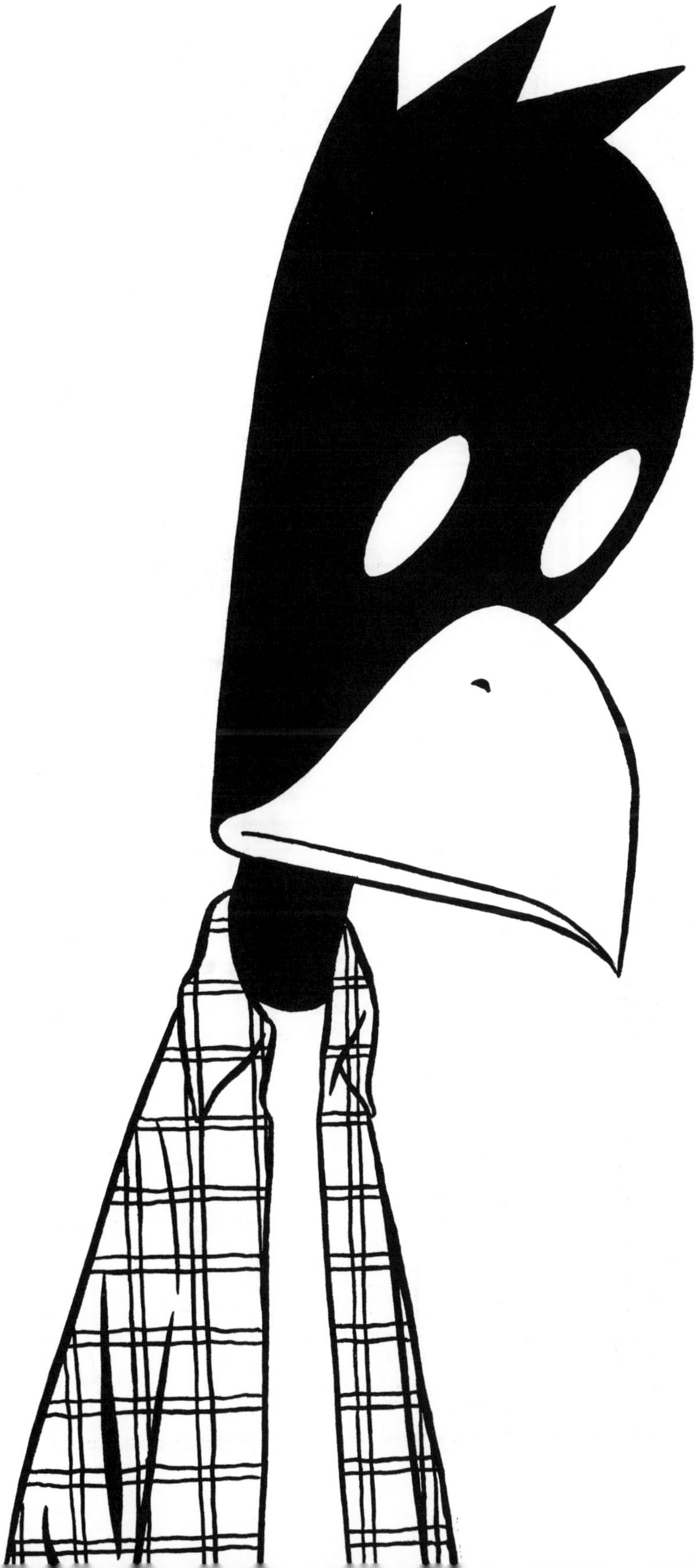

3

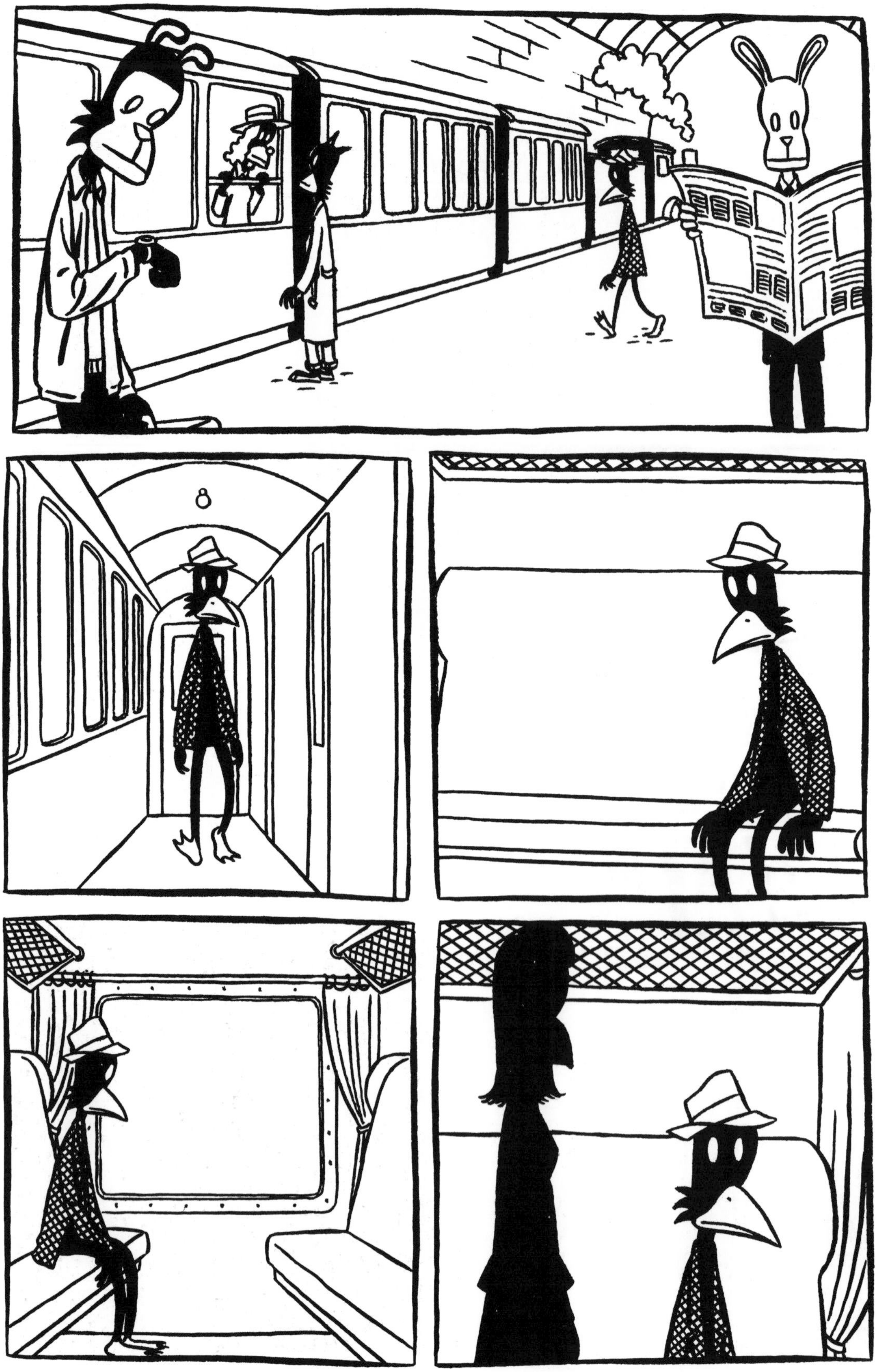

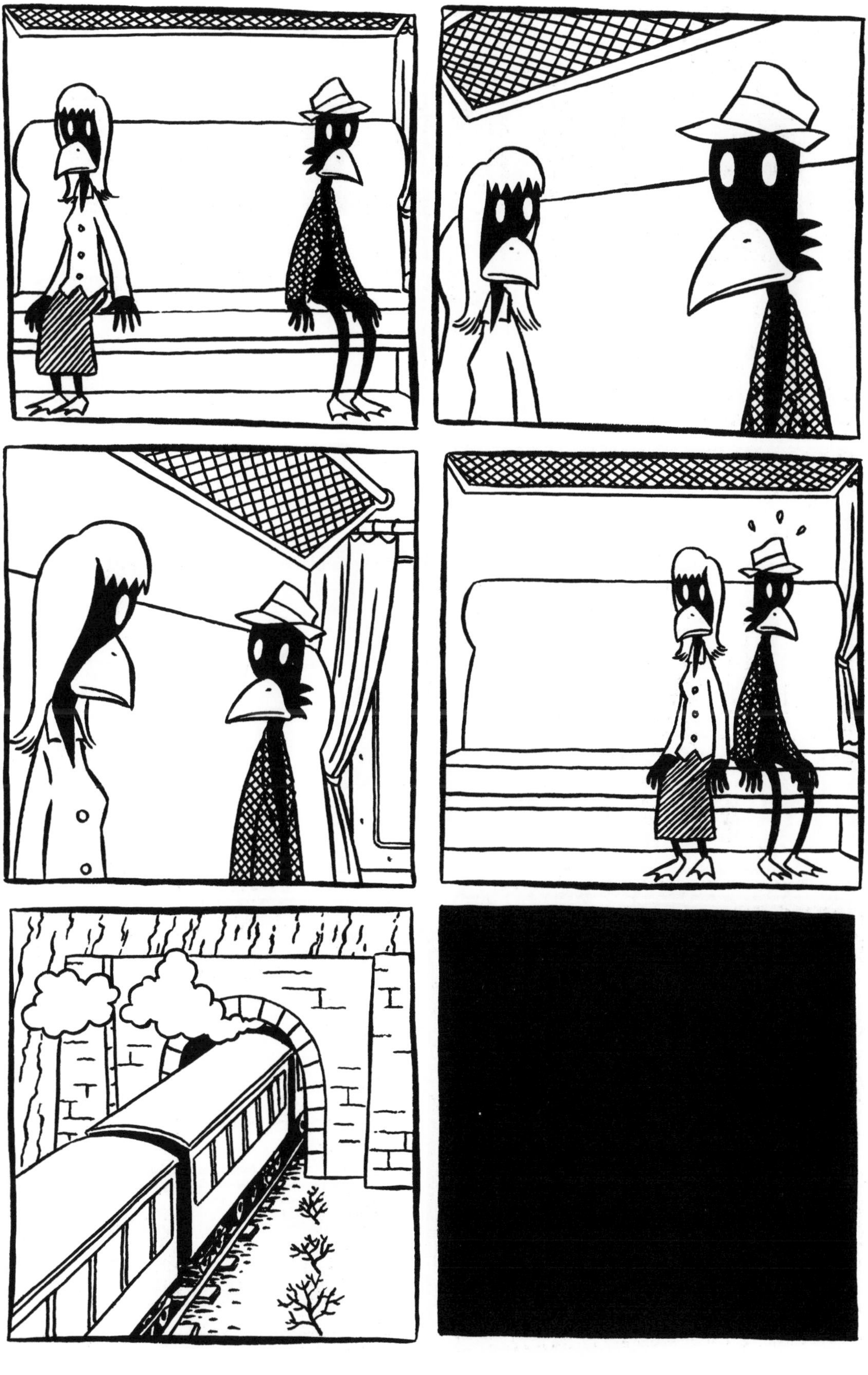

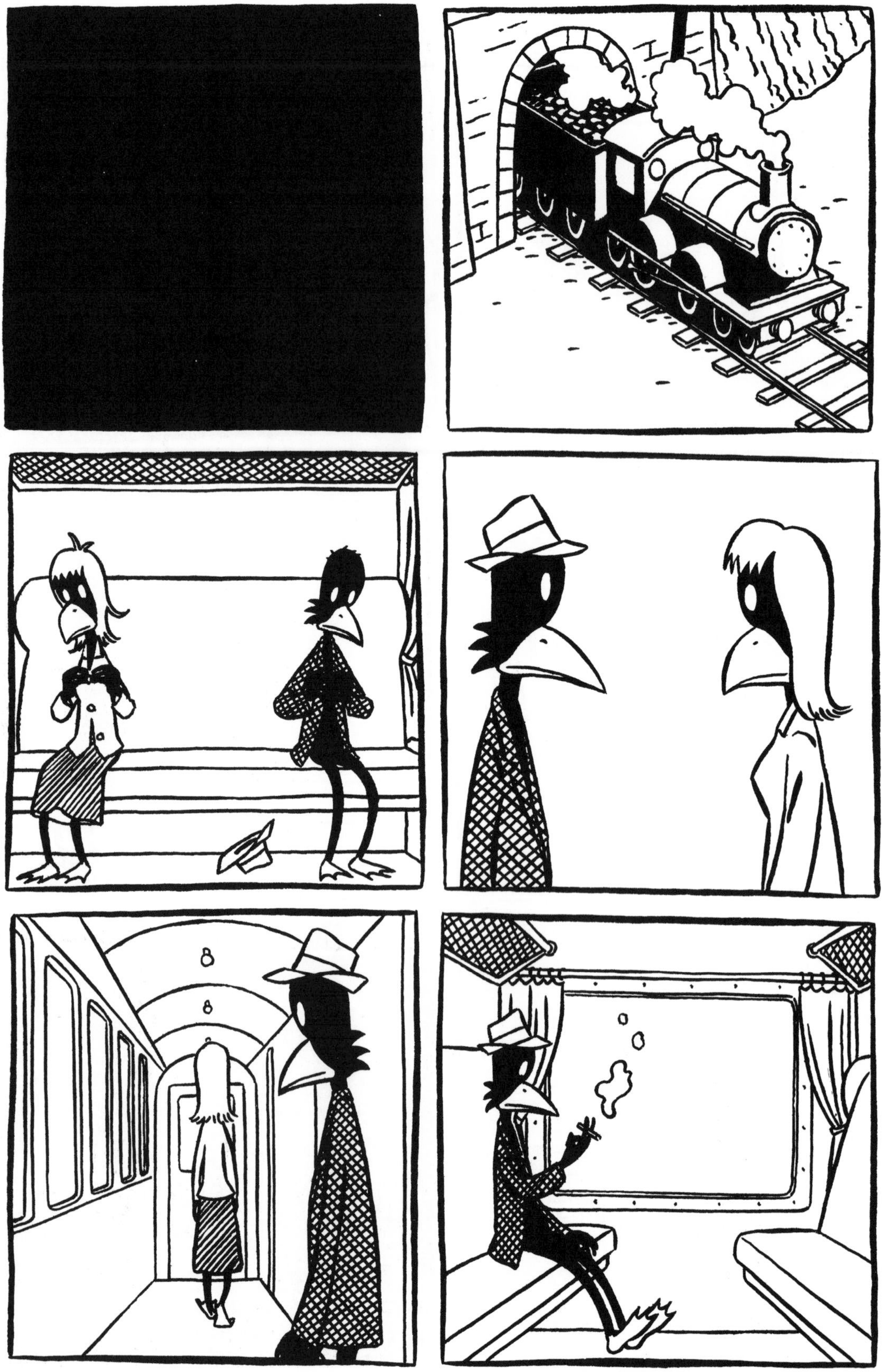

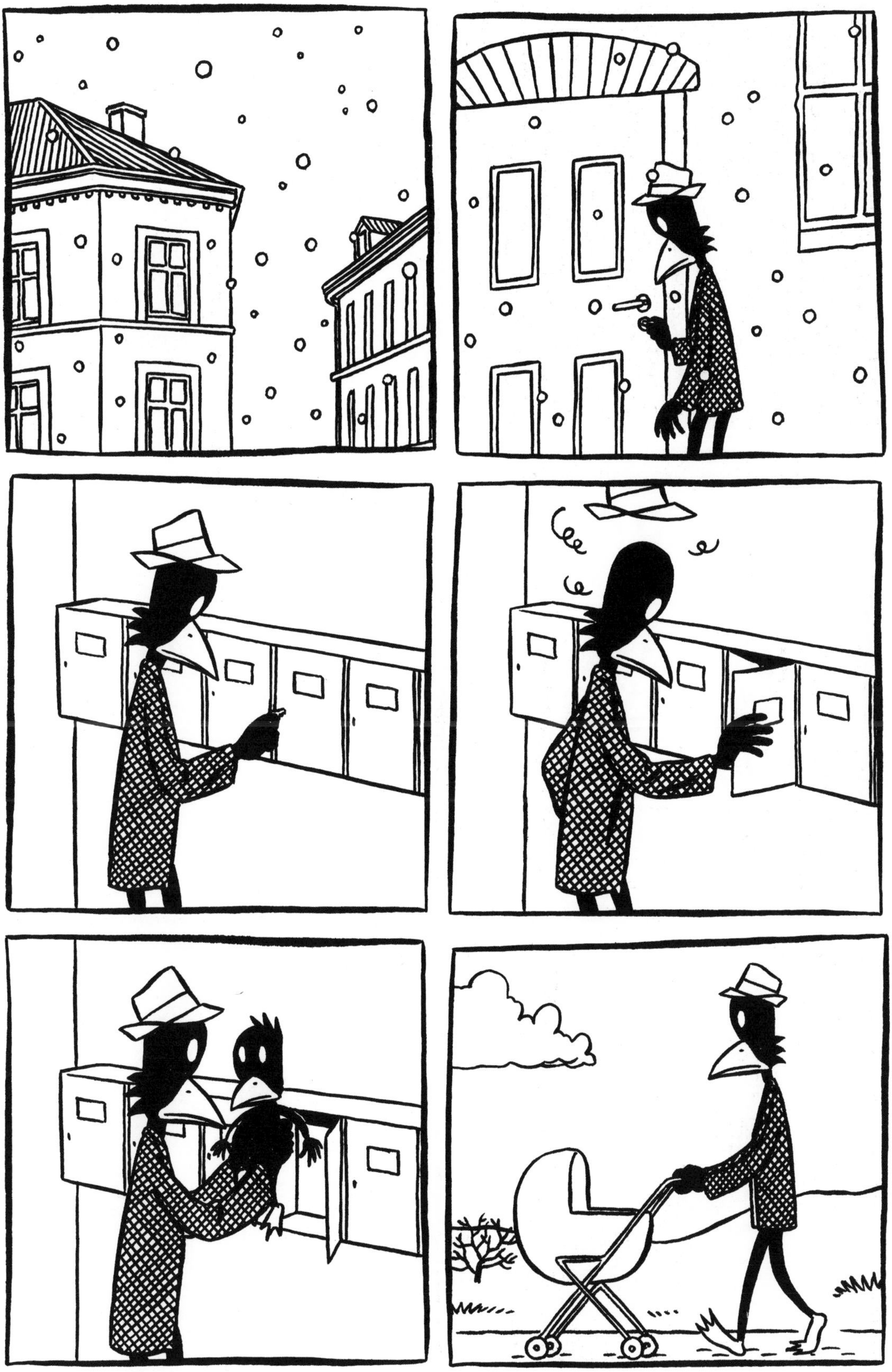

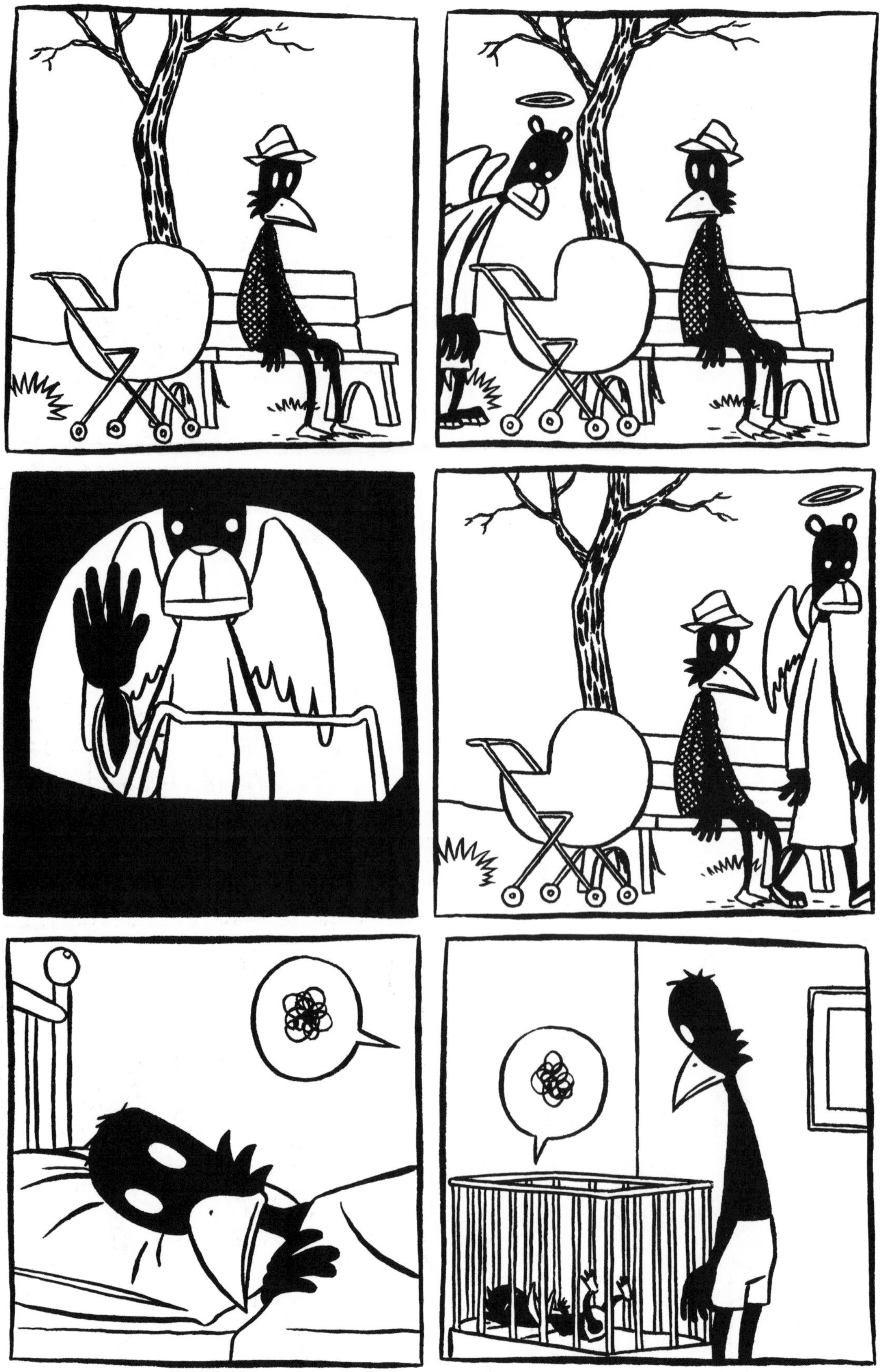

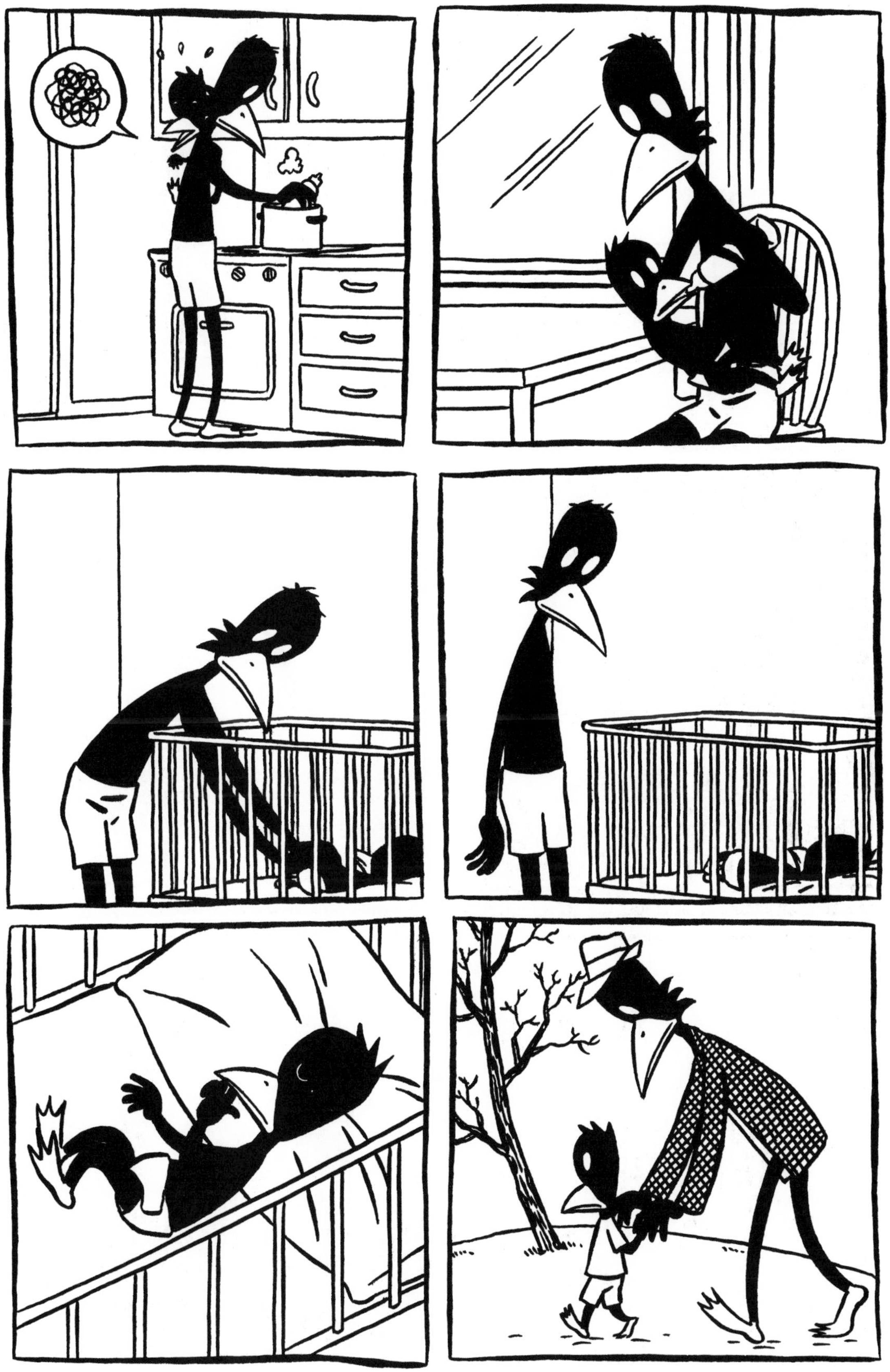

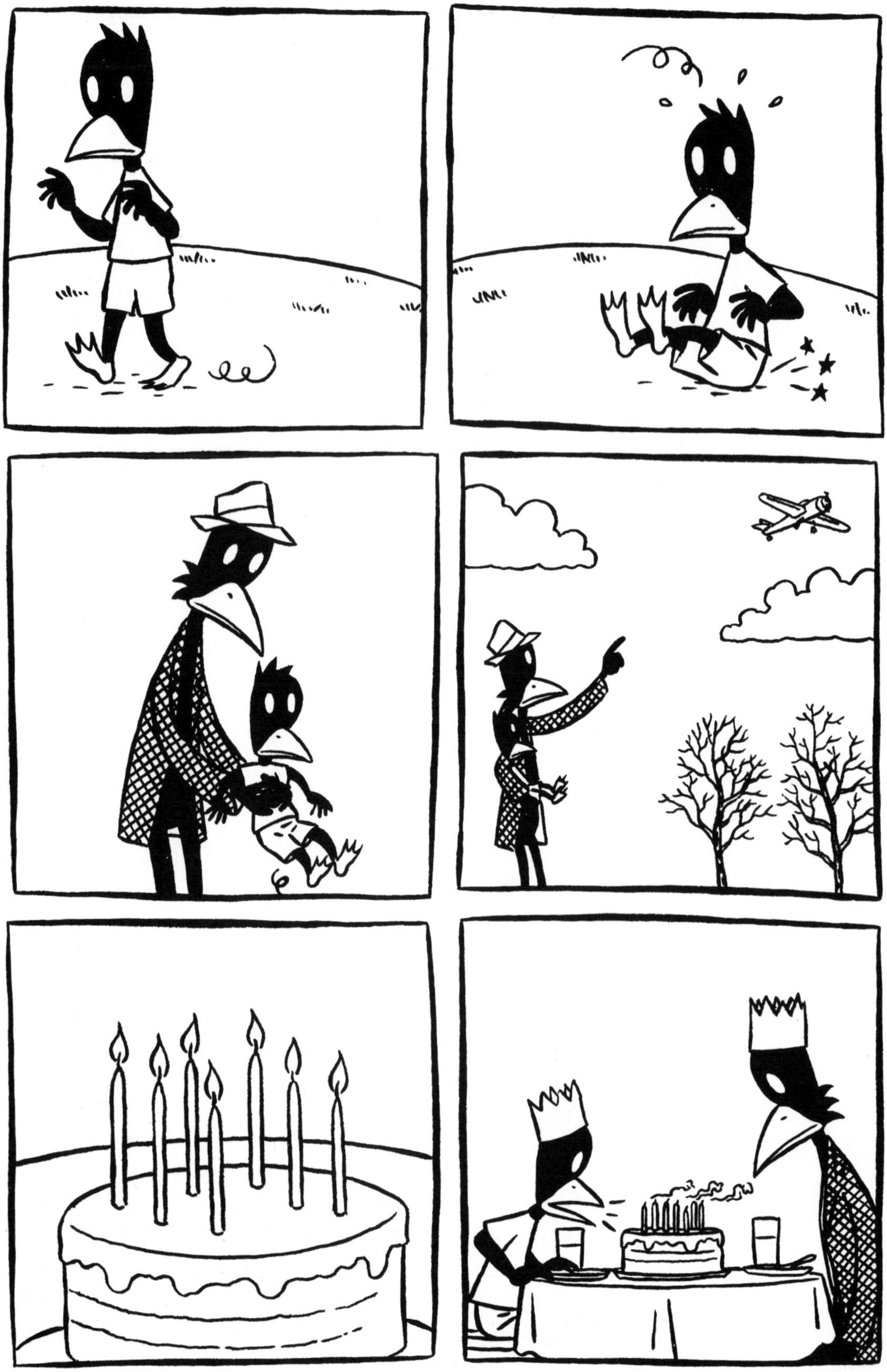

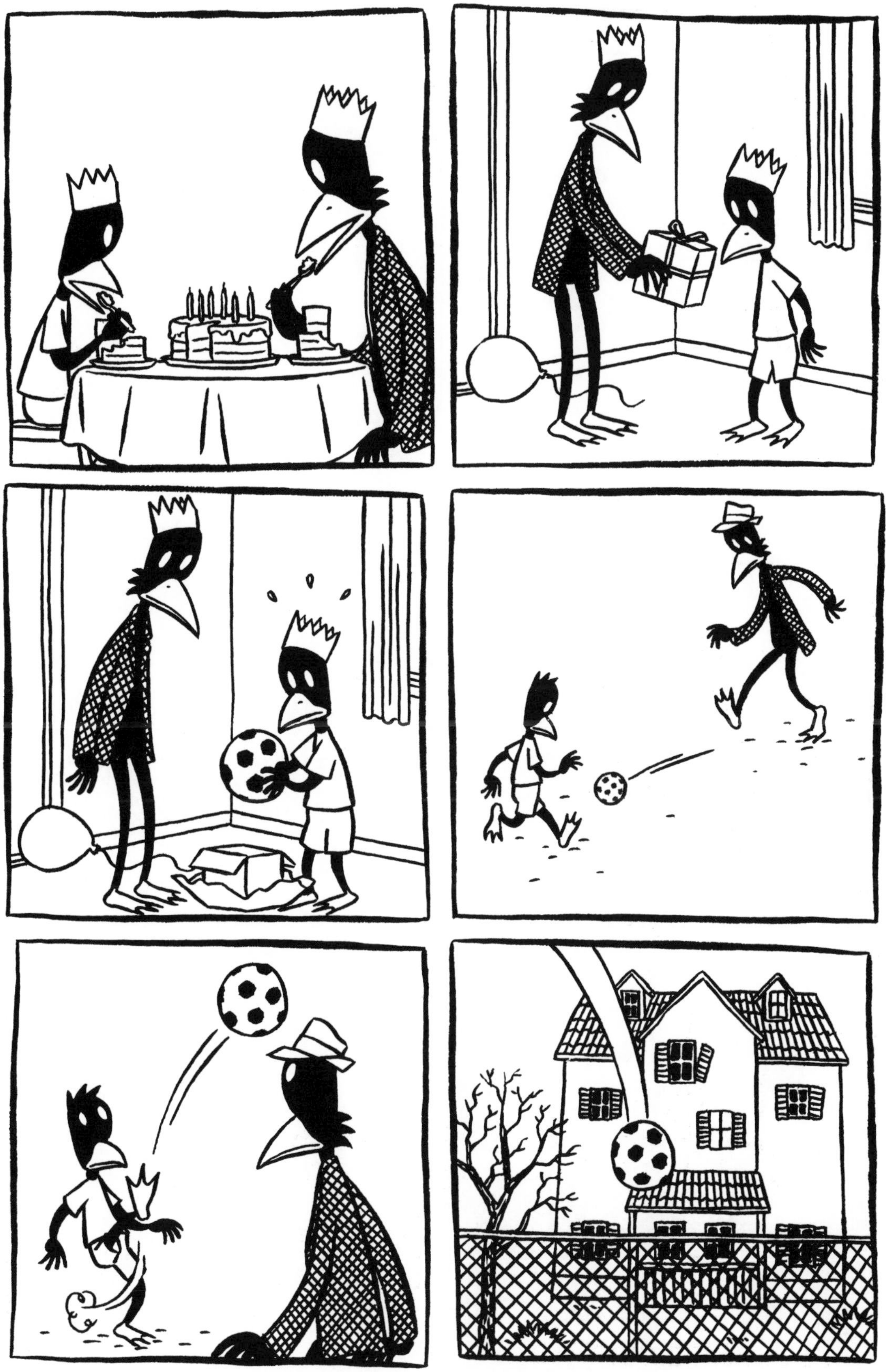

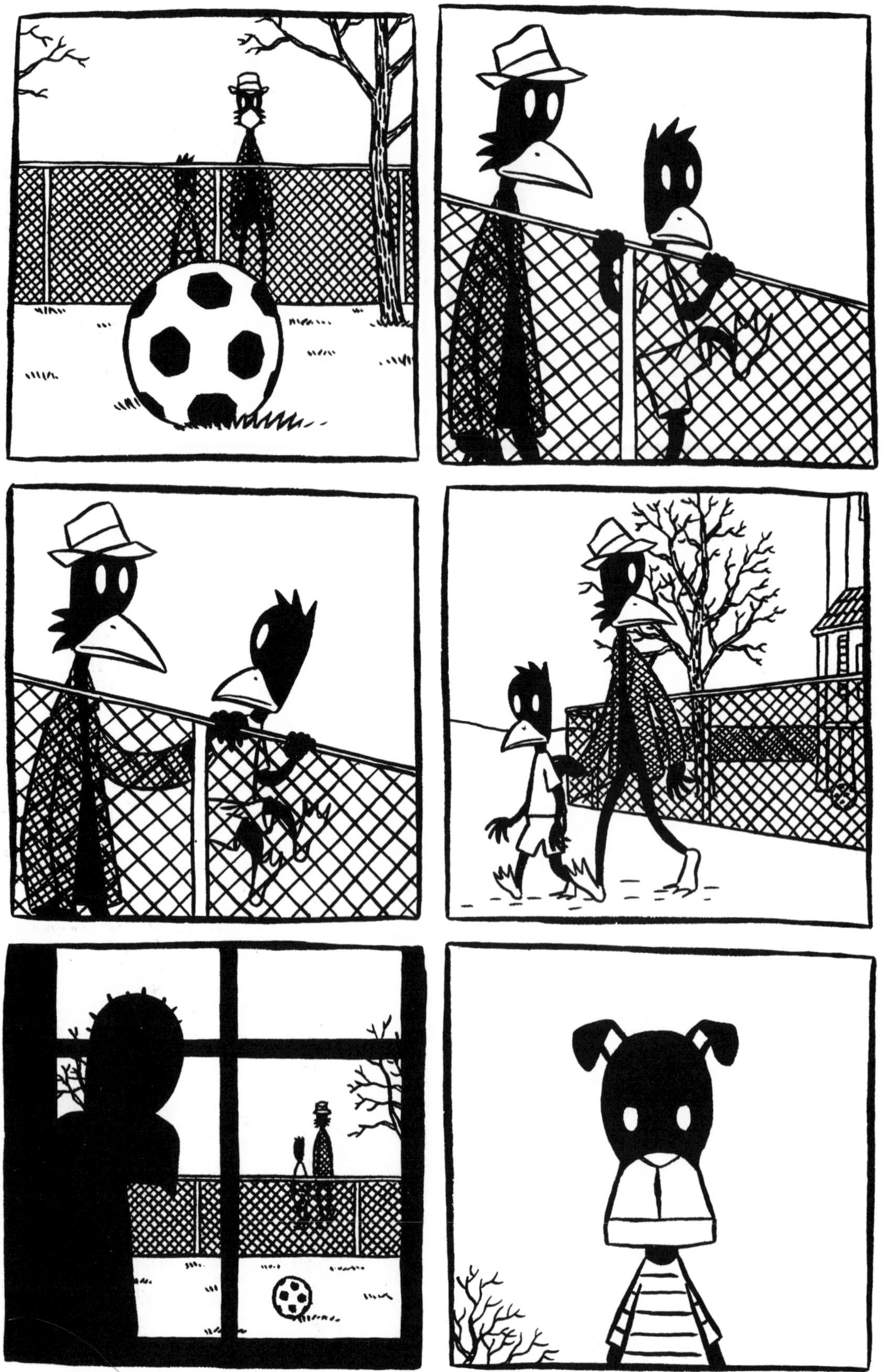

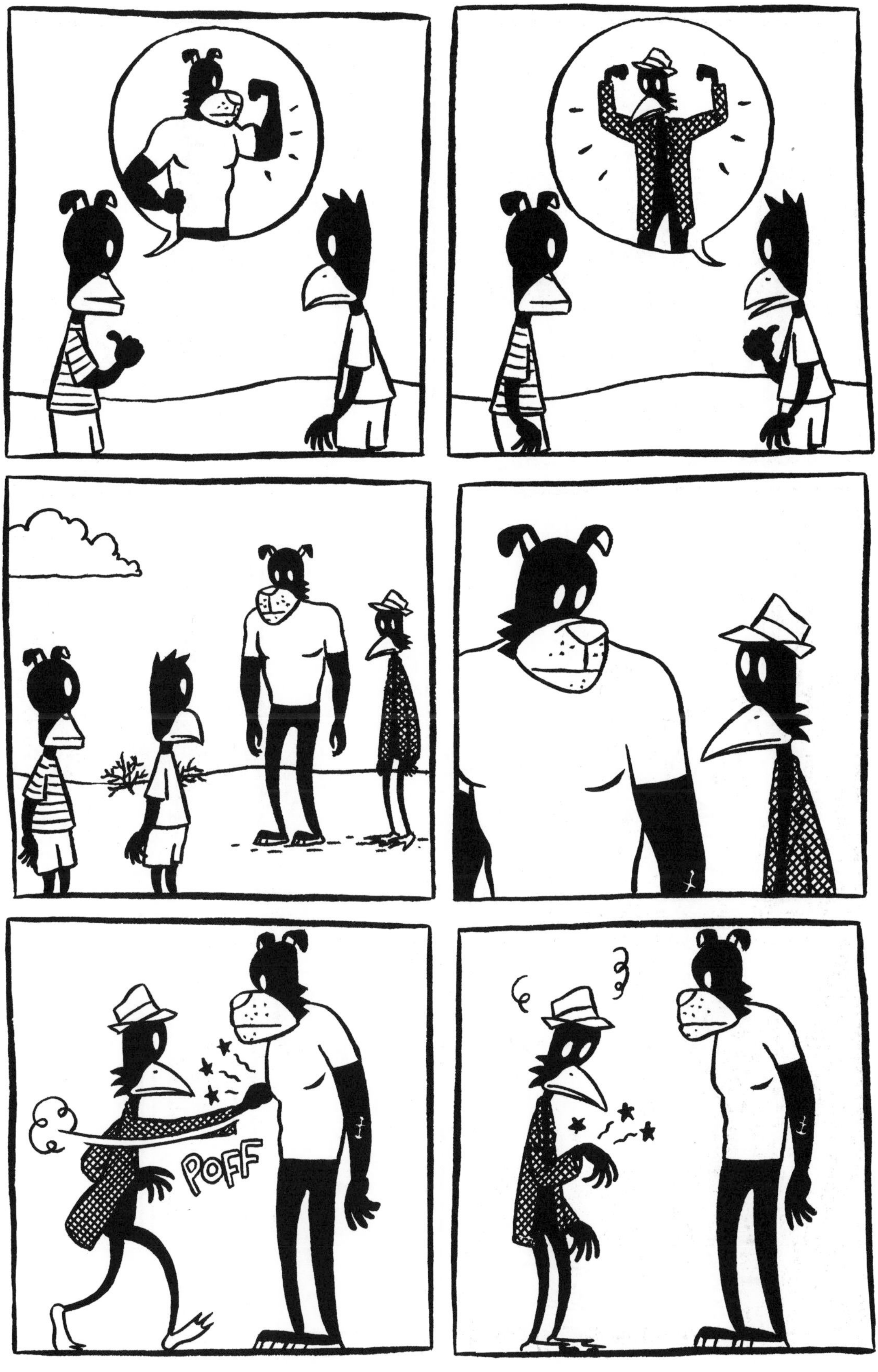
POFF

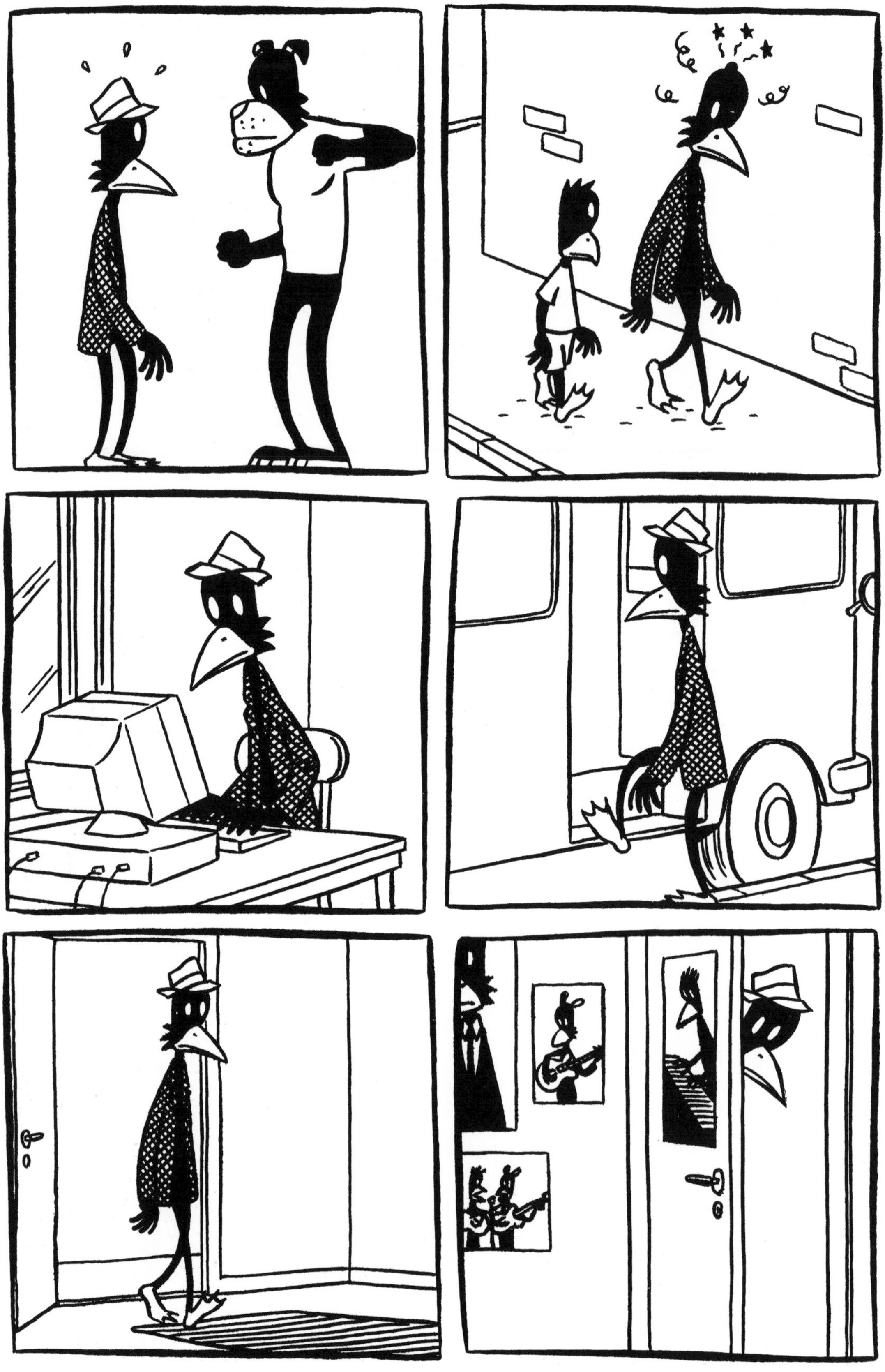

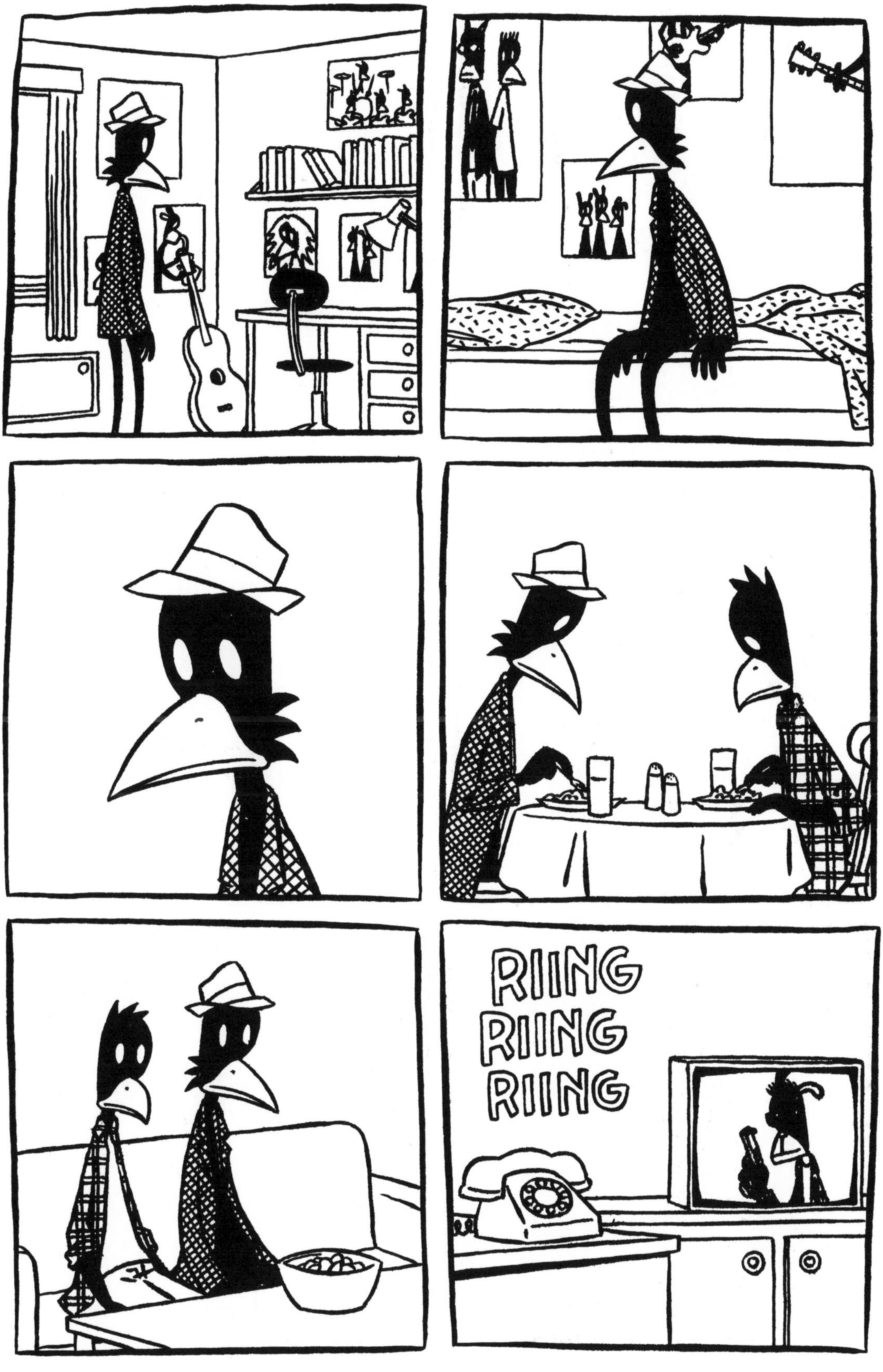
RIING
RIING
RIING

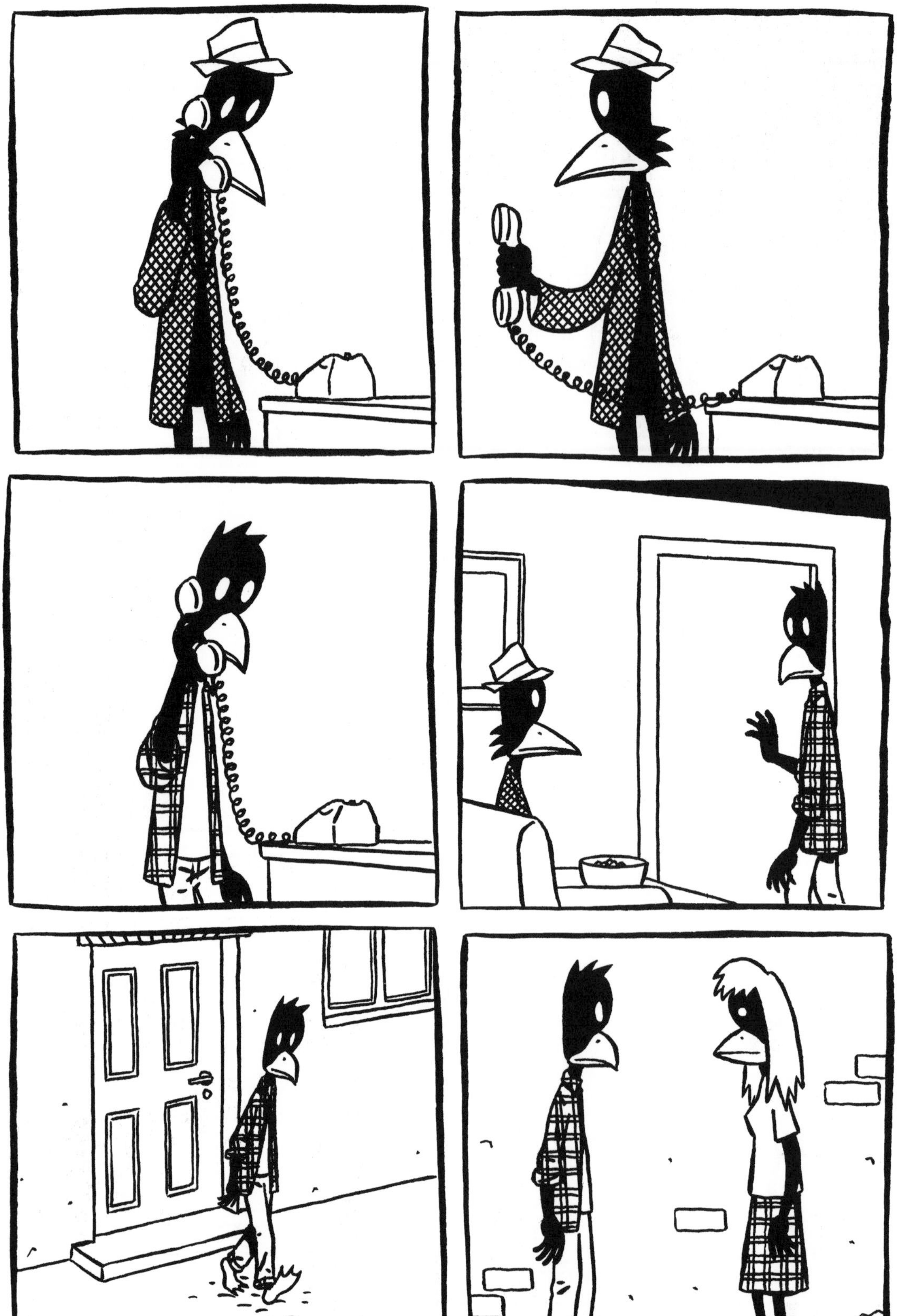

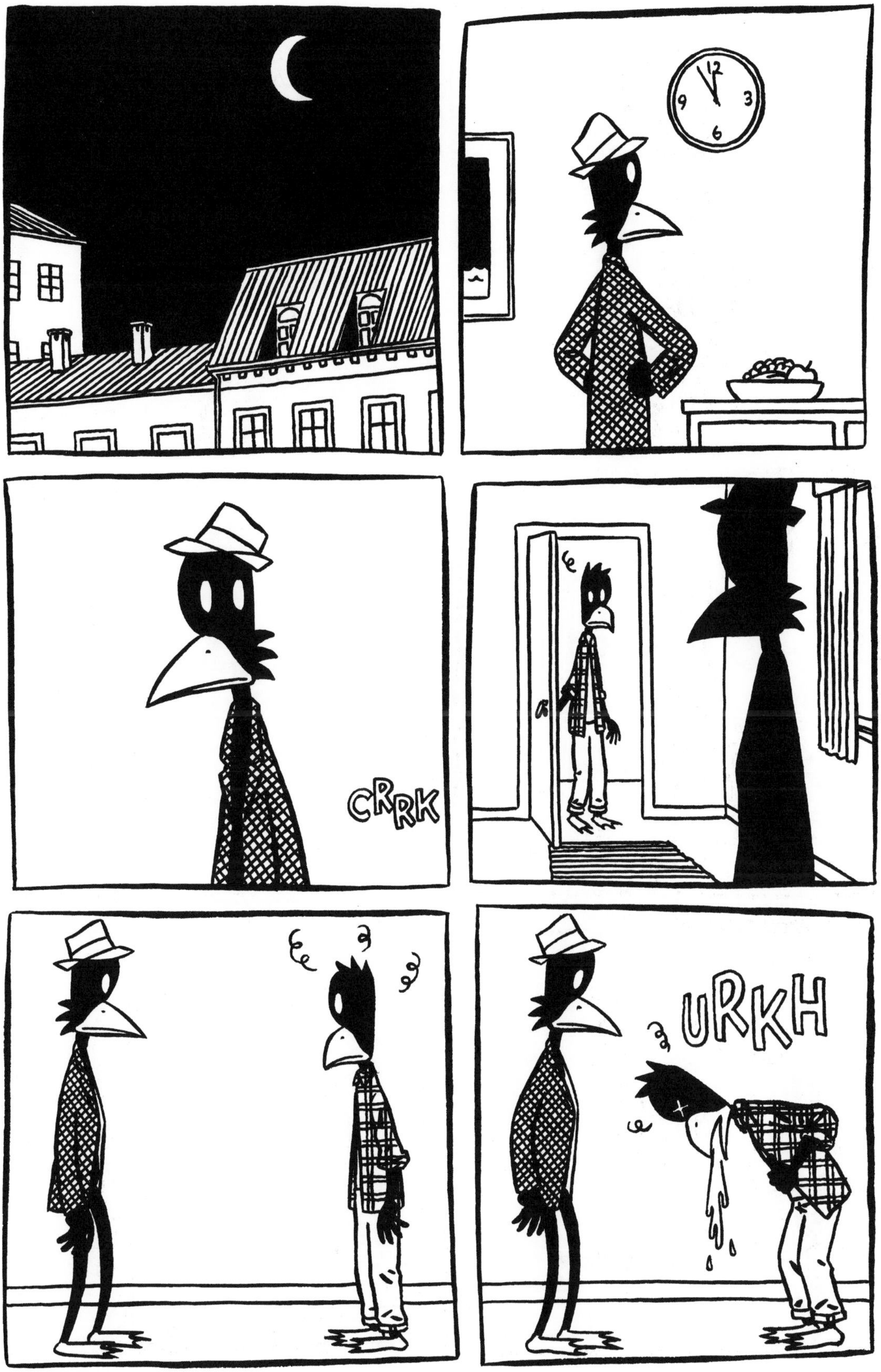
CRRK
URKH

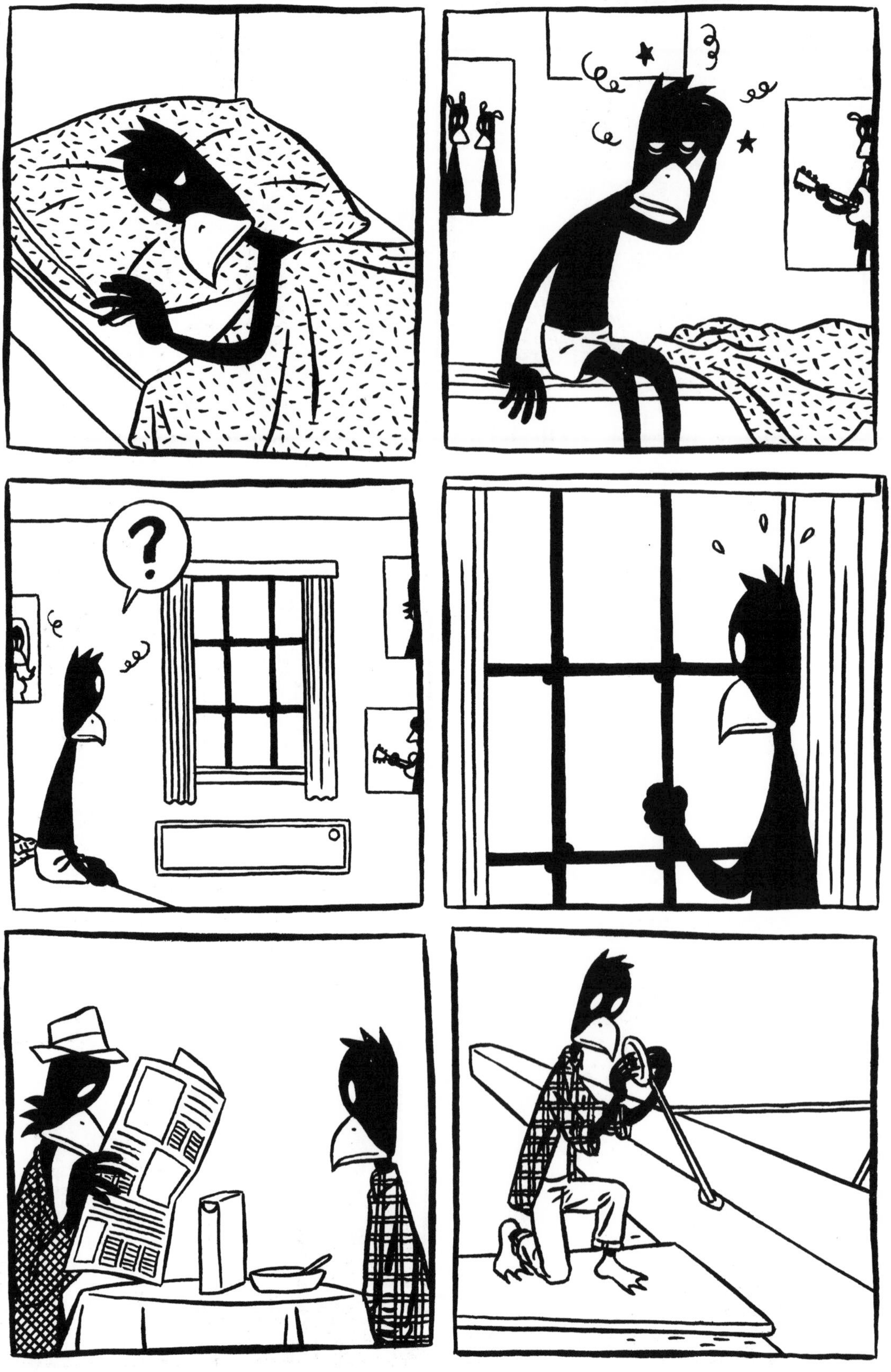
?

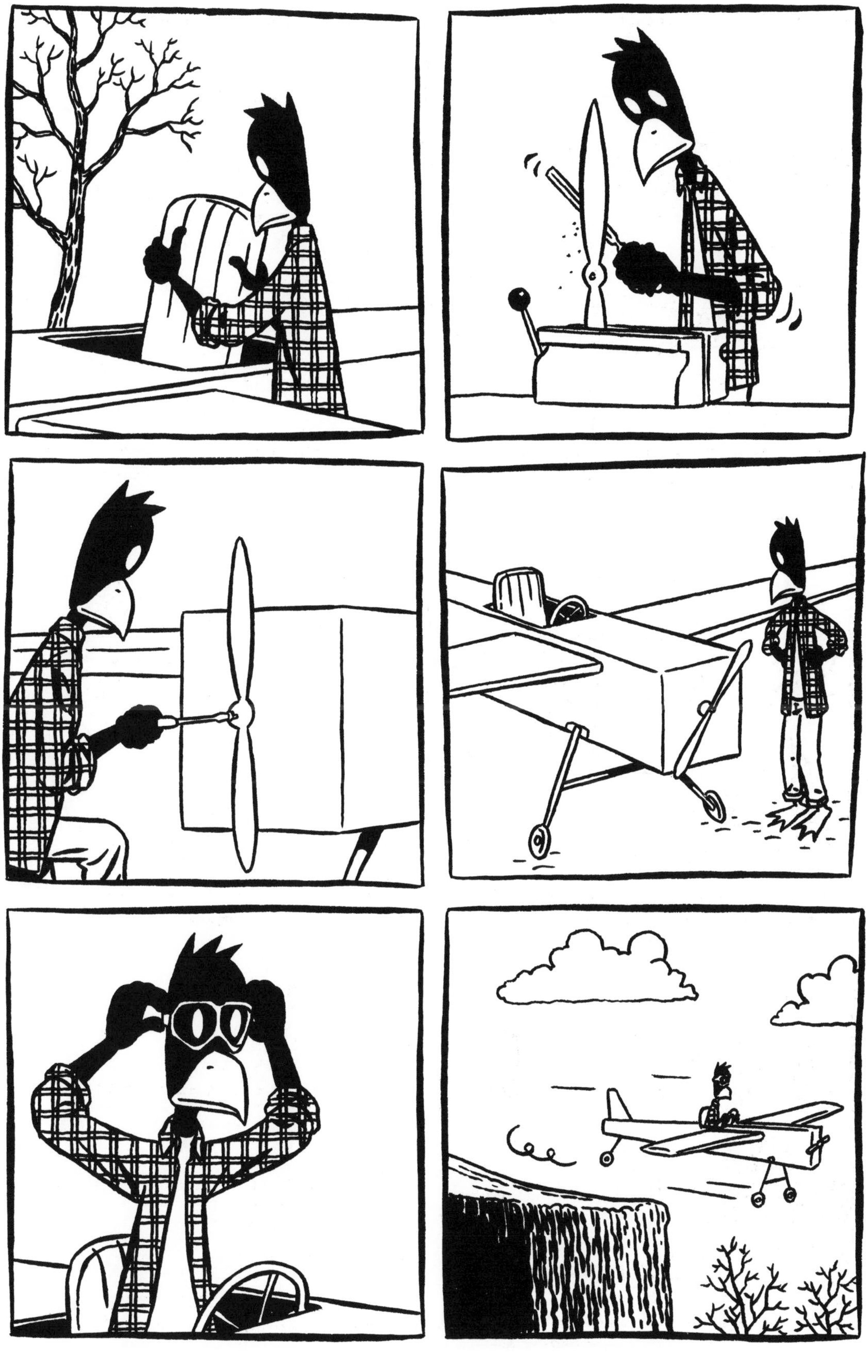

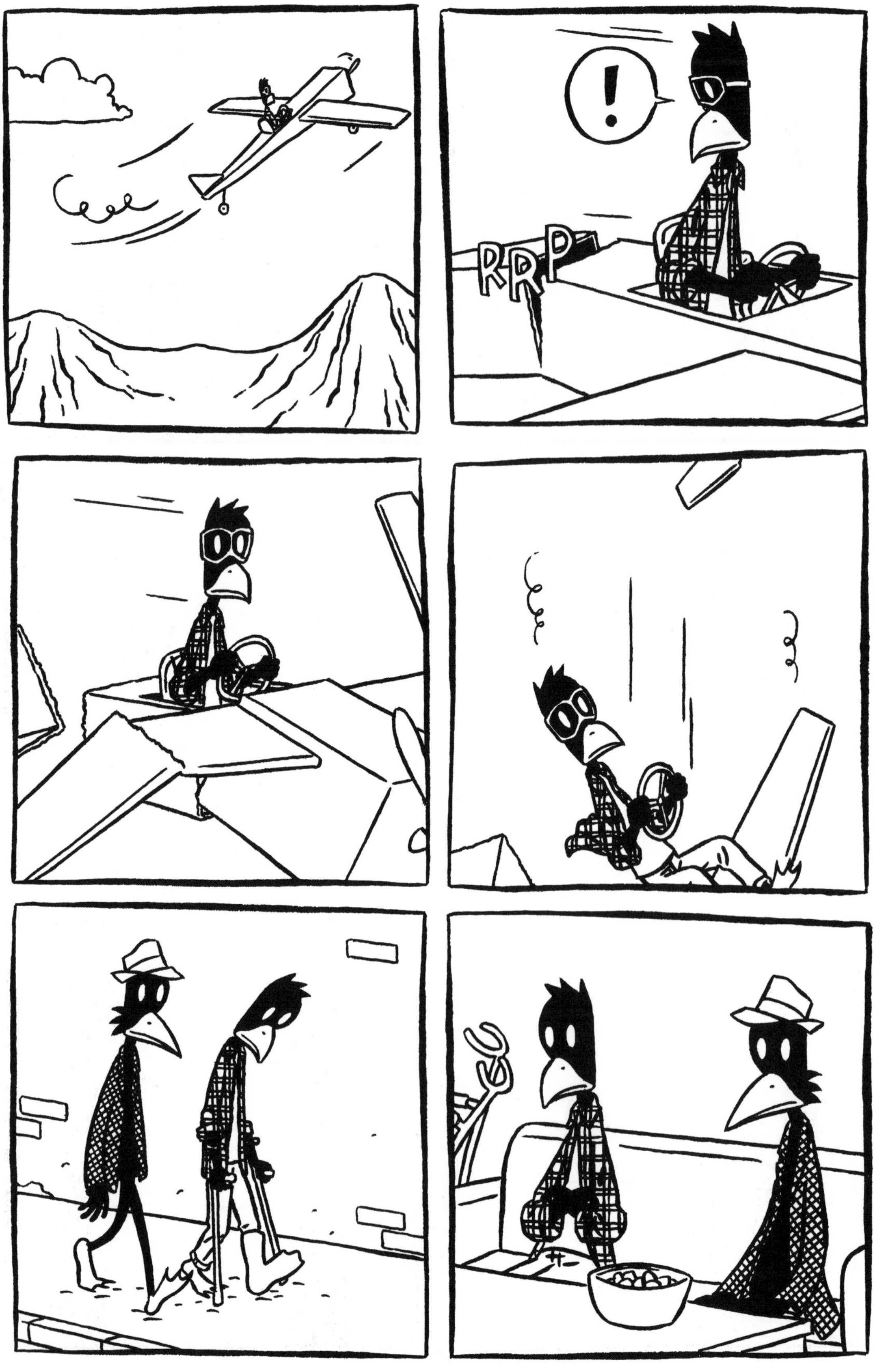
!
RRP

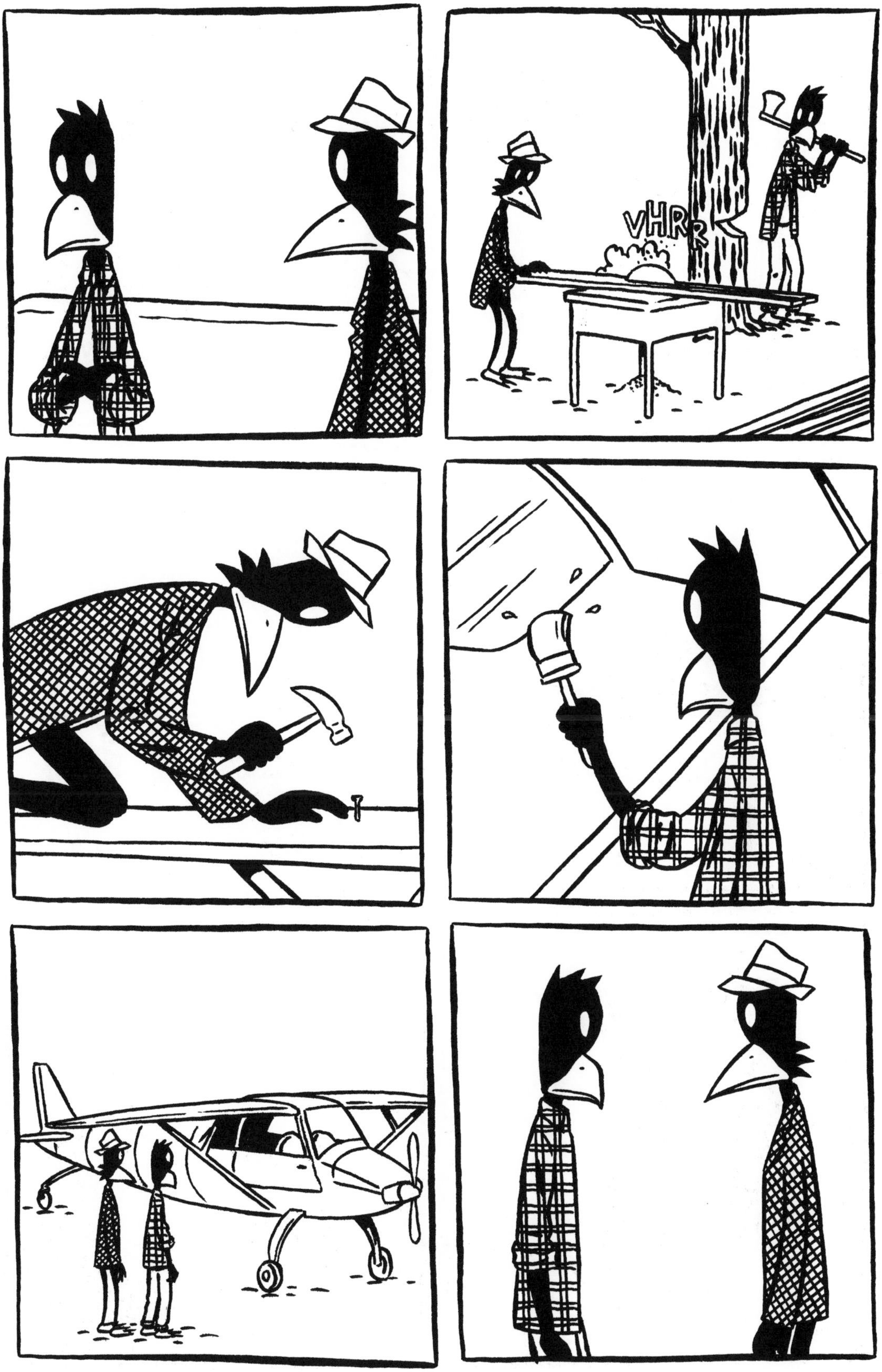
VHRR

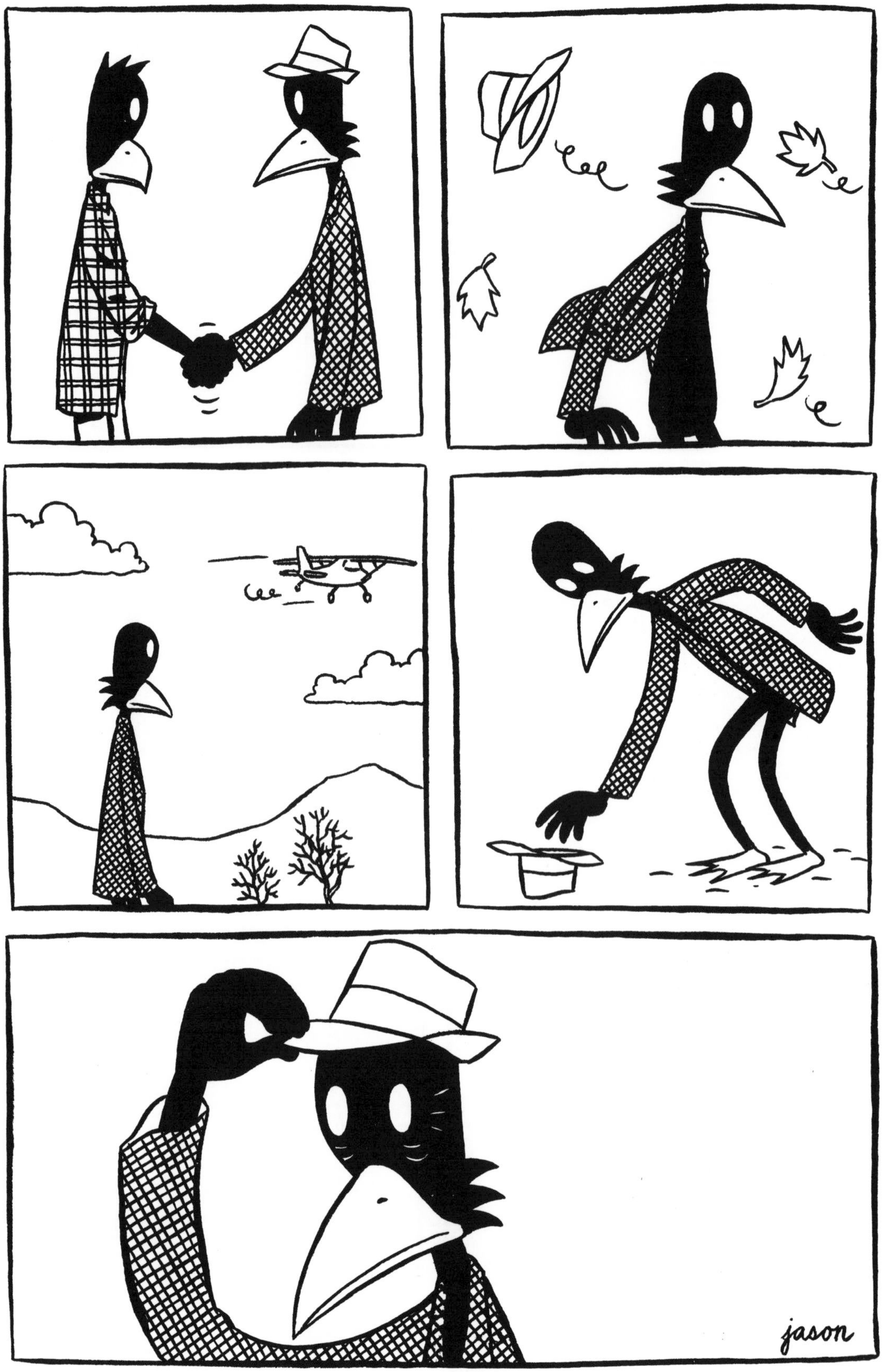
jason

4

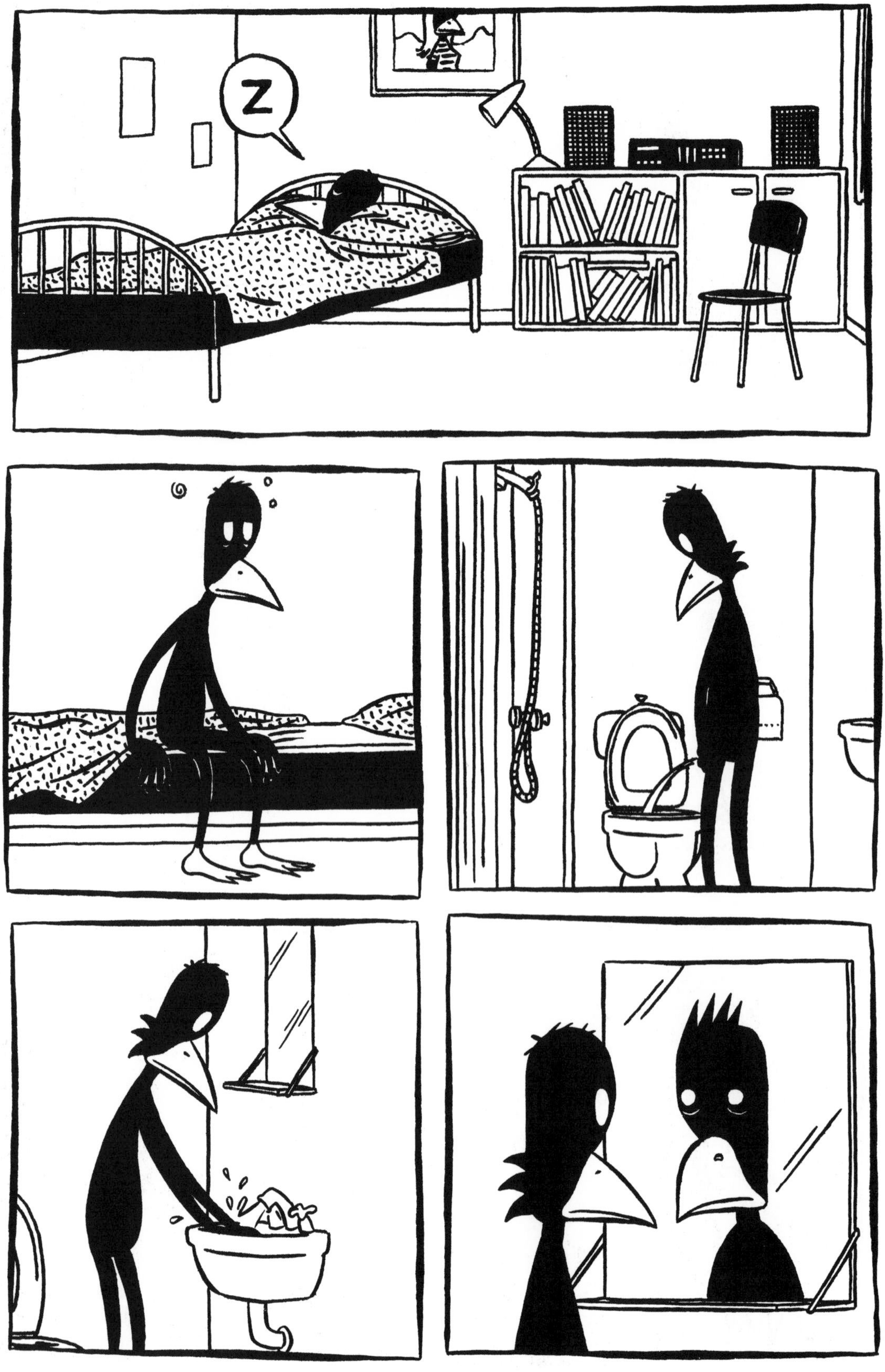
Z

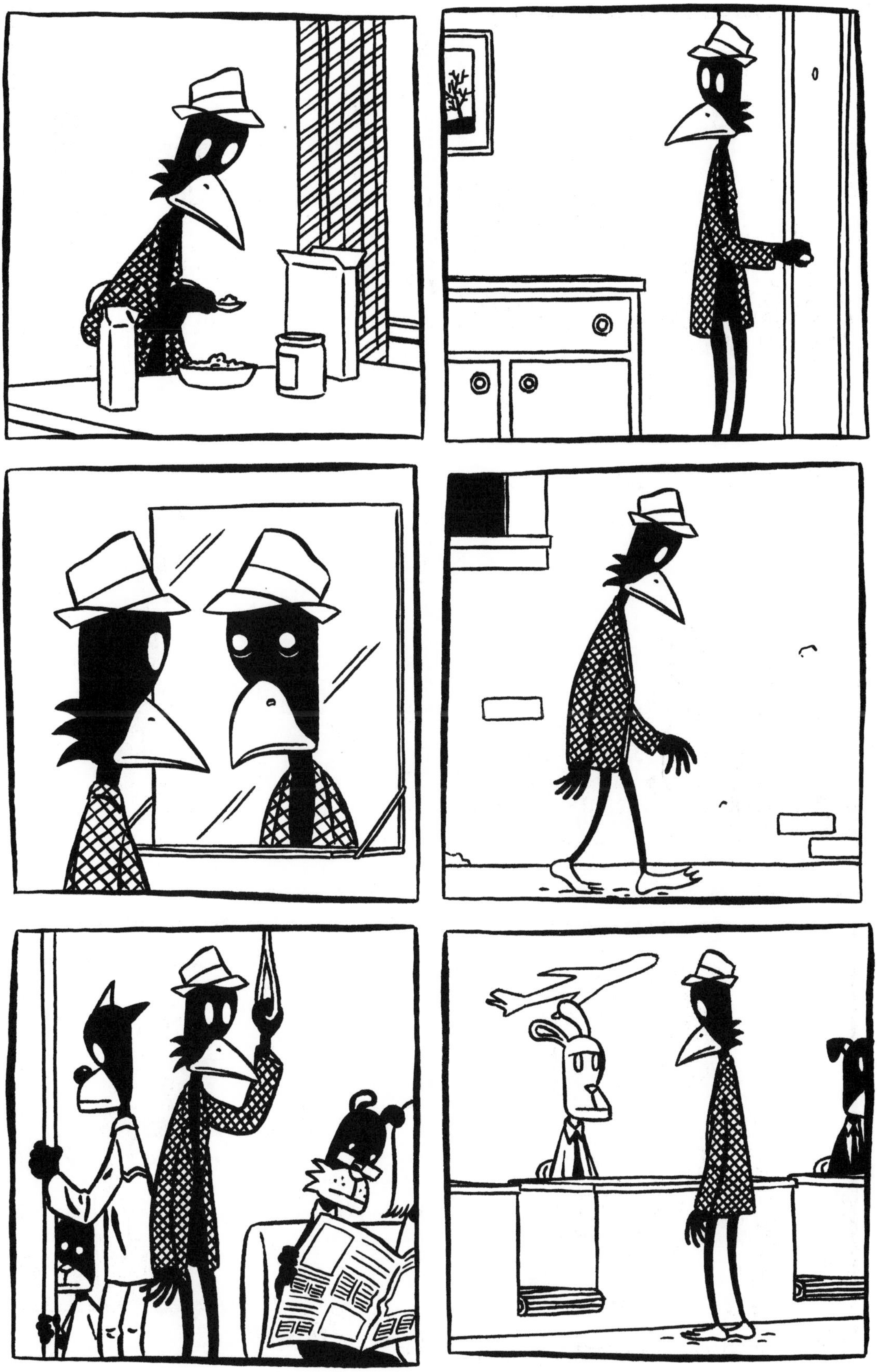

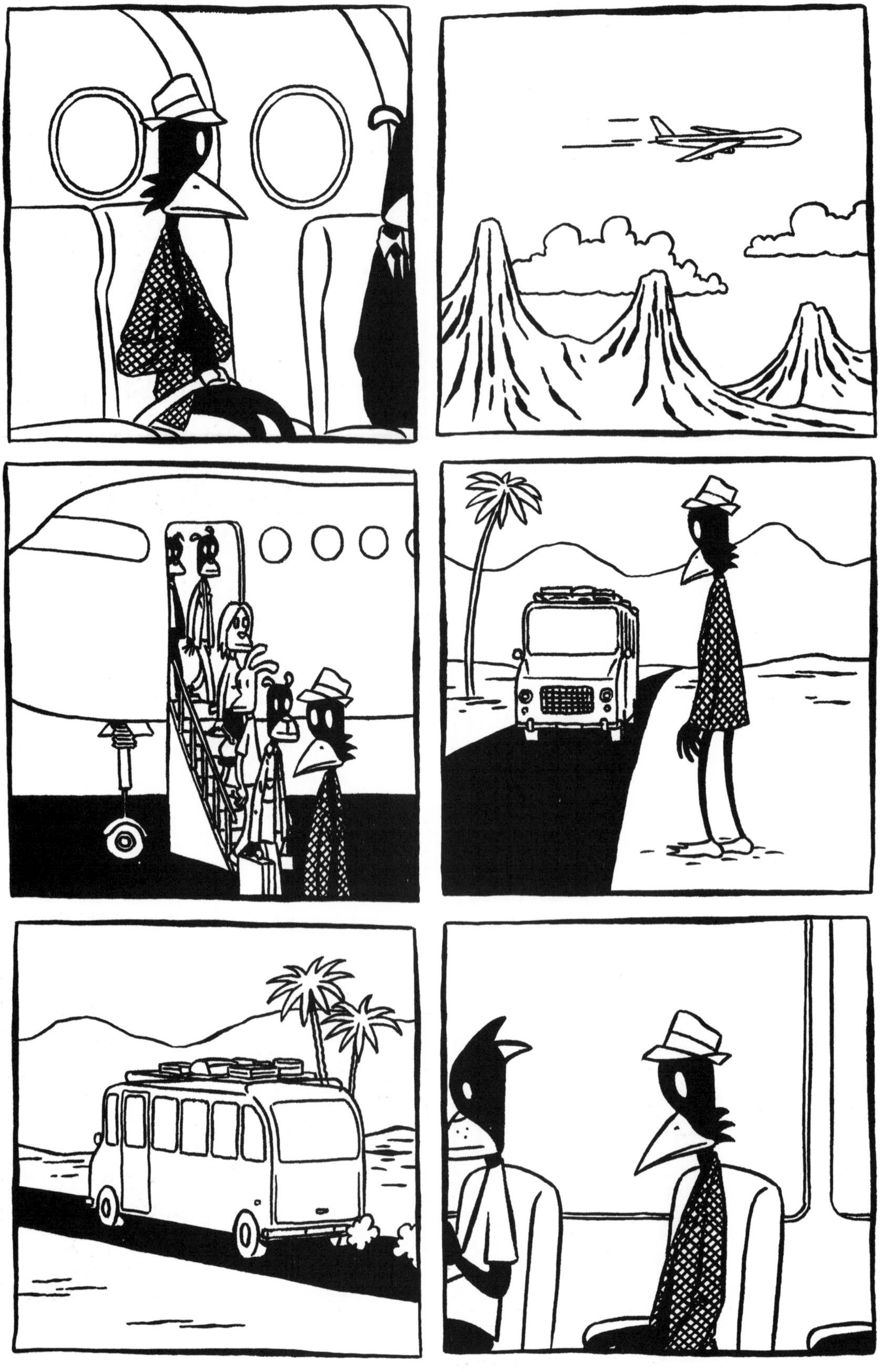

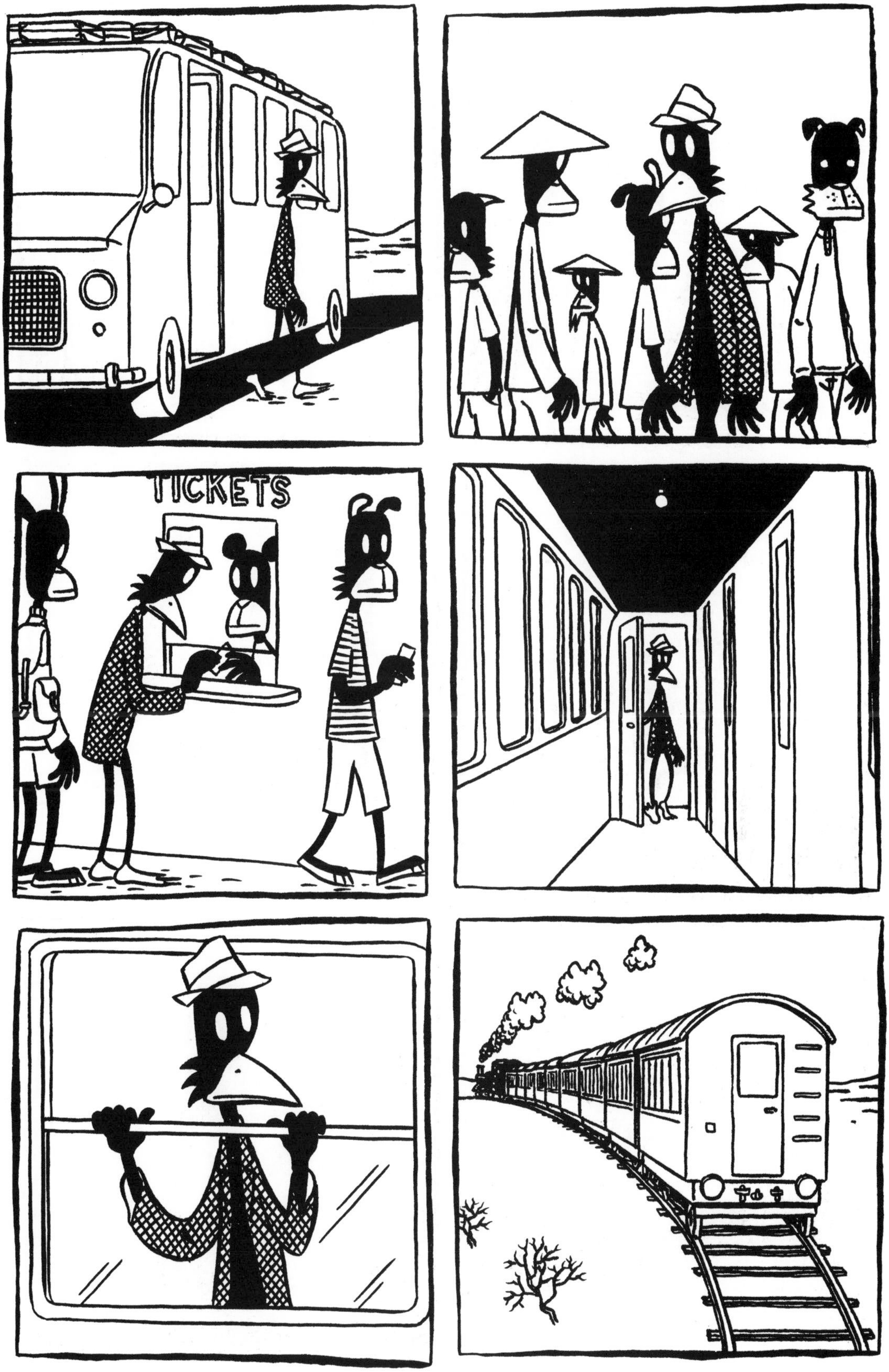
TICKETS

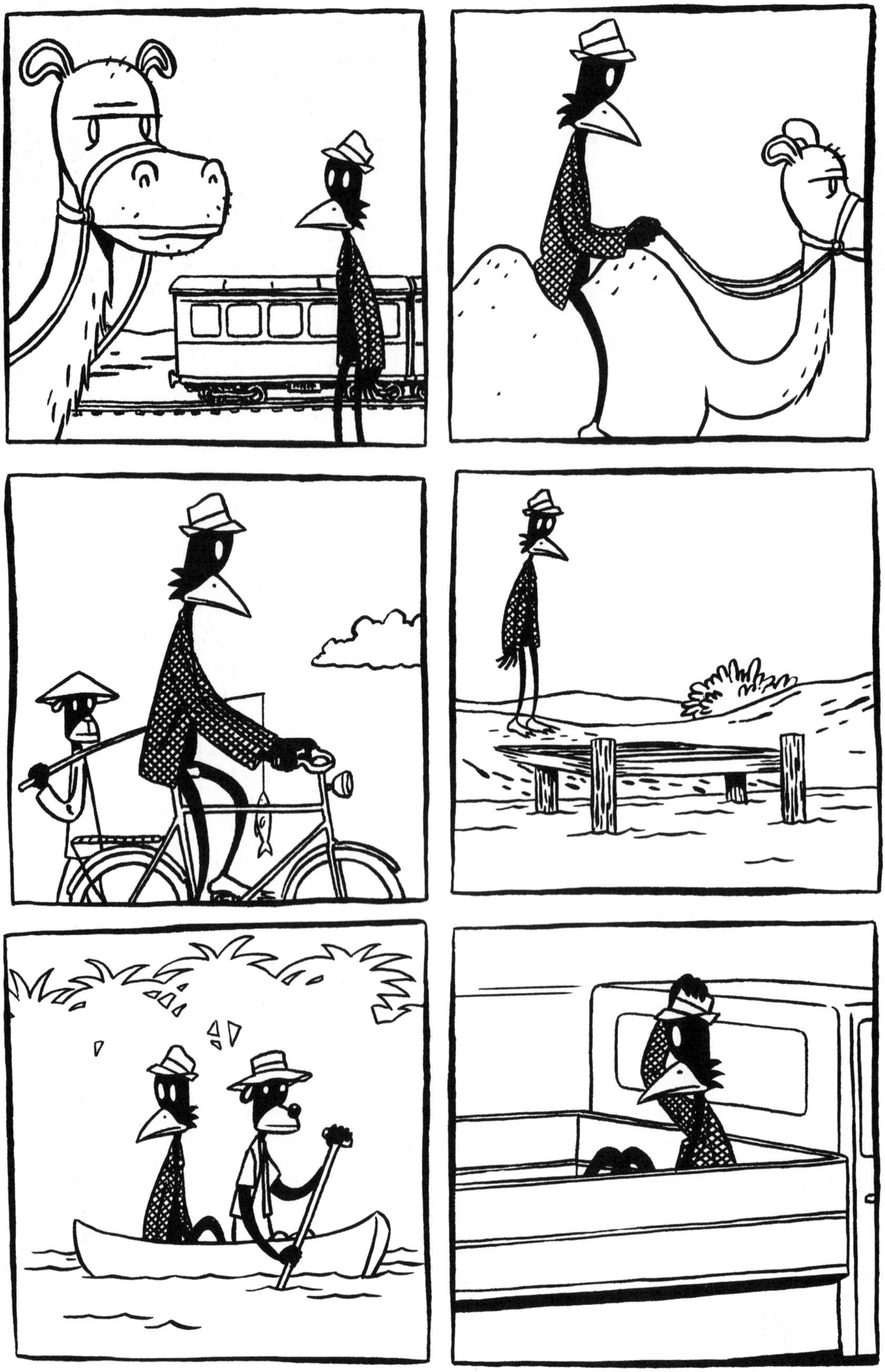

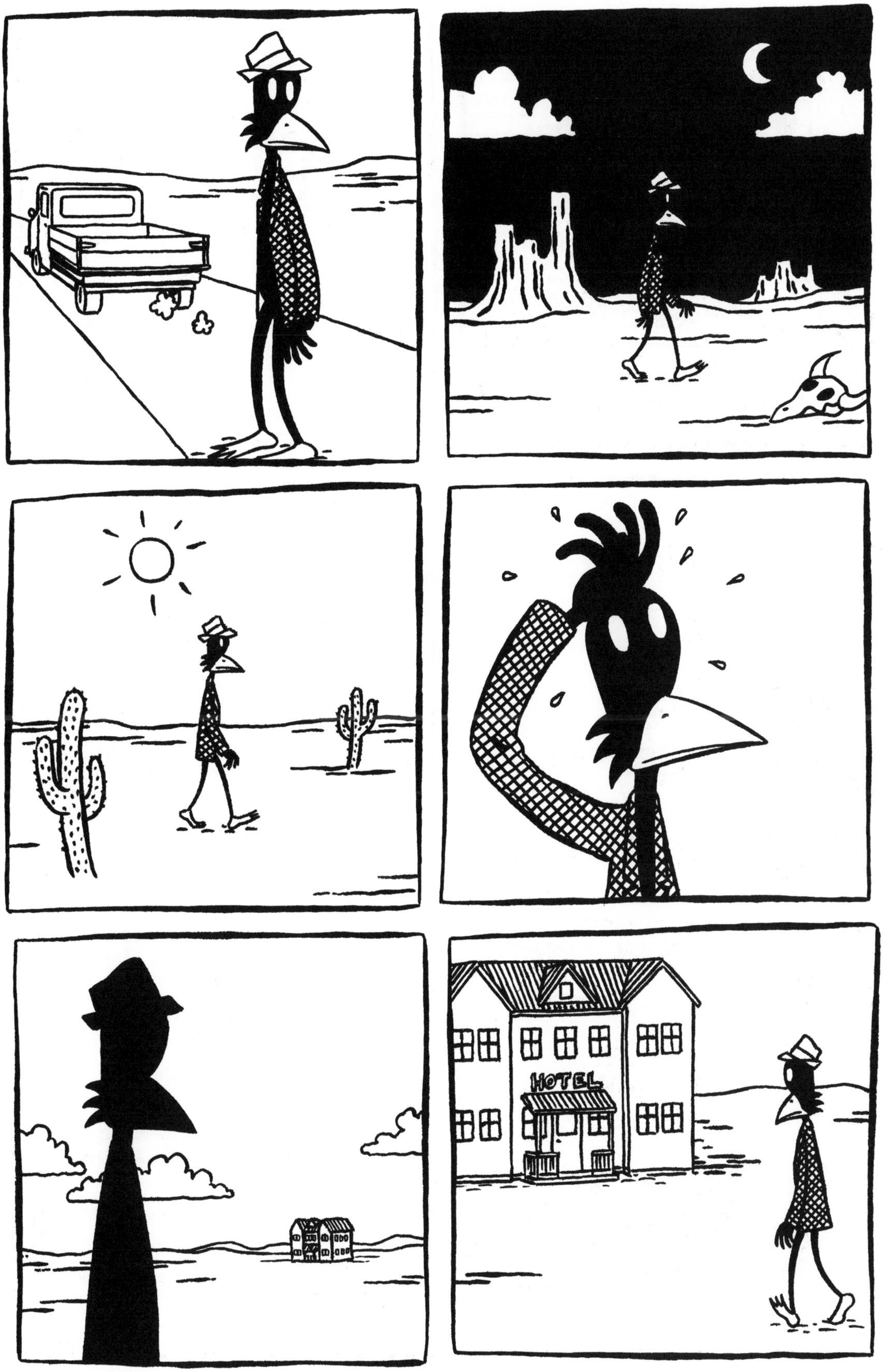
HOTEL

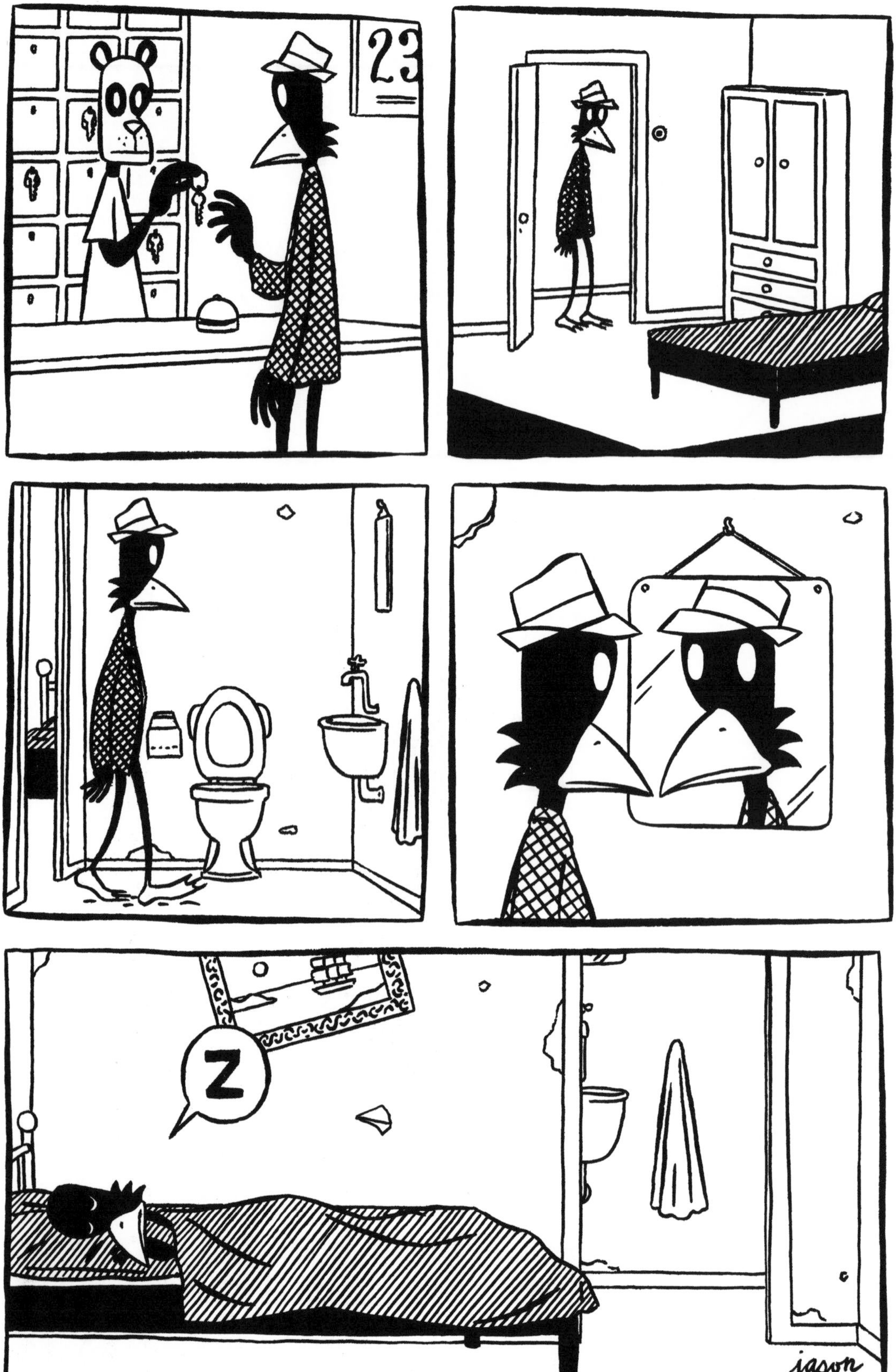
23
Z
jason

5

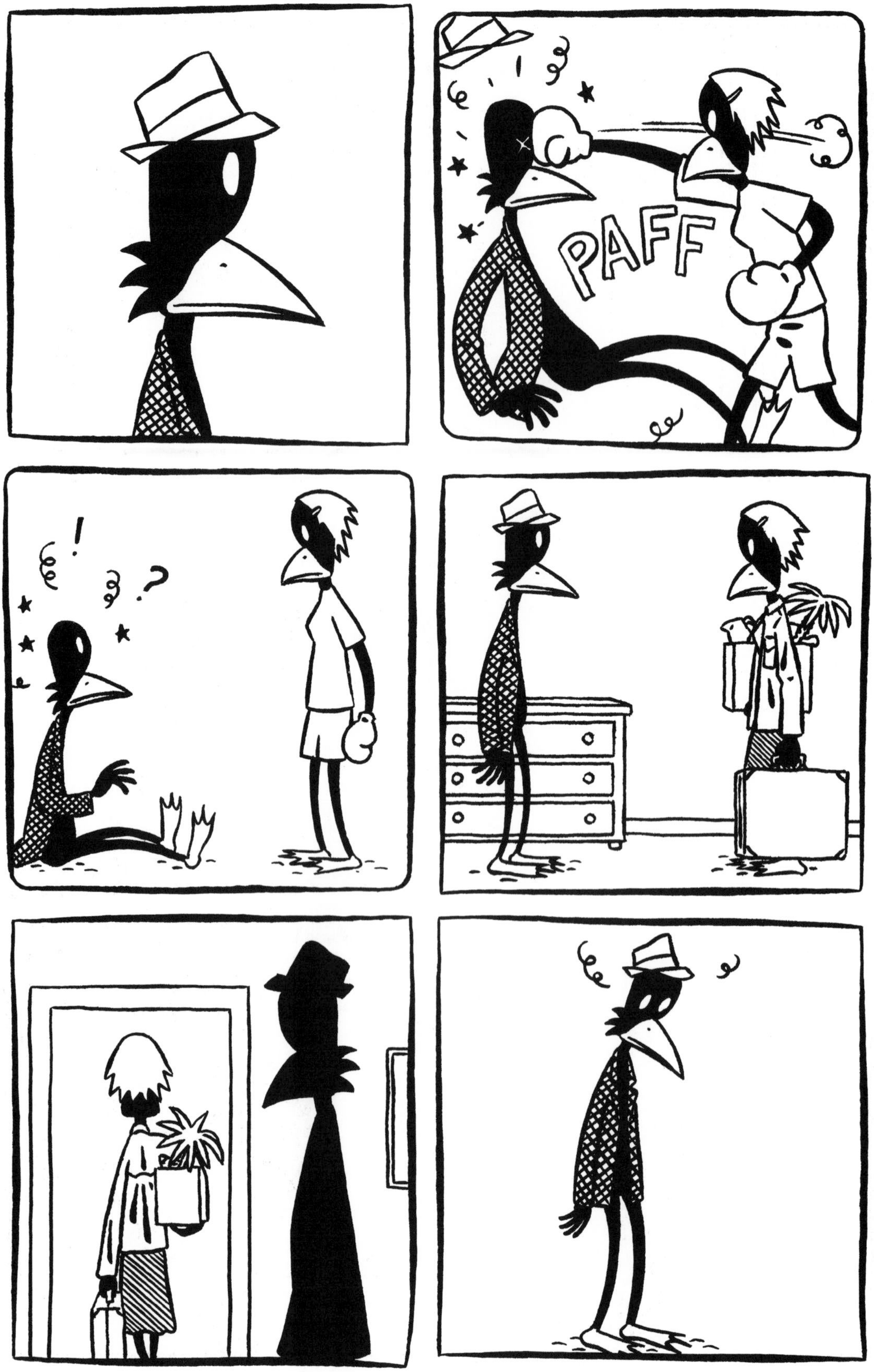
PAFF
!
?

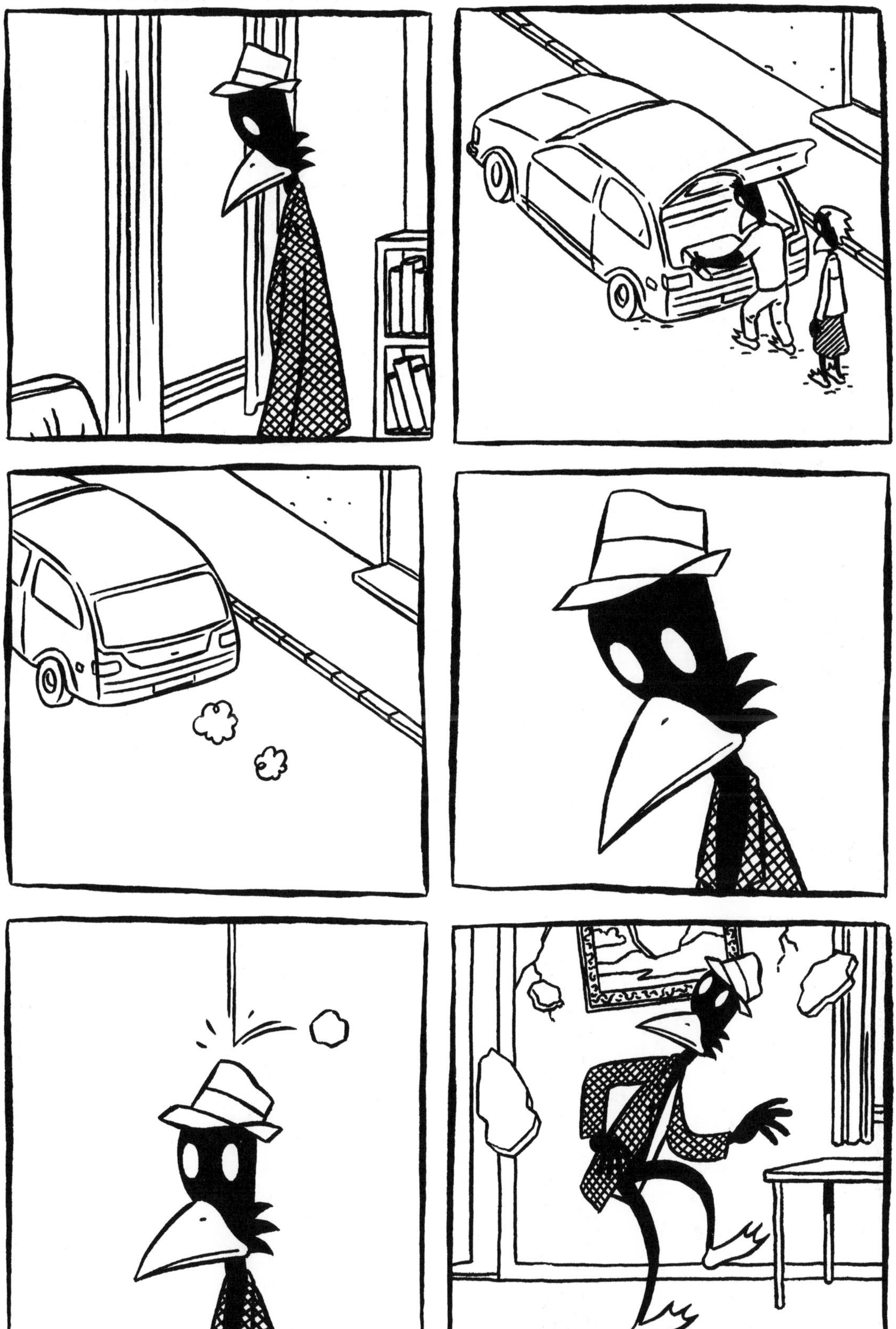

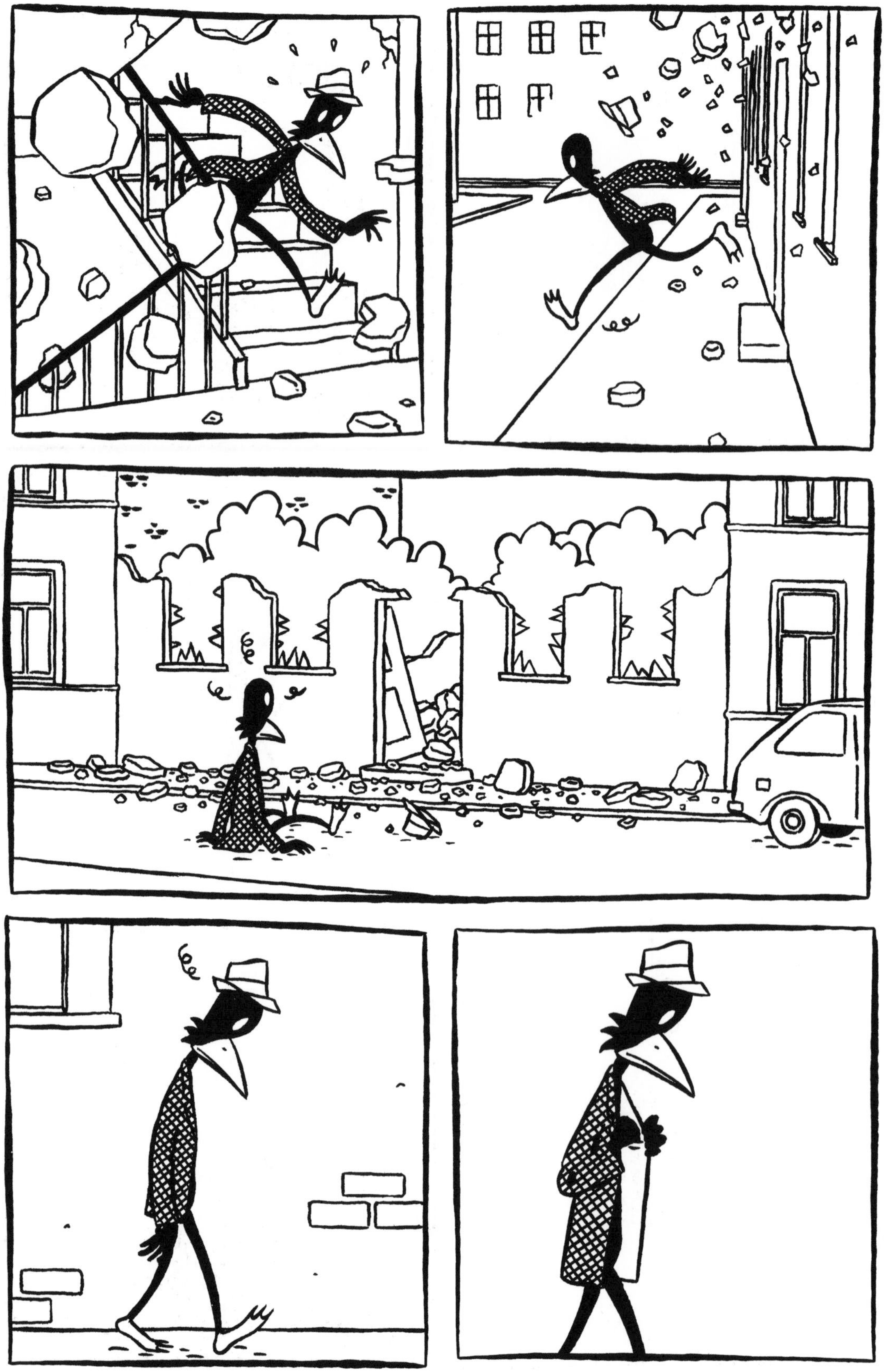

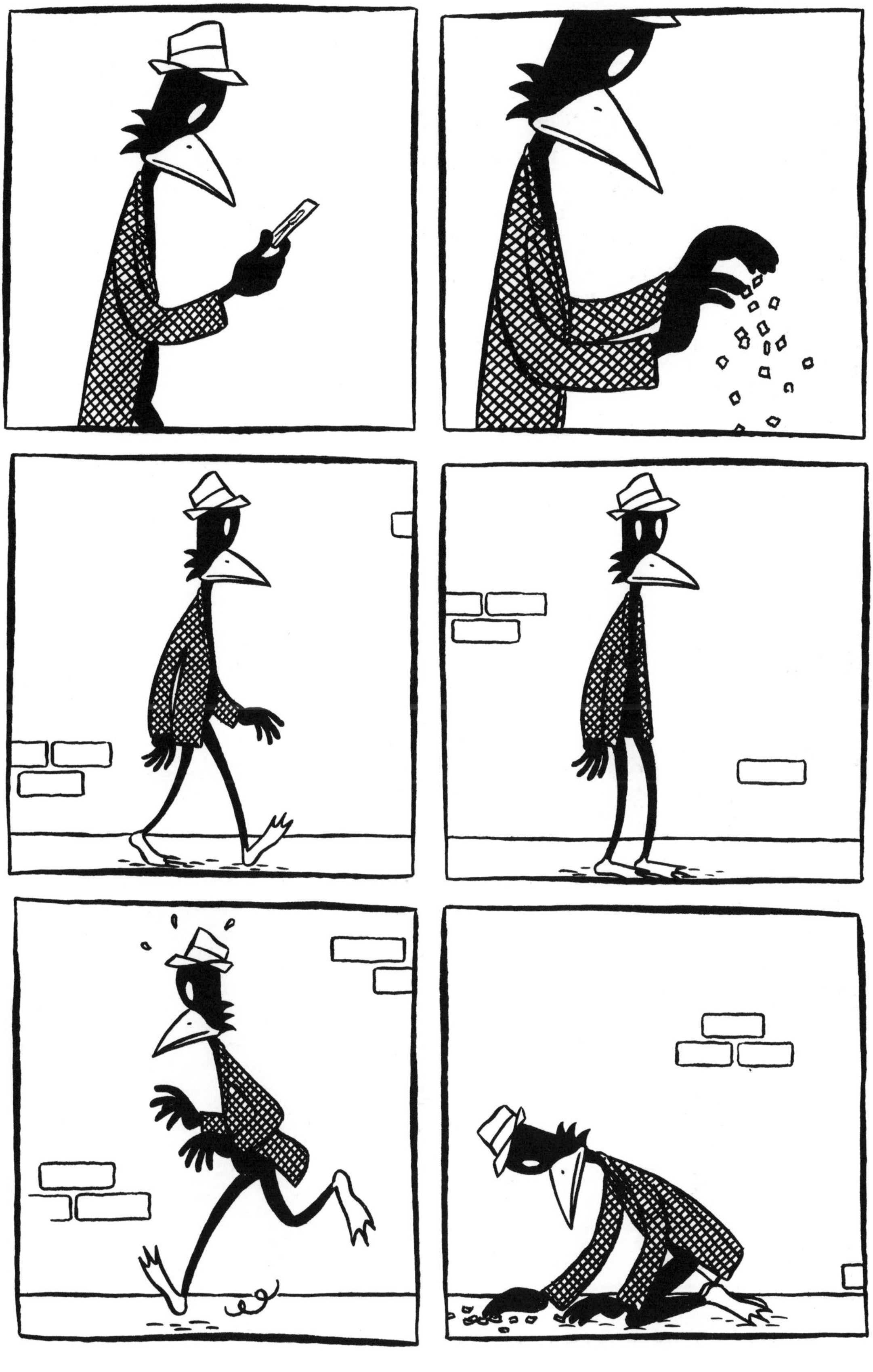

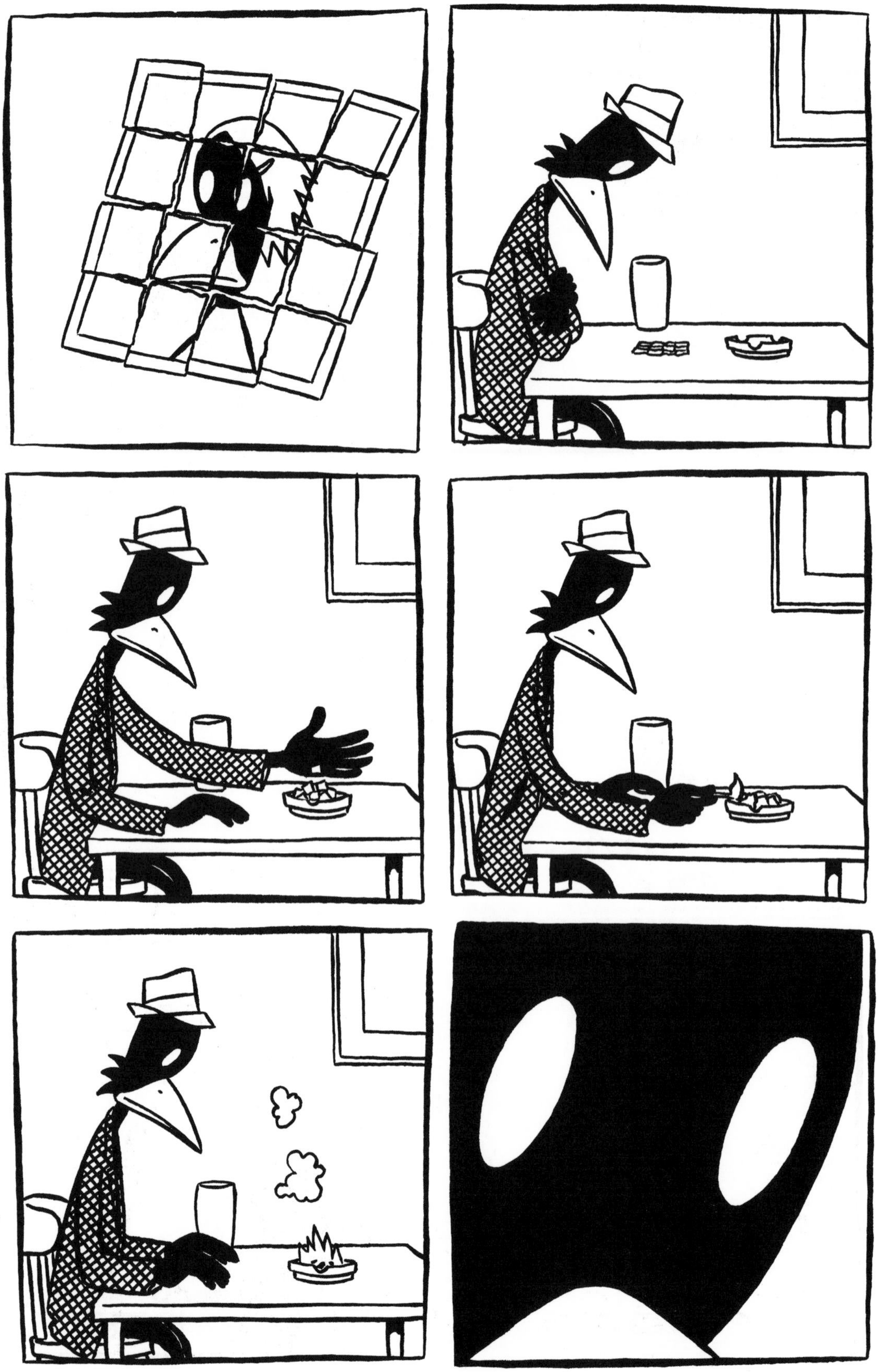

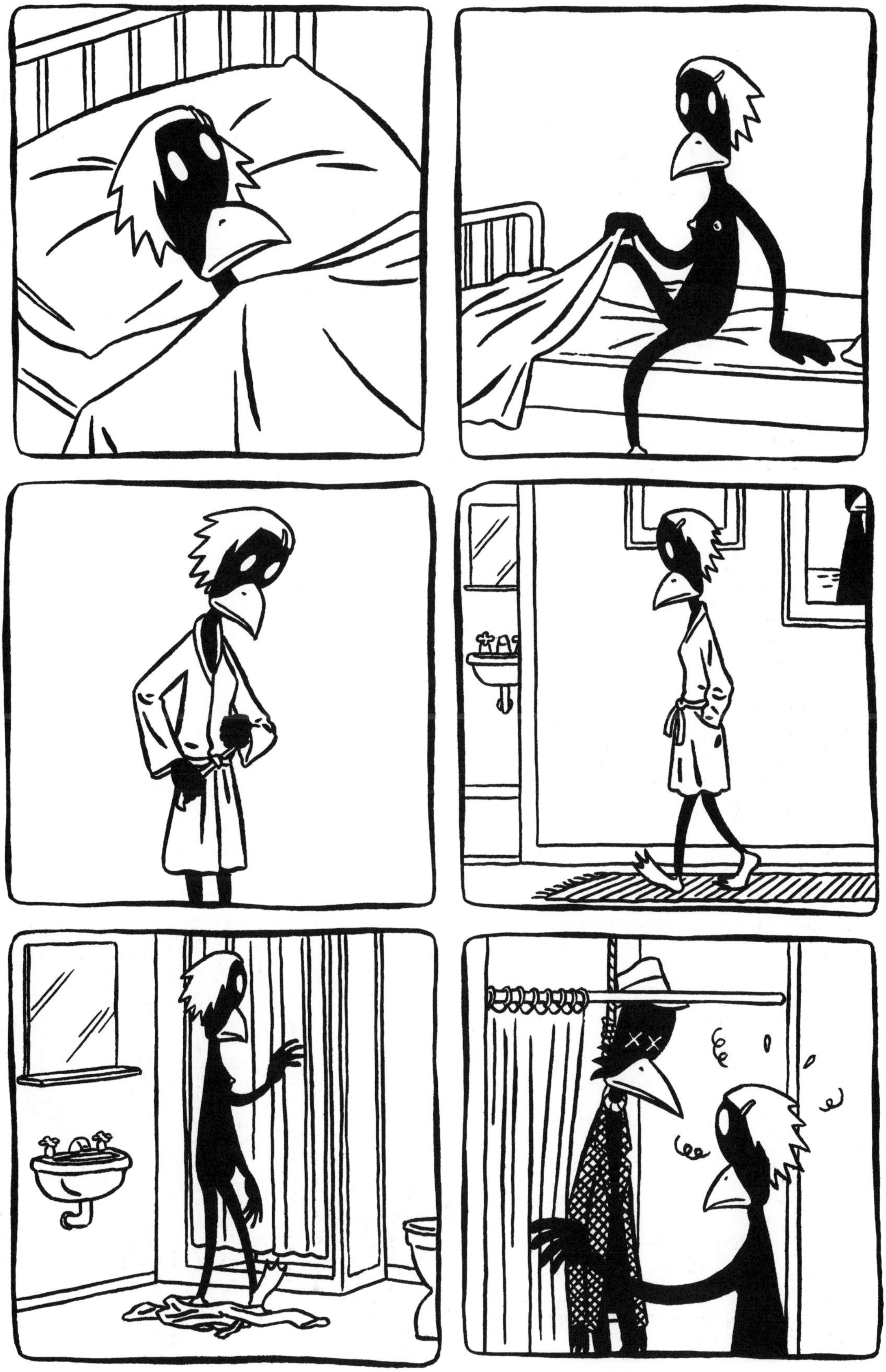

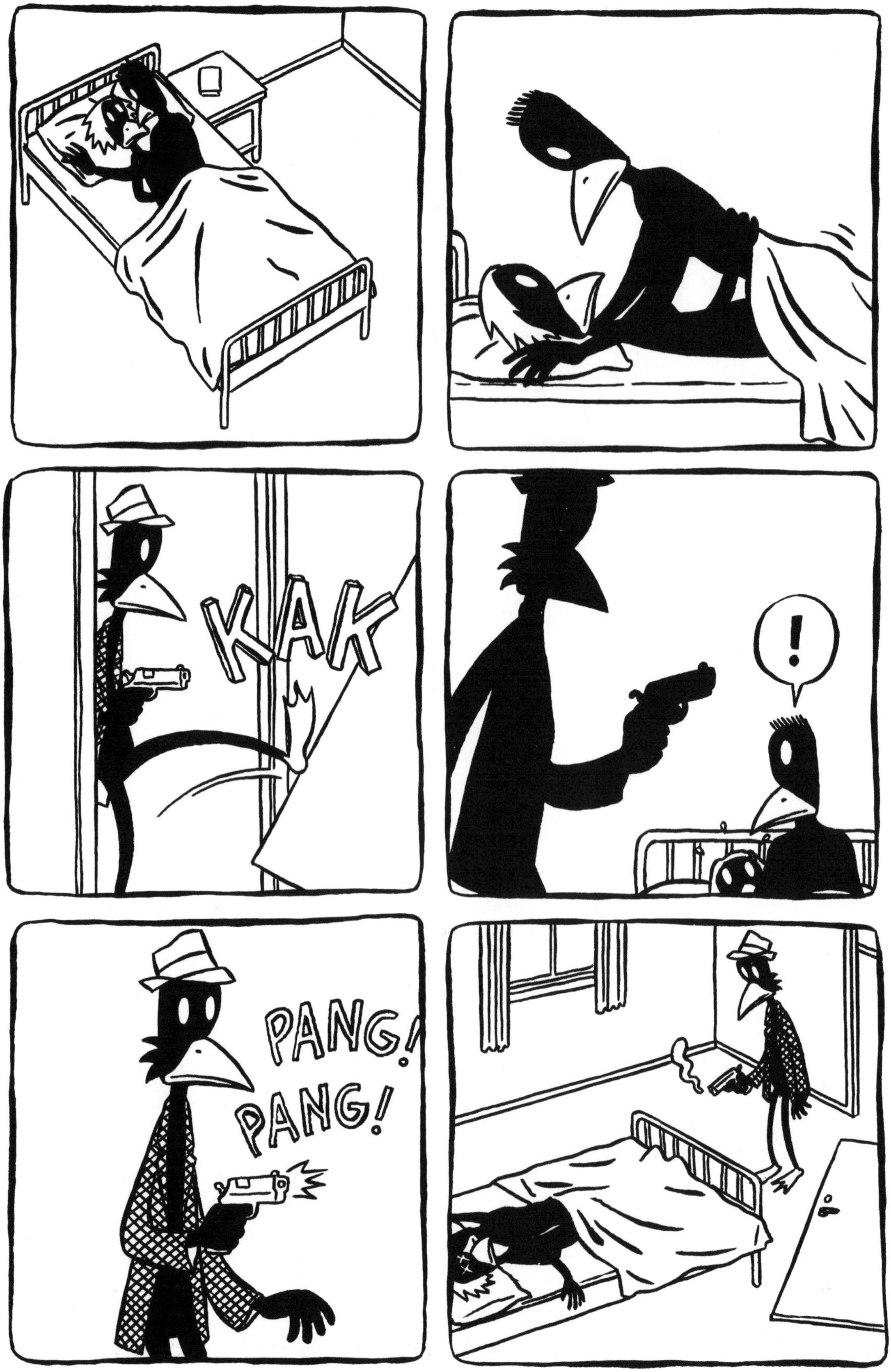
KAK
!
PANG!
PANG!

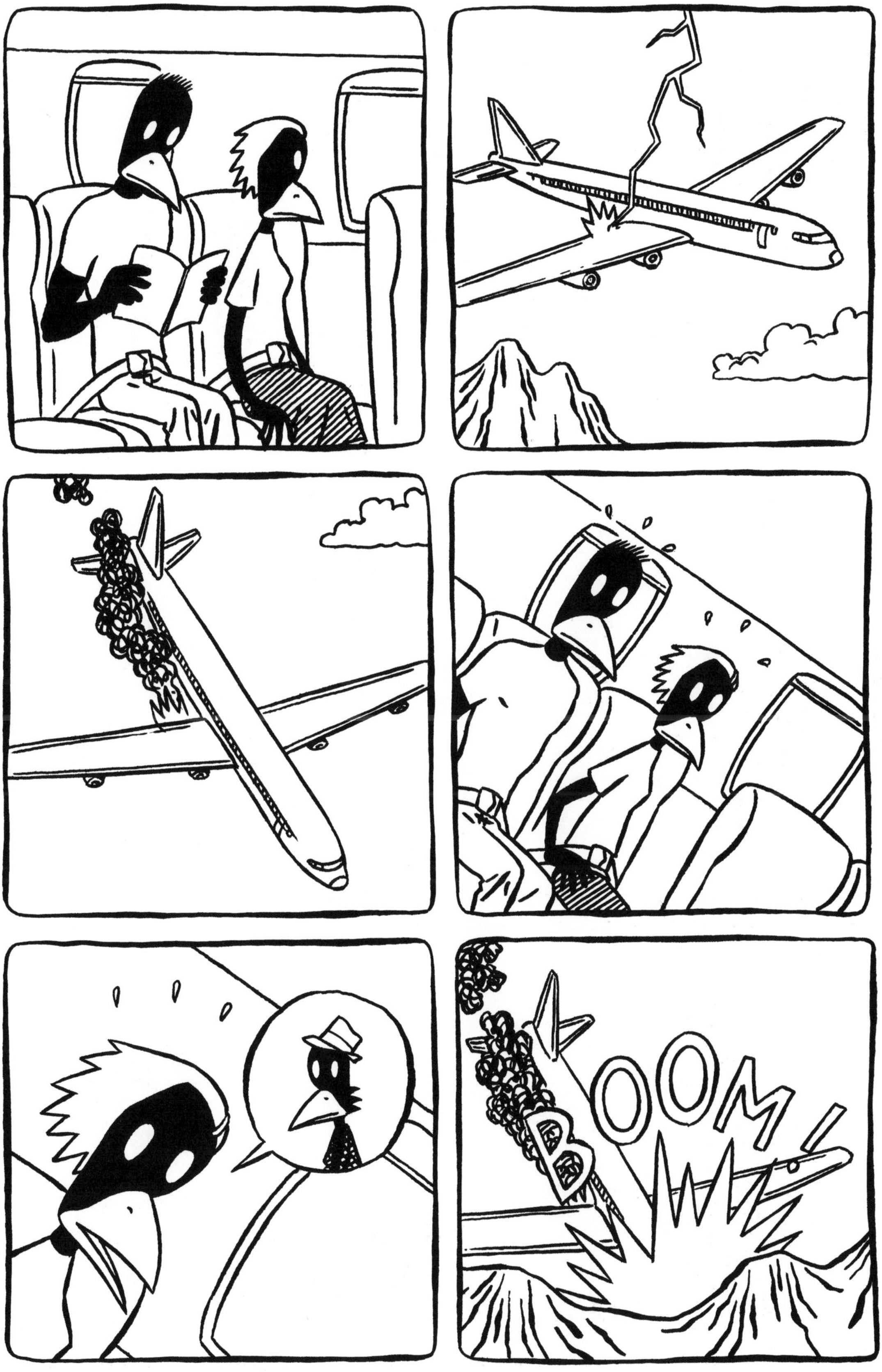
BOOM!

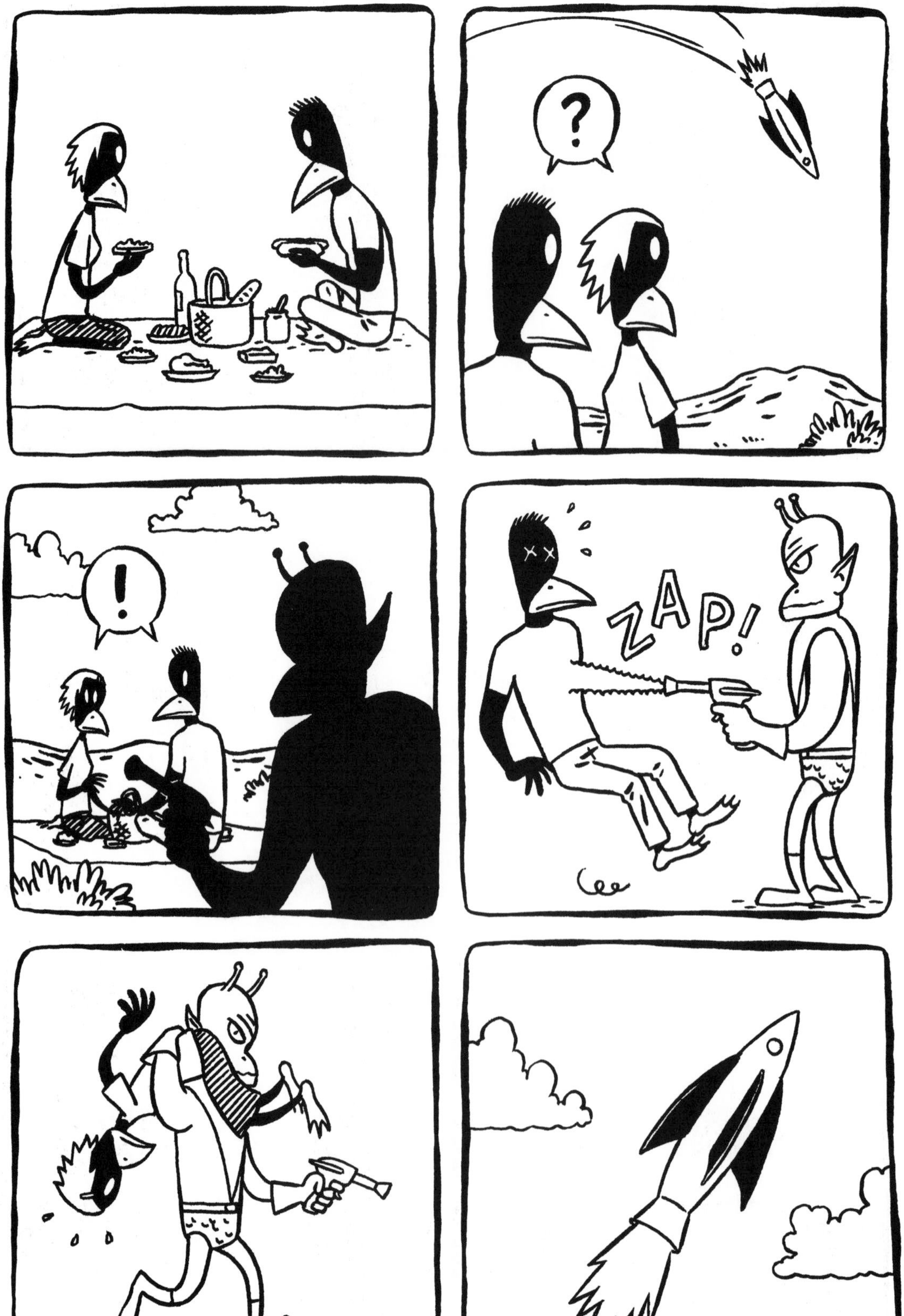
?
!
ZAP!
Lee
Lee

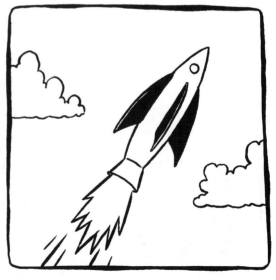

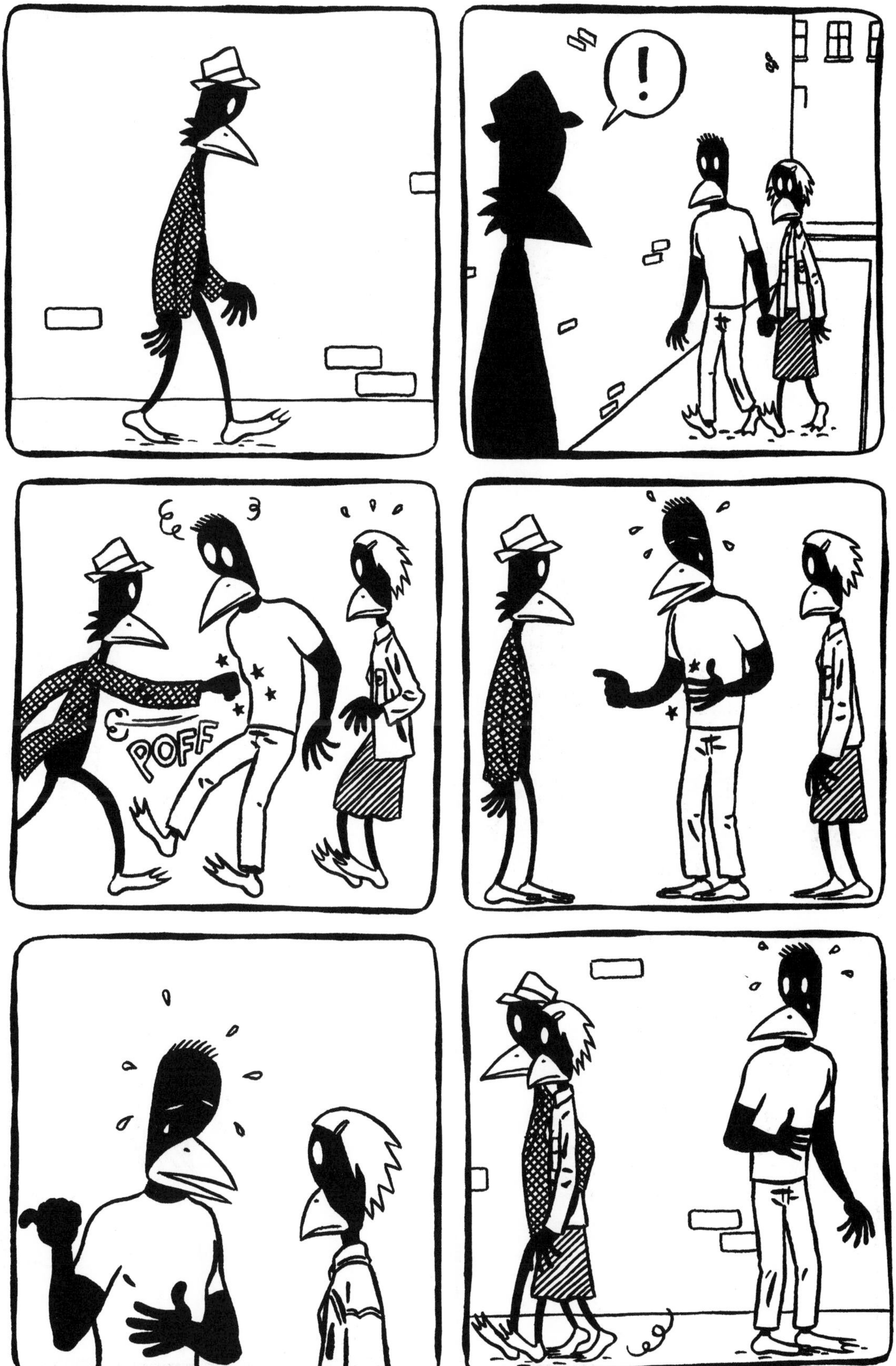
!
POFF

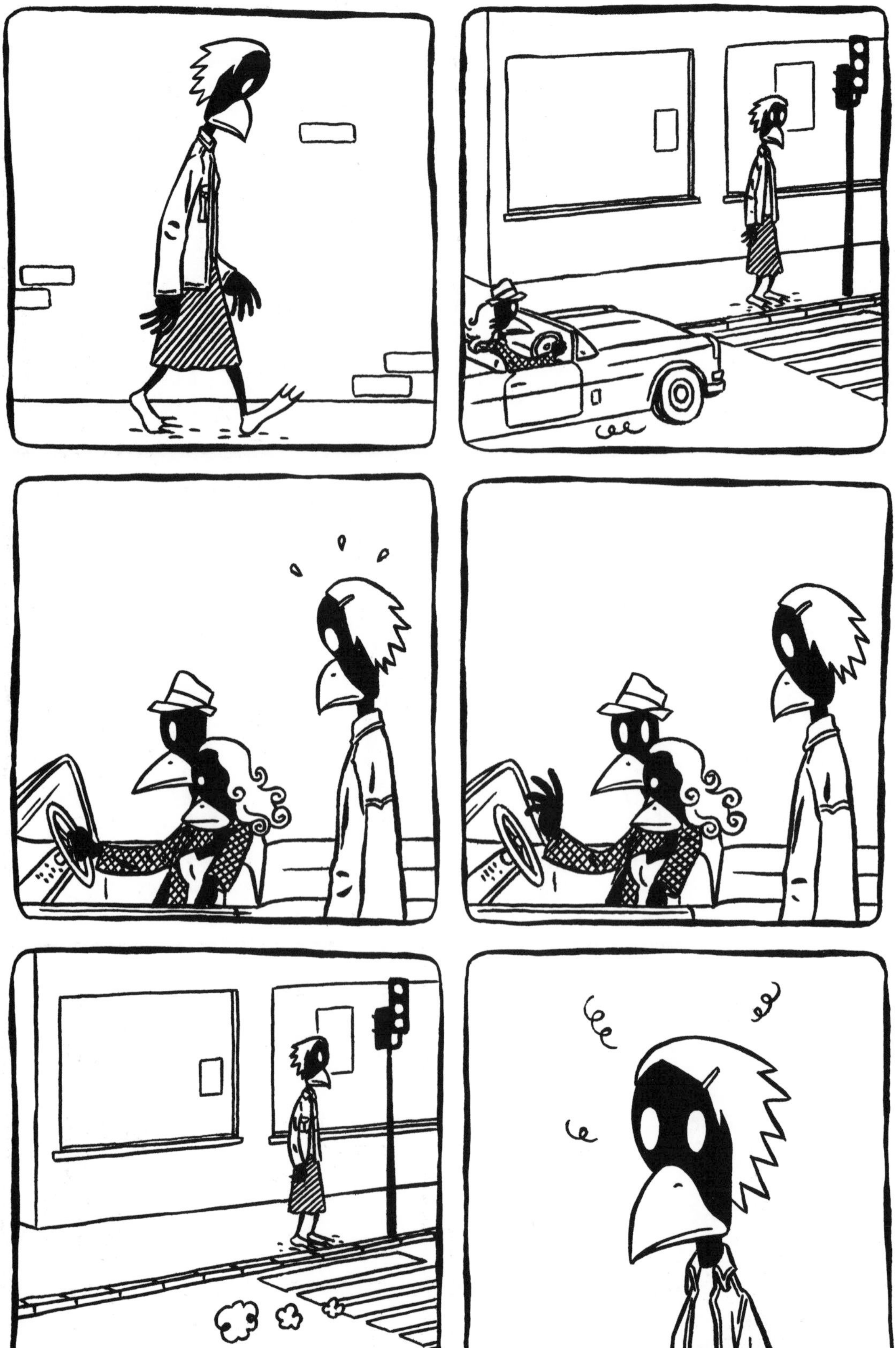

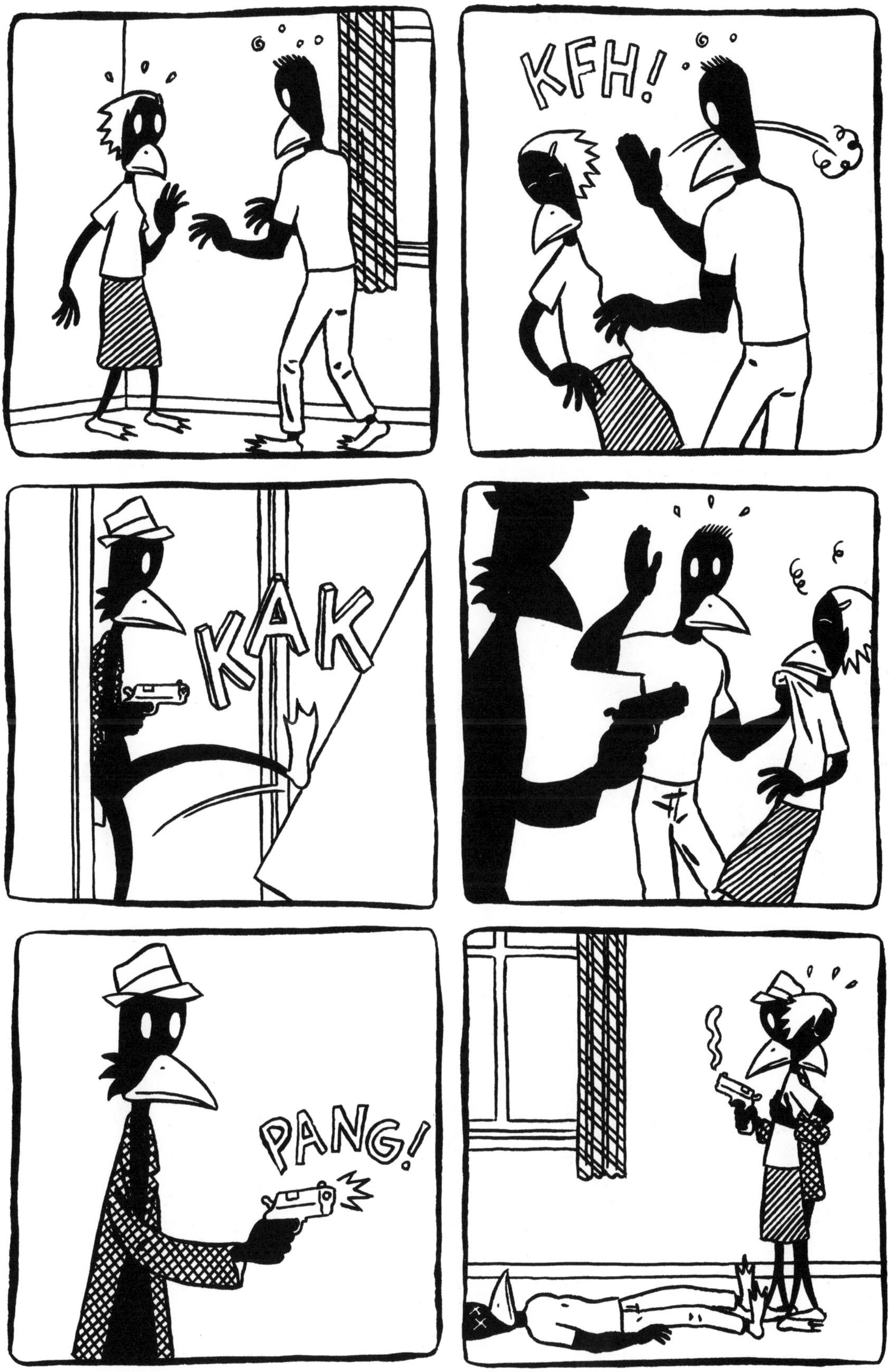
KFH!
KAK
PANG!

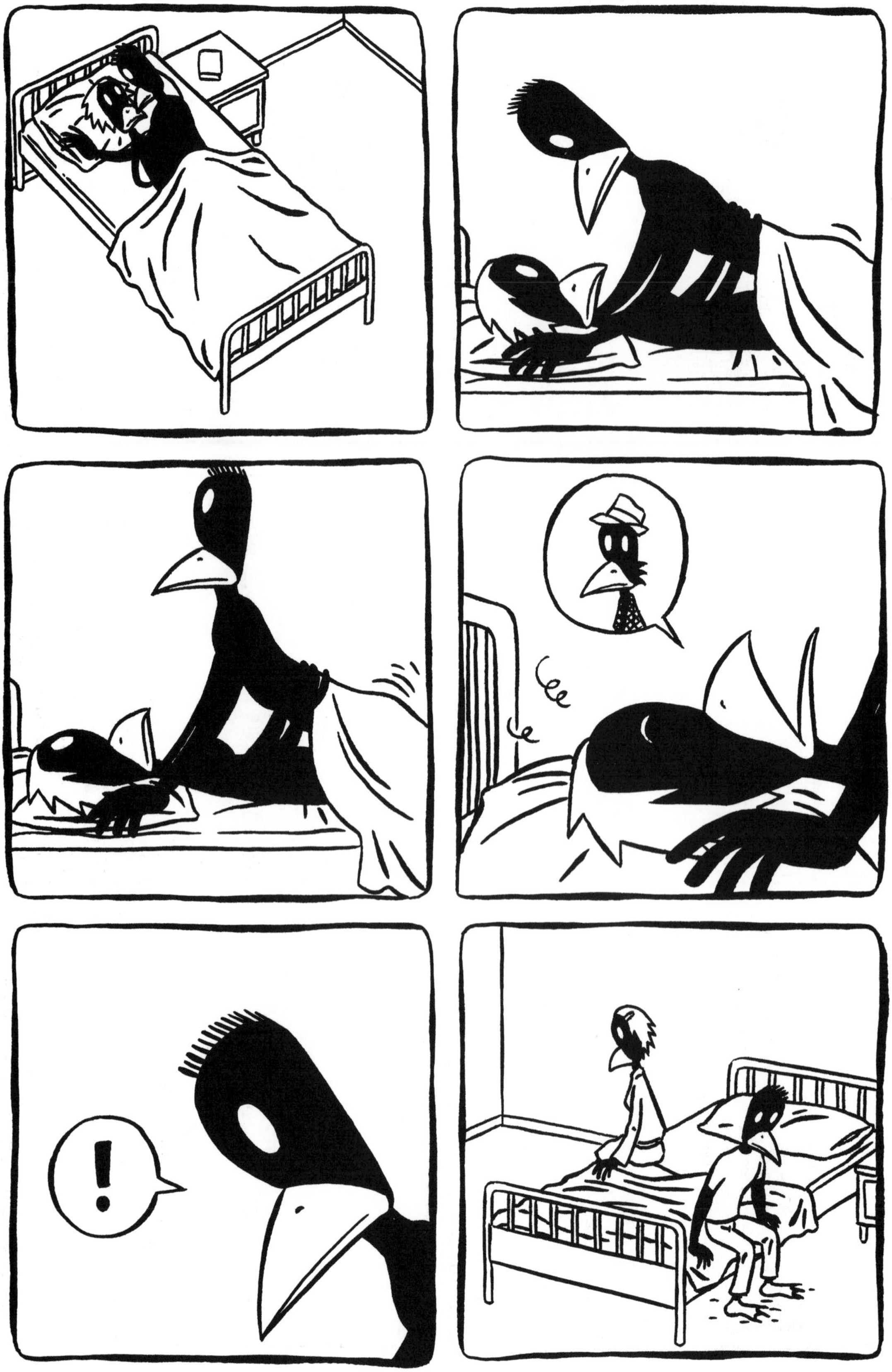
!

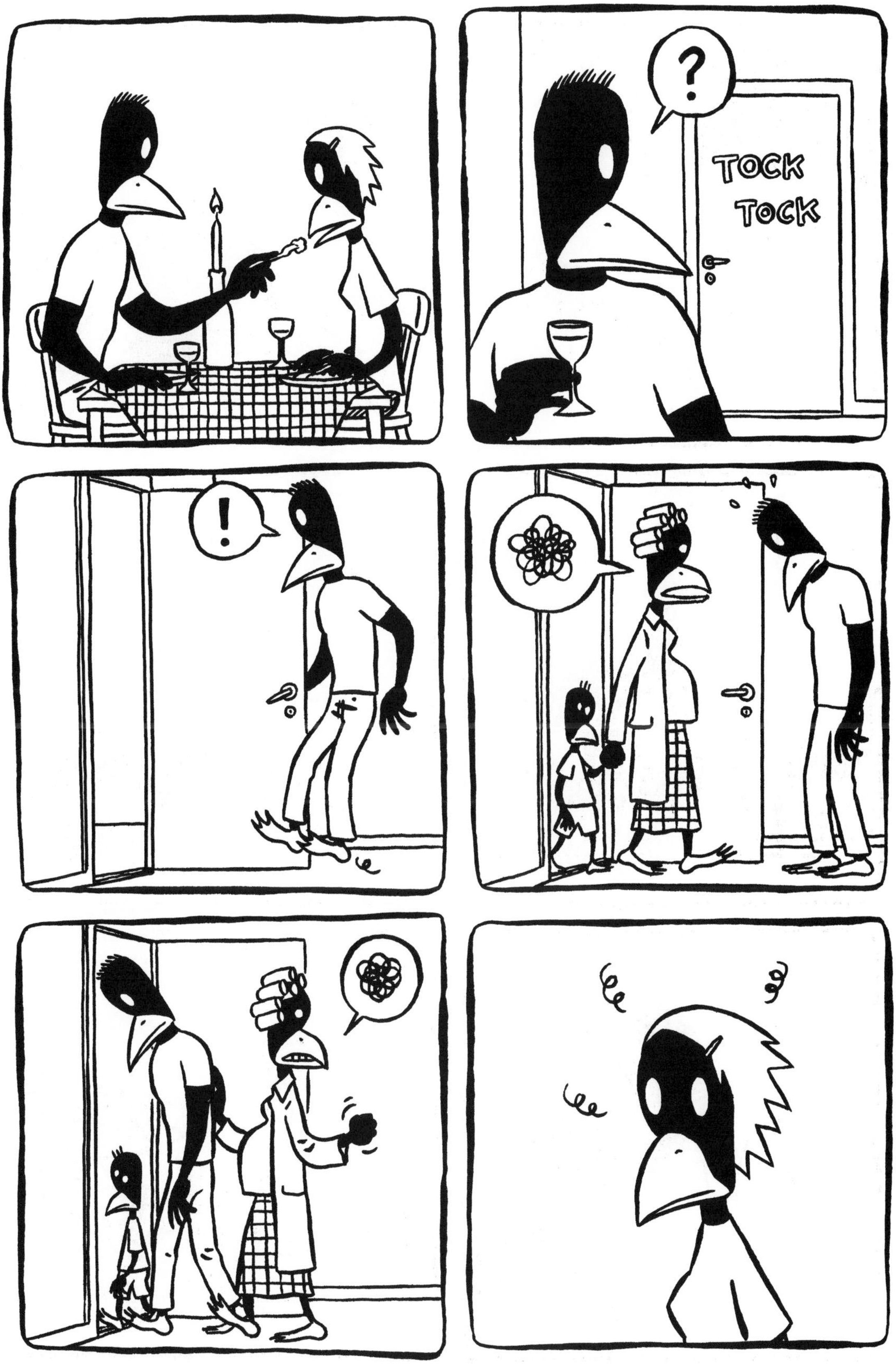
?
TOCK
TOCK
!

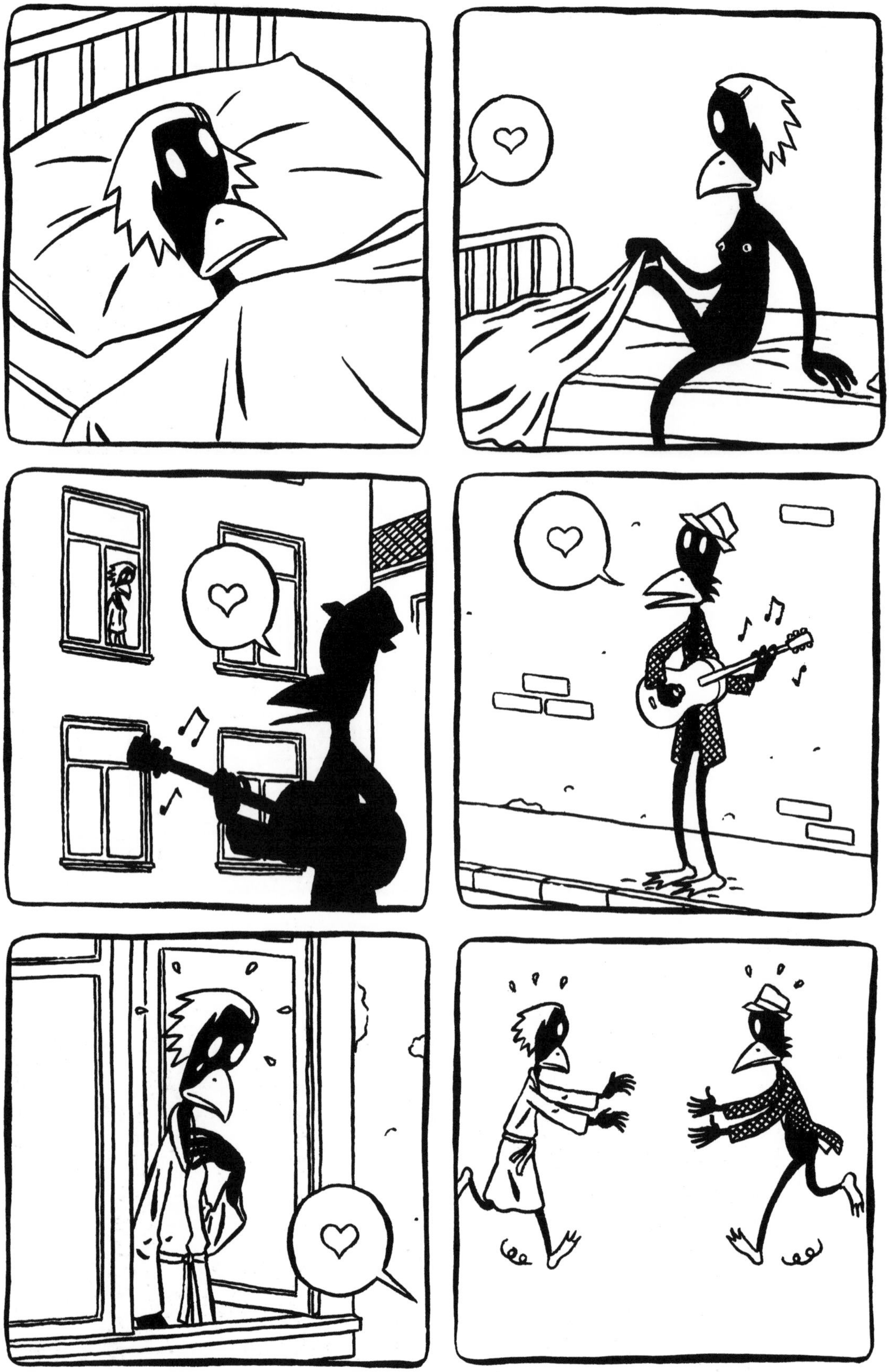

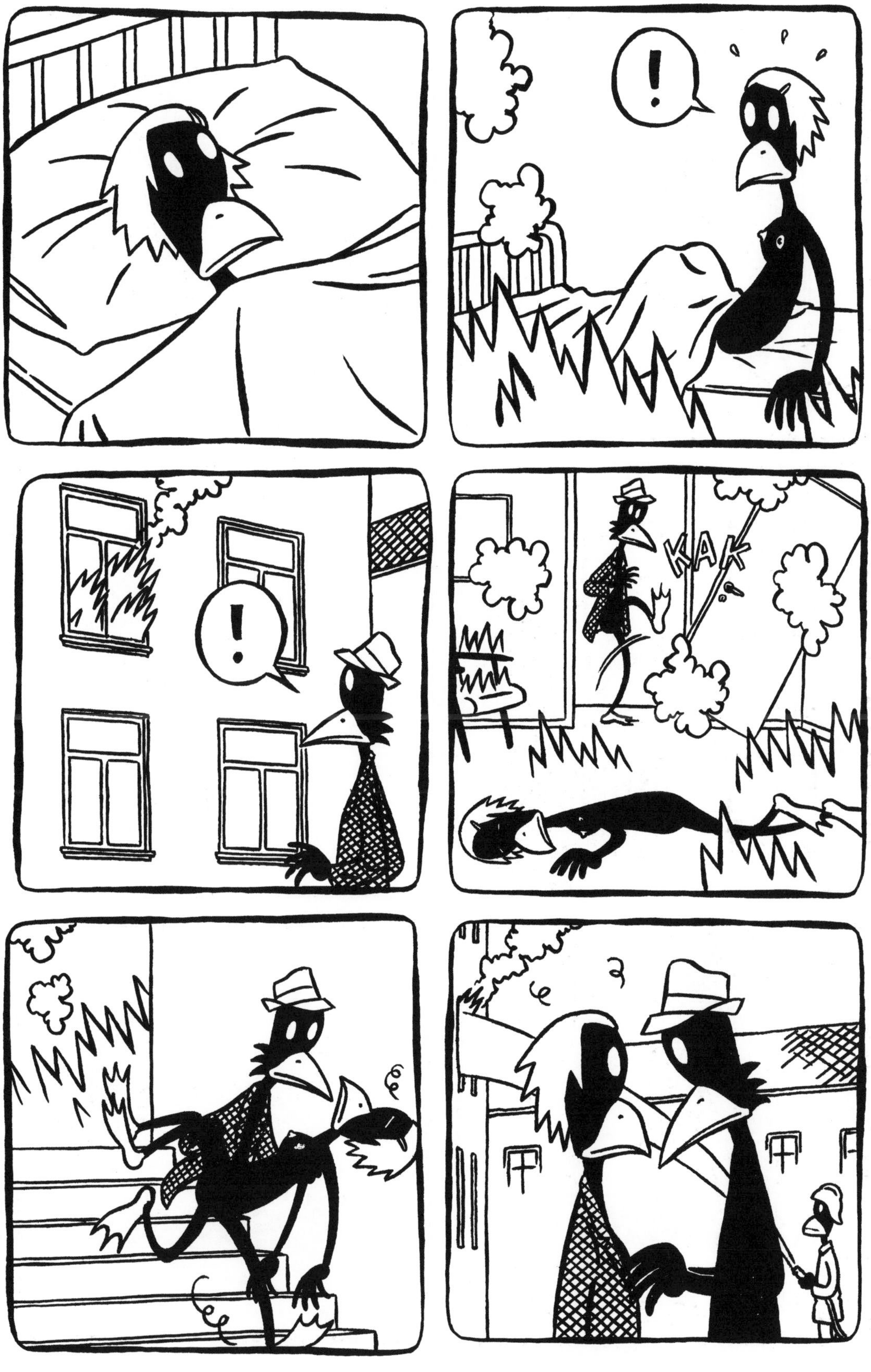
!
!
KAK

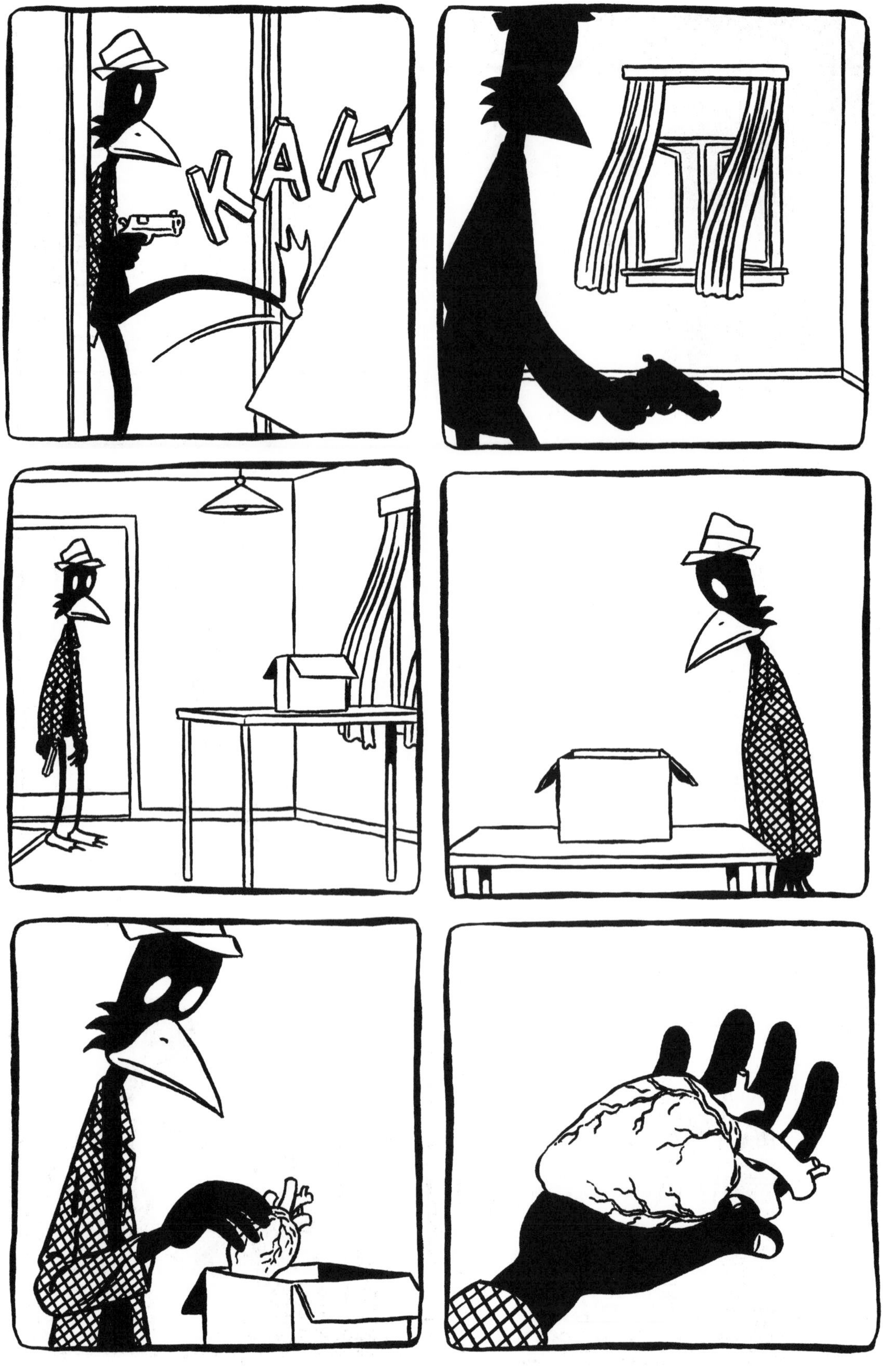
KAK

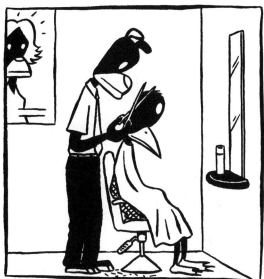

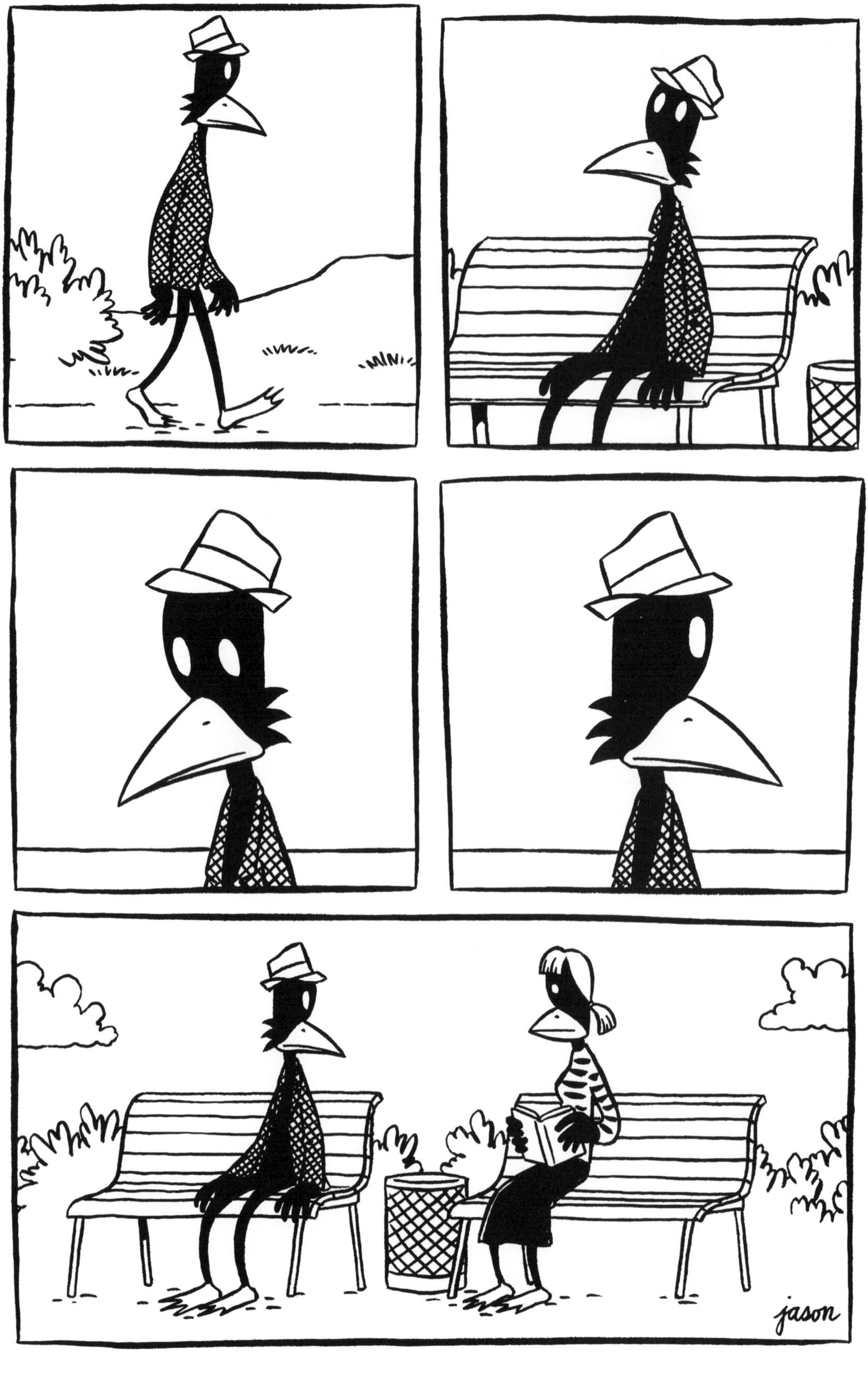
jason

6

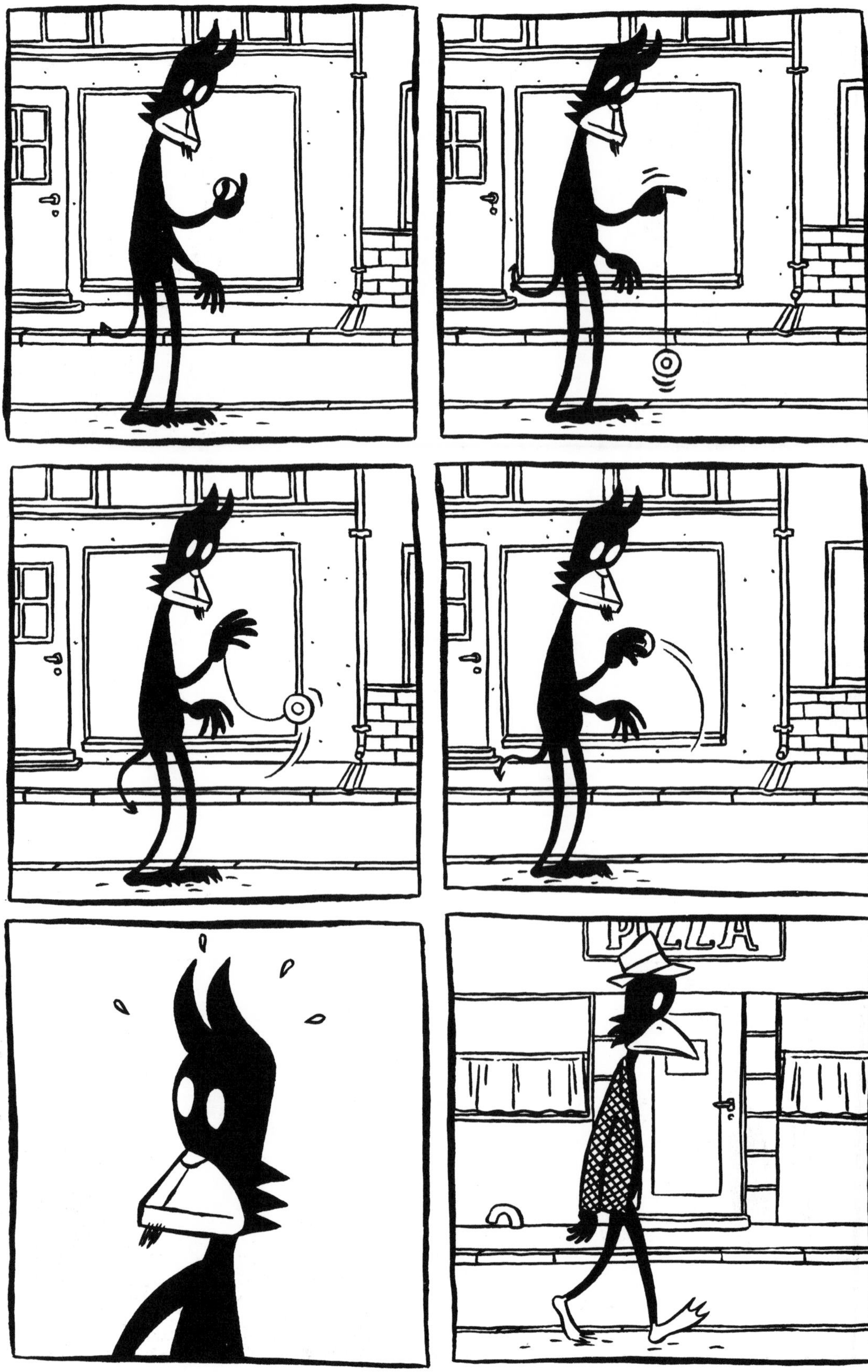
PIZZA

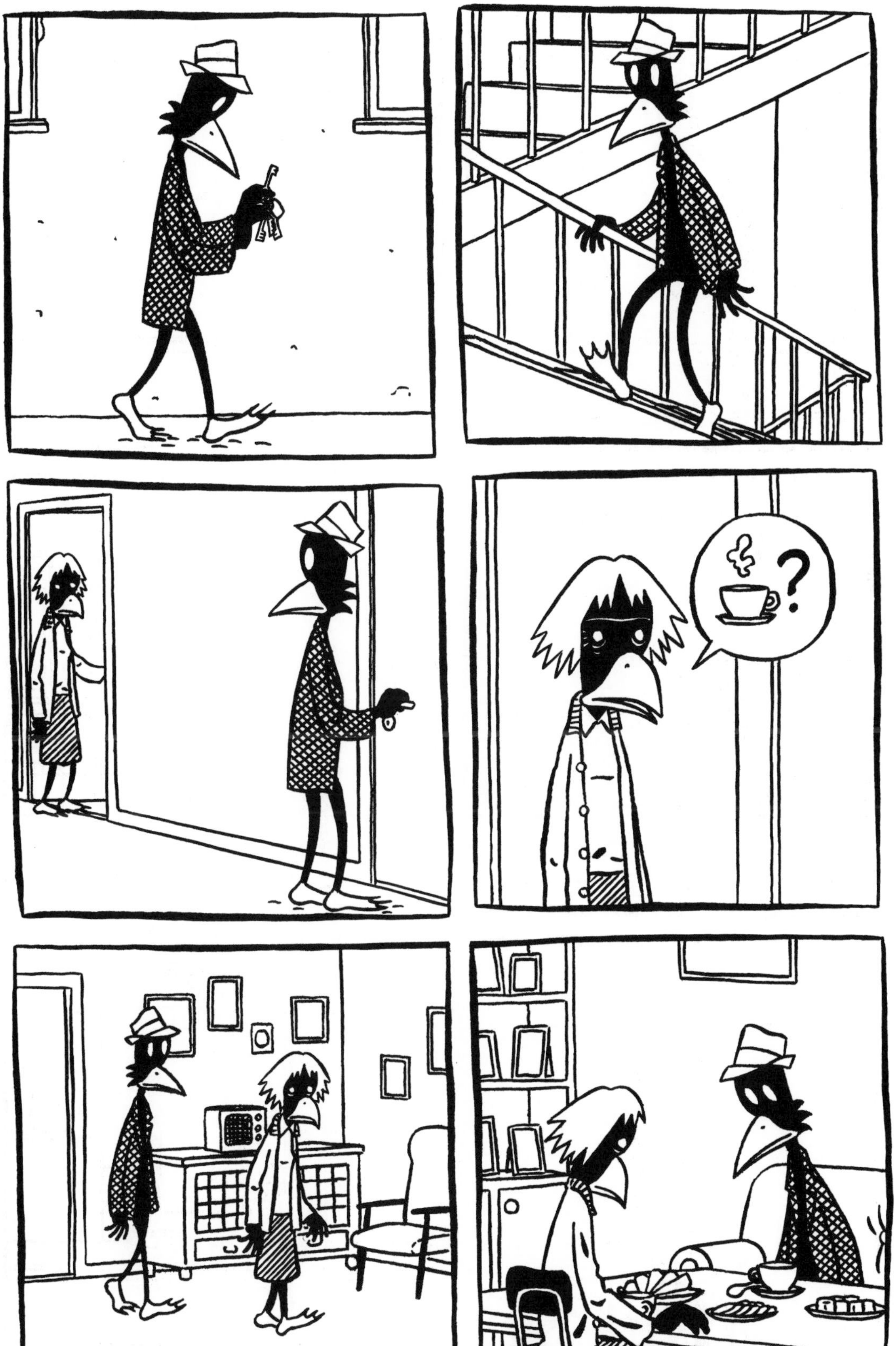
?

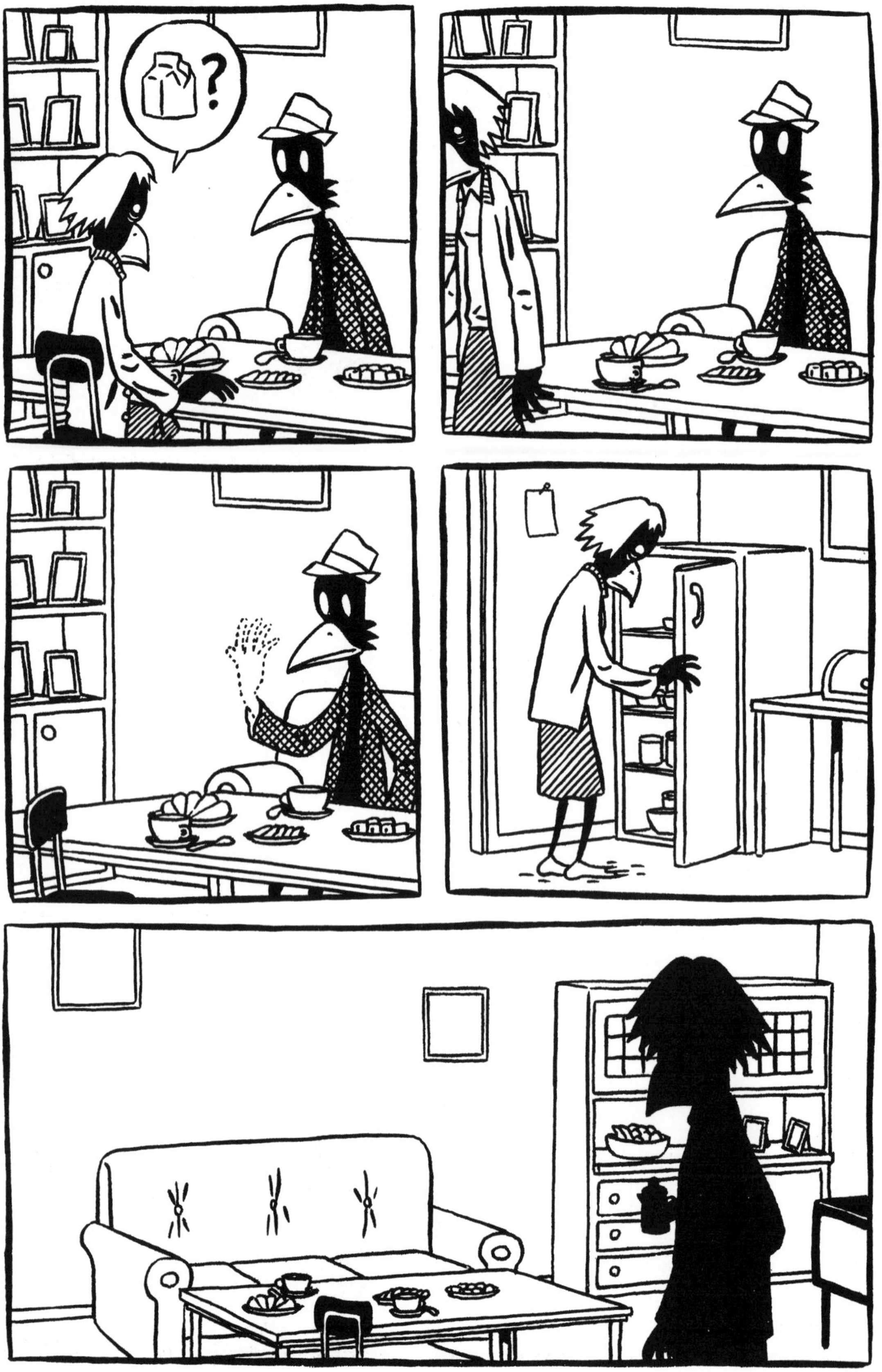
?

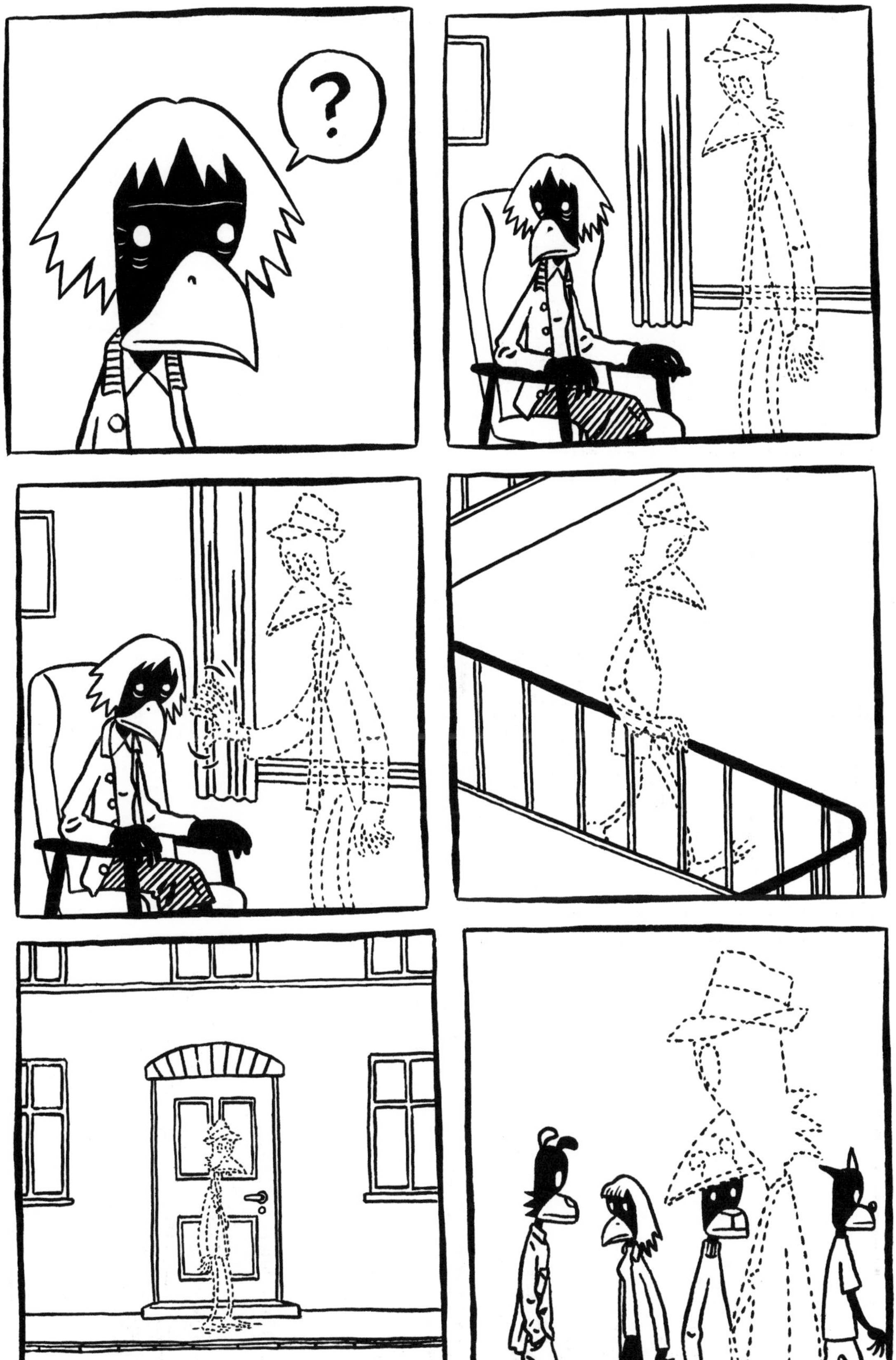
?

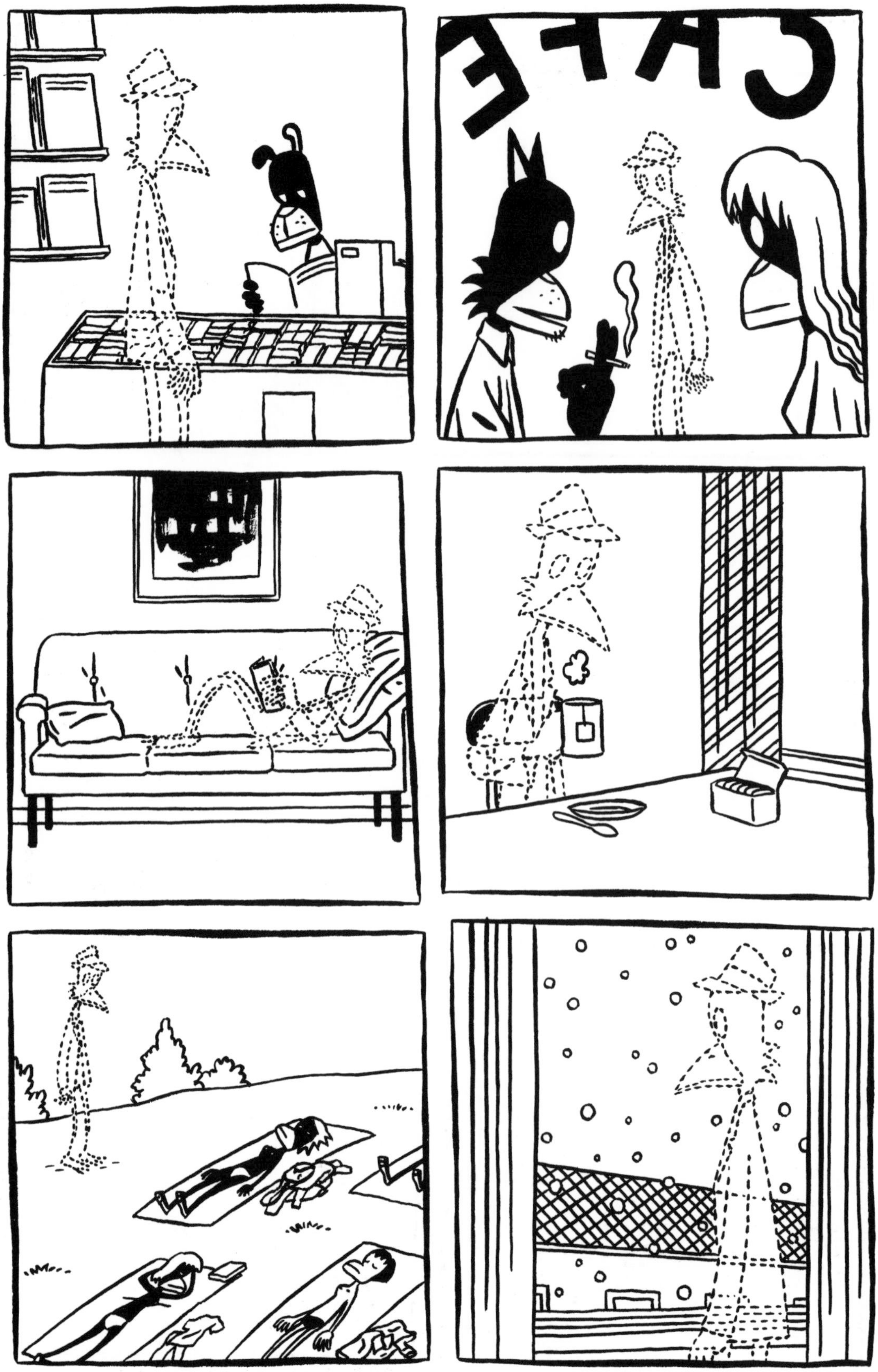
CAFE

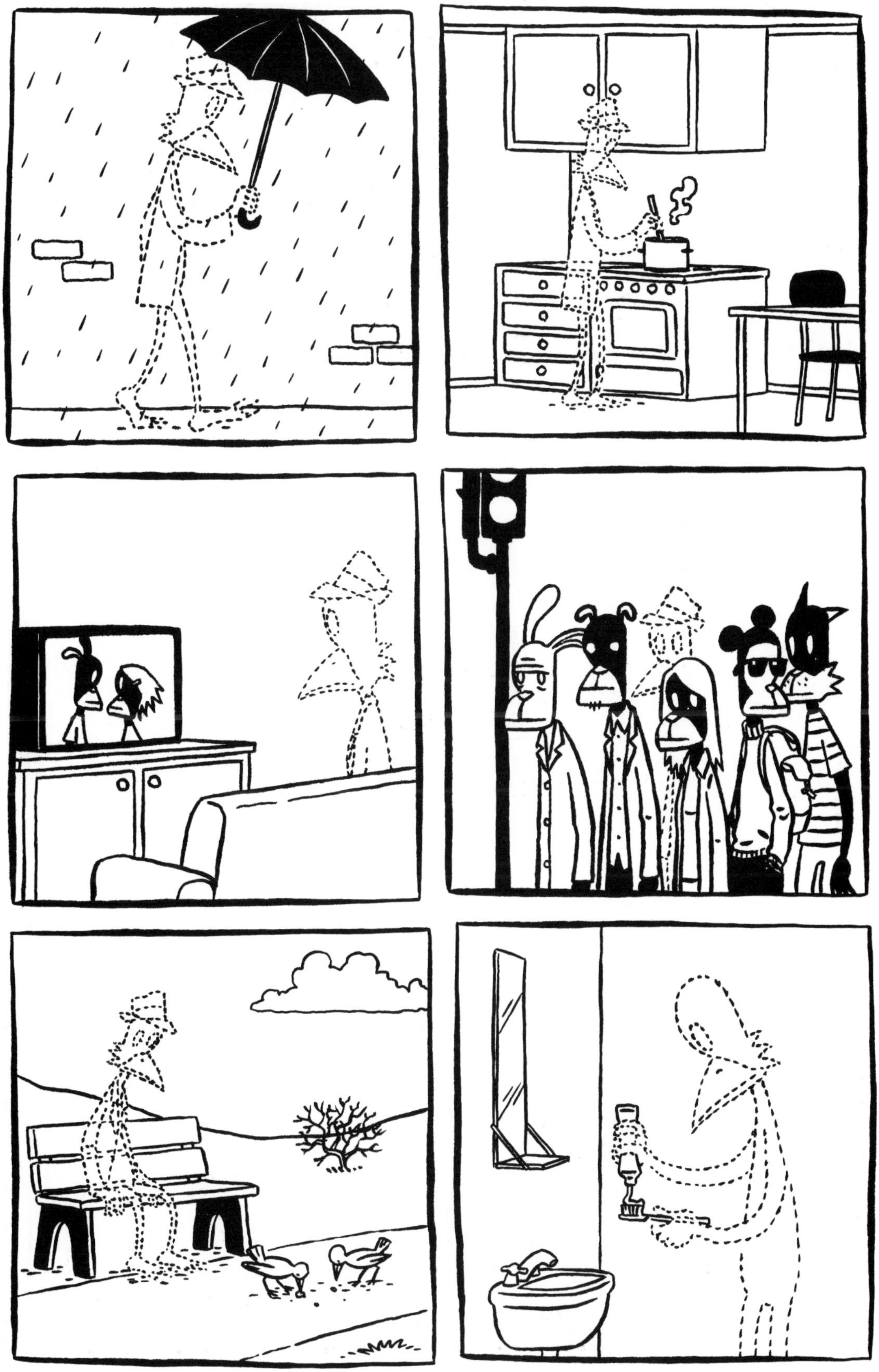

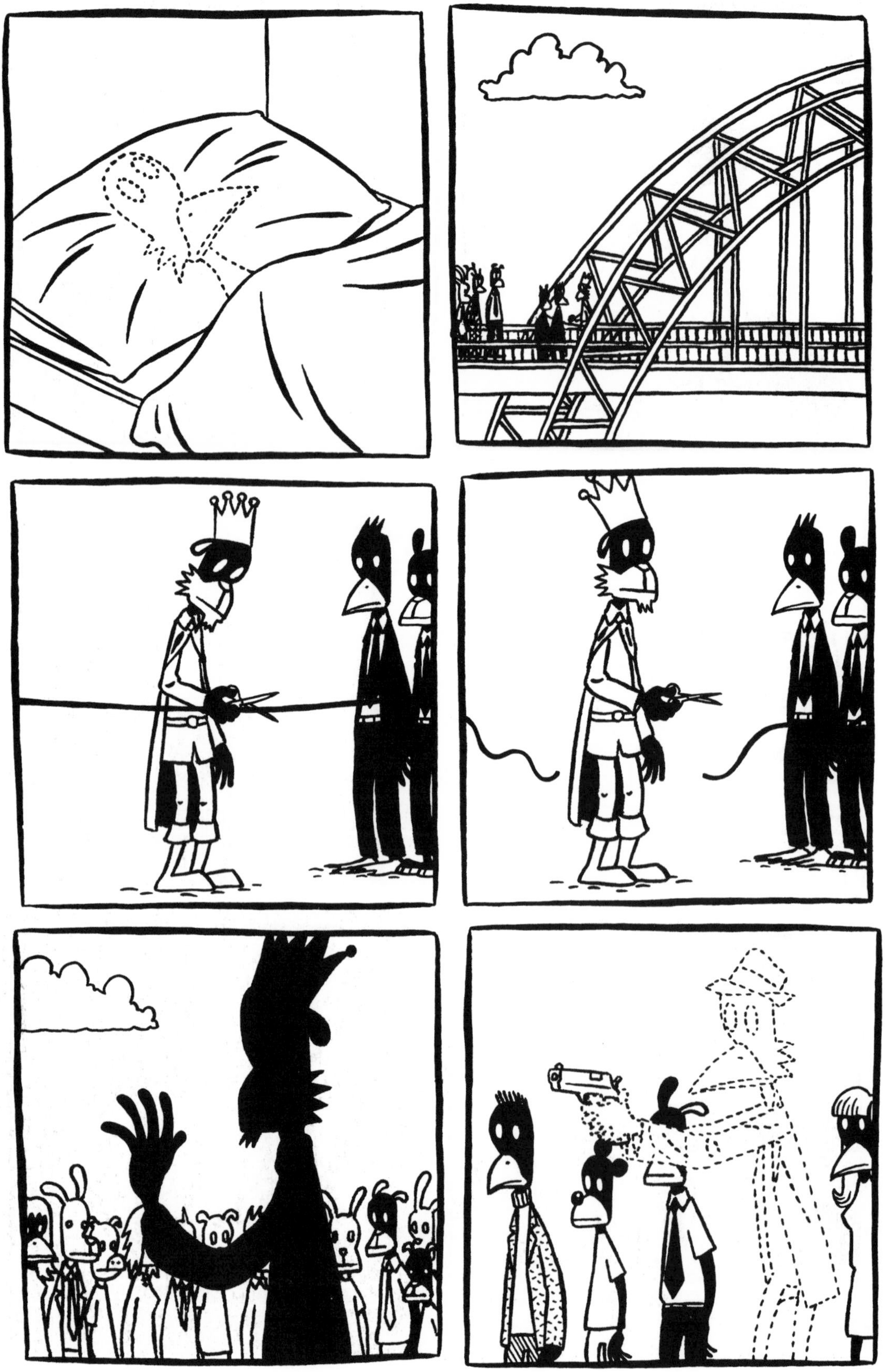

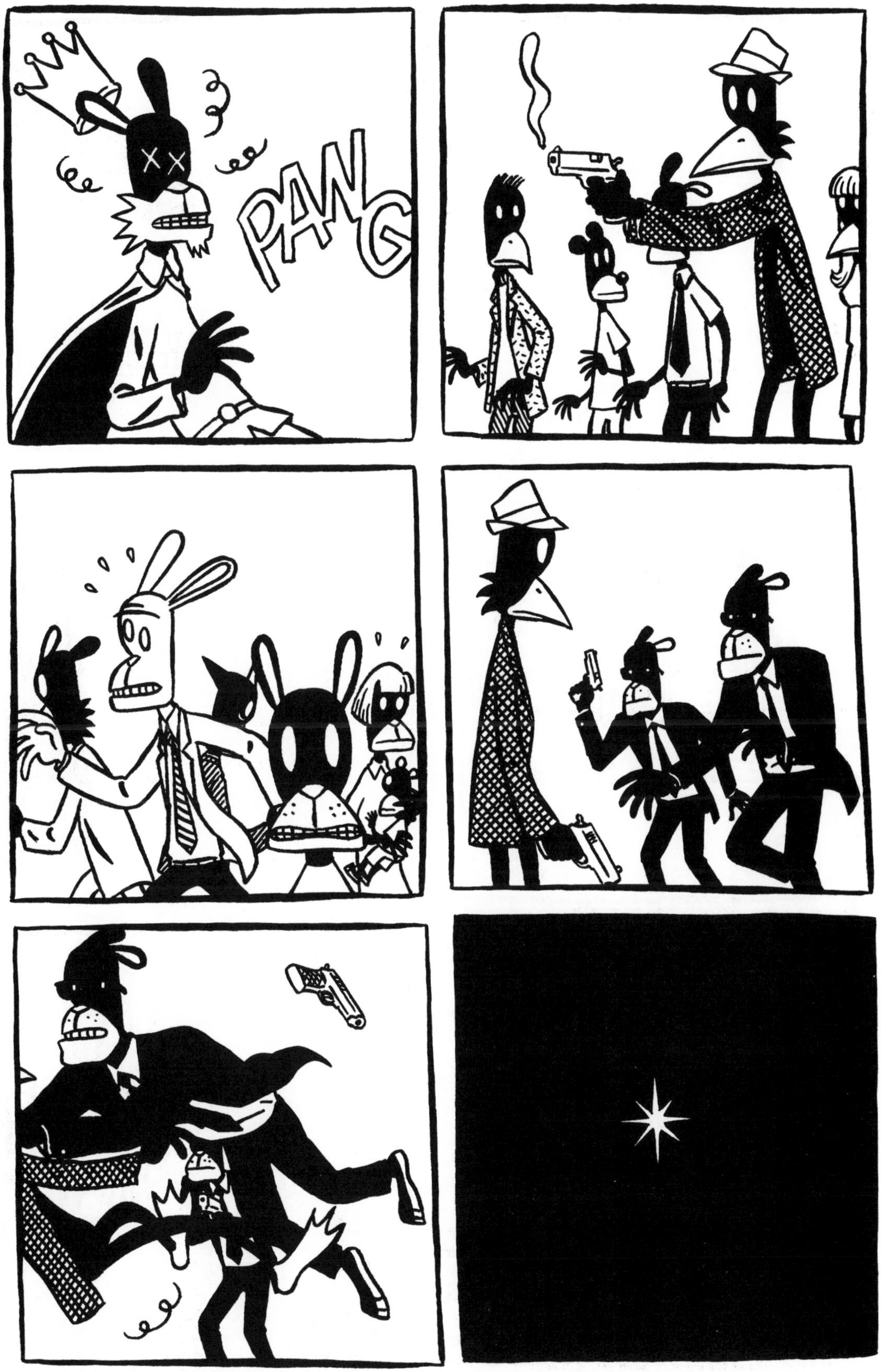
PANG

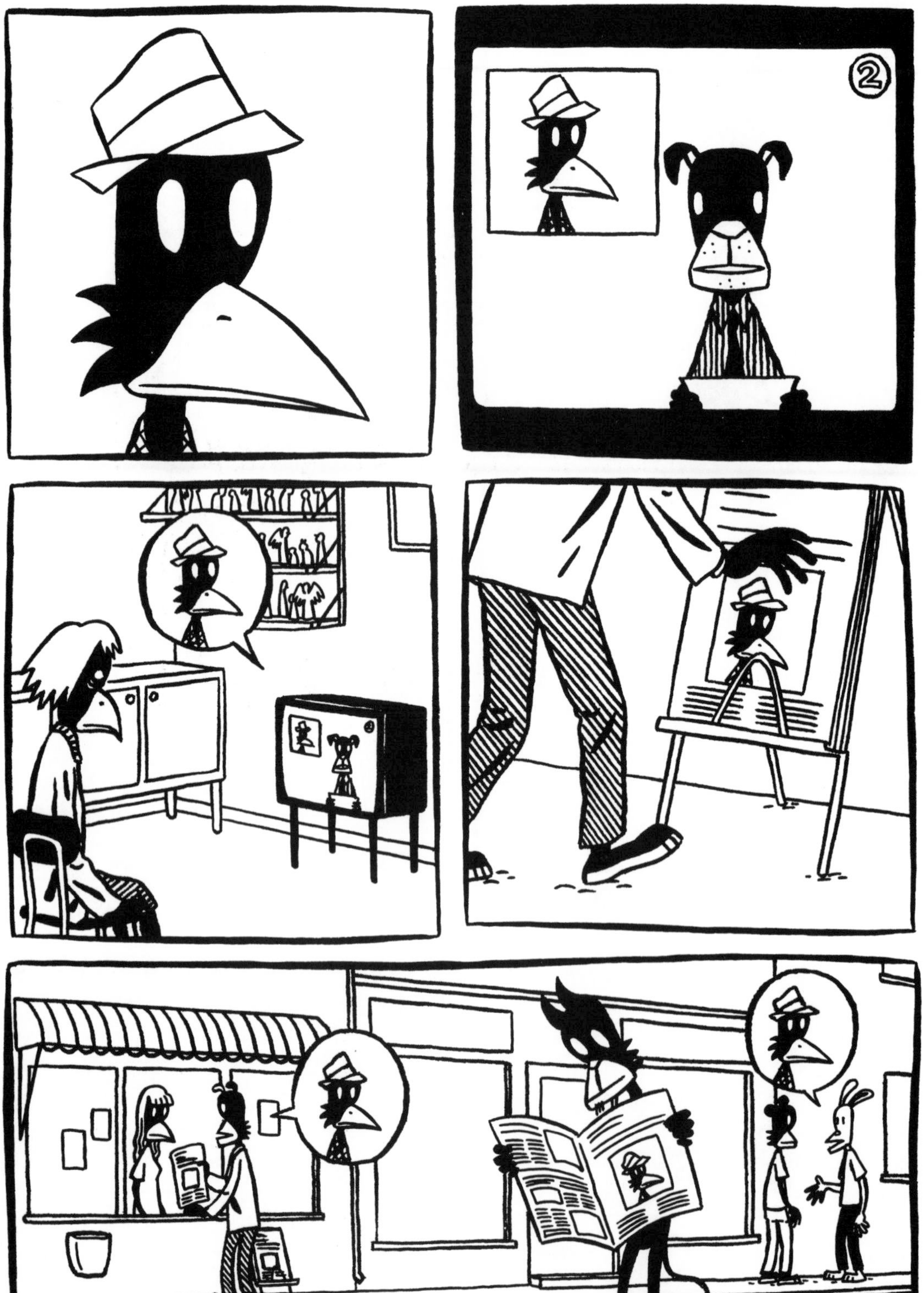
2
jason

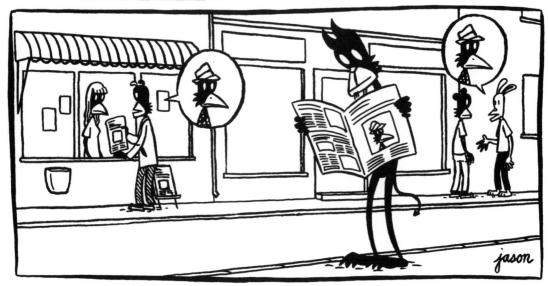

7

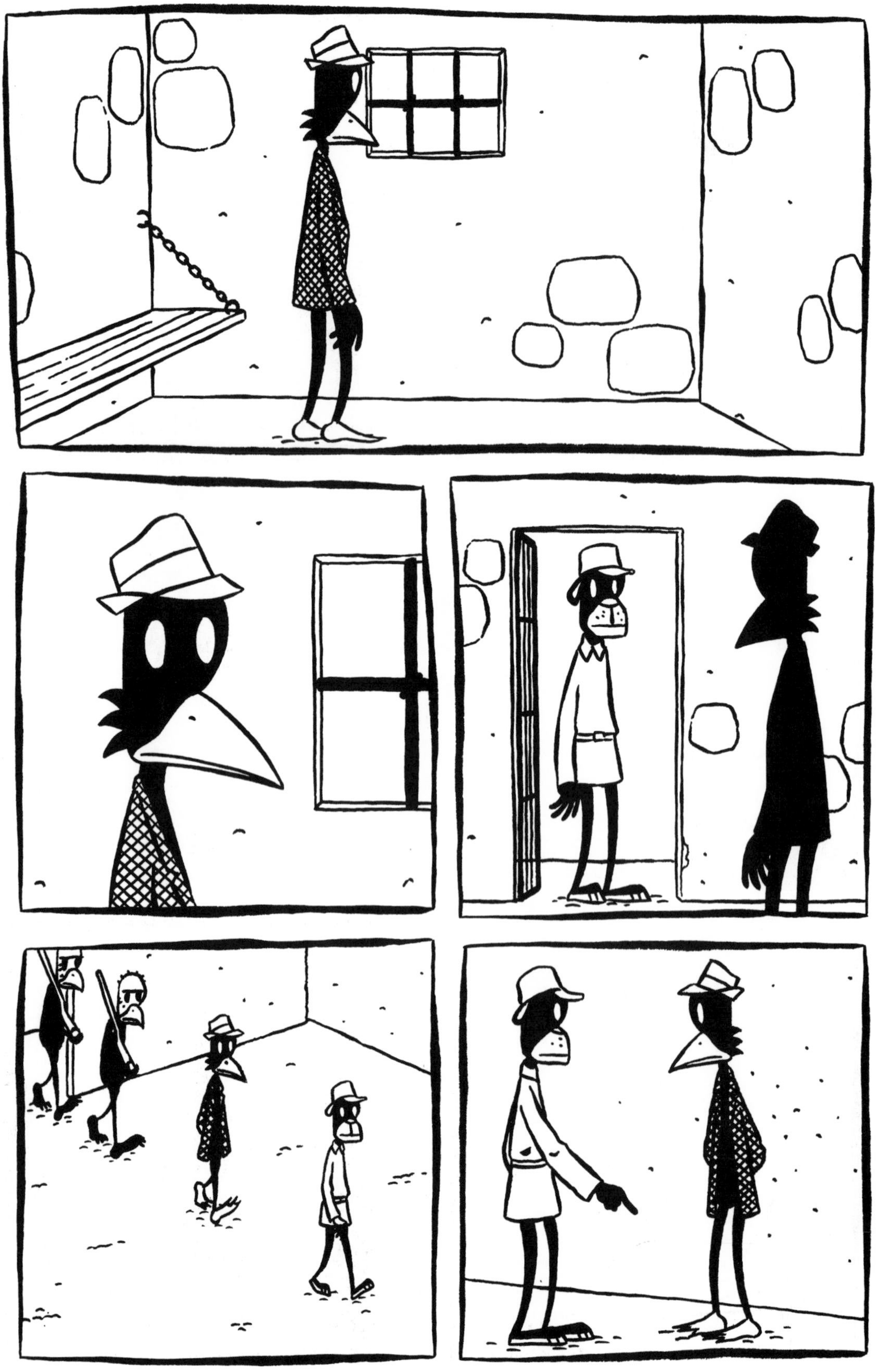

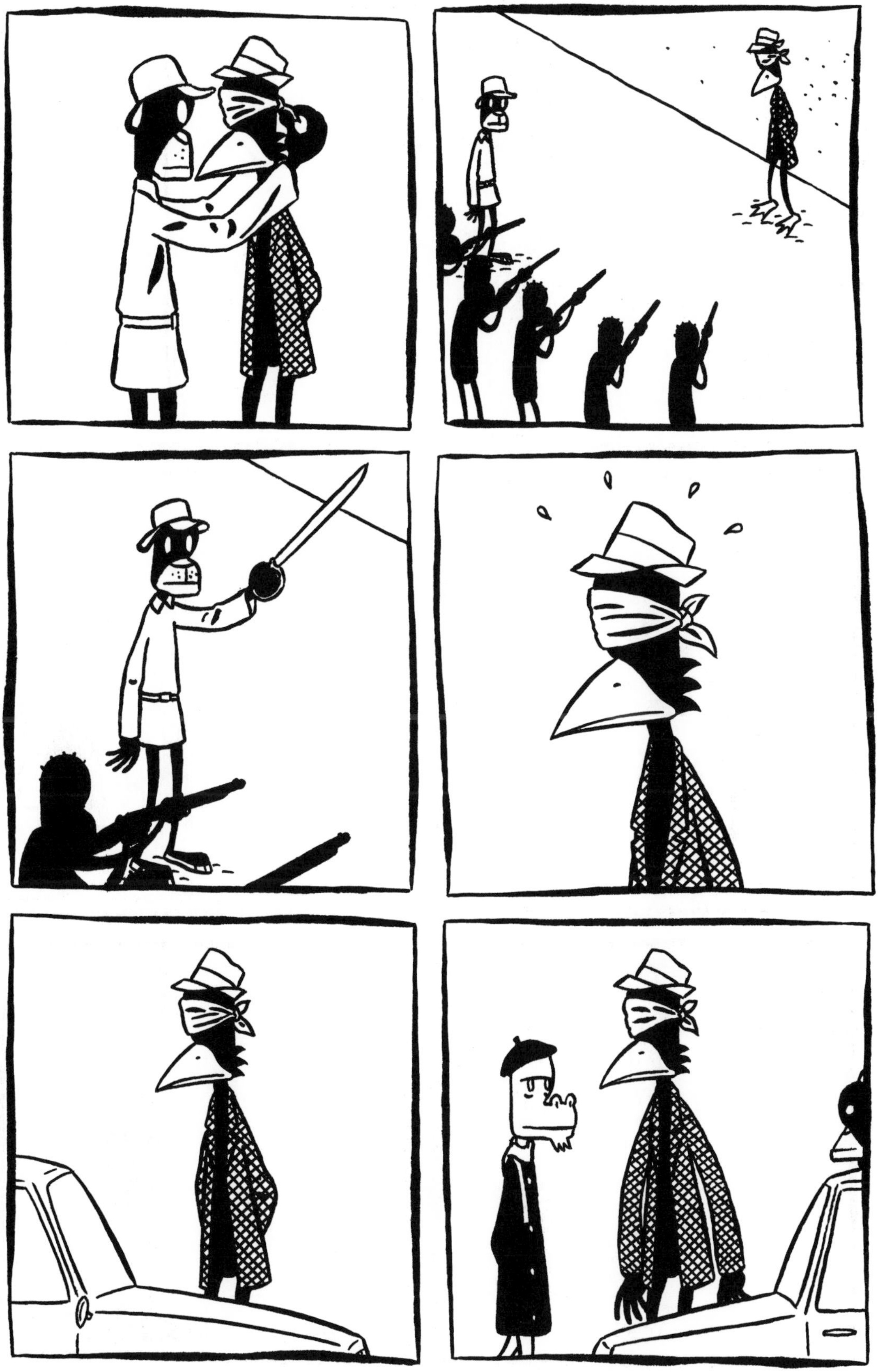

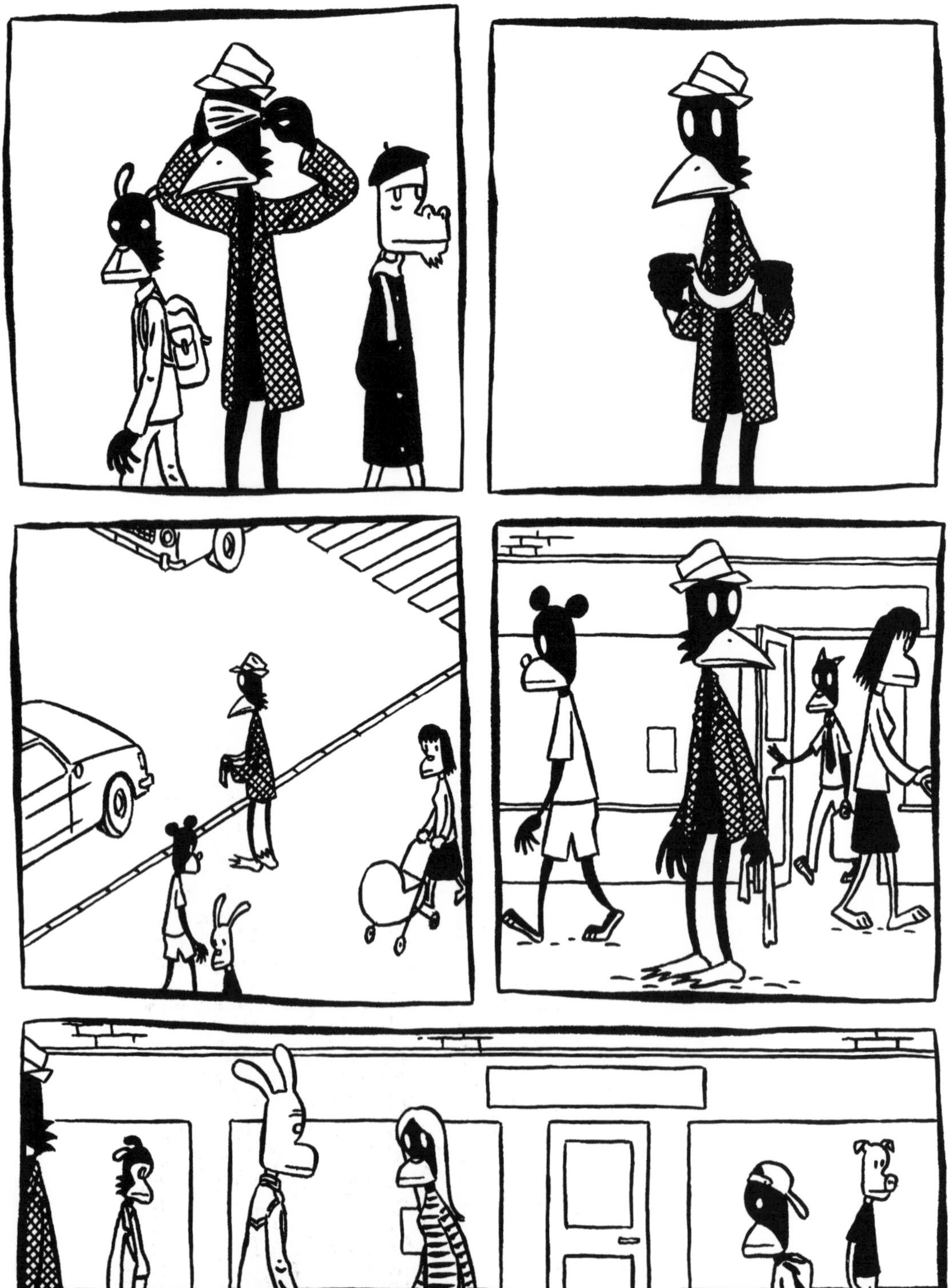
jason

8

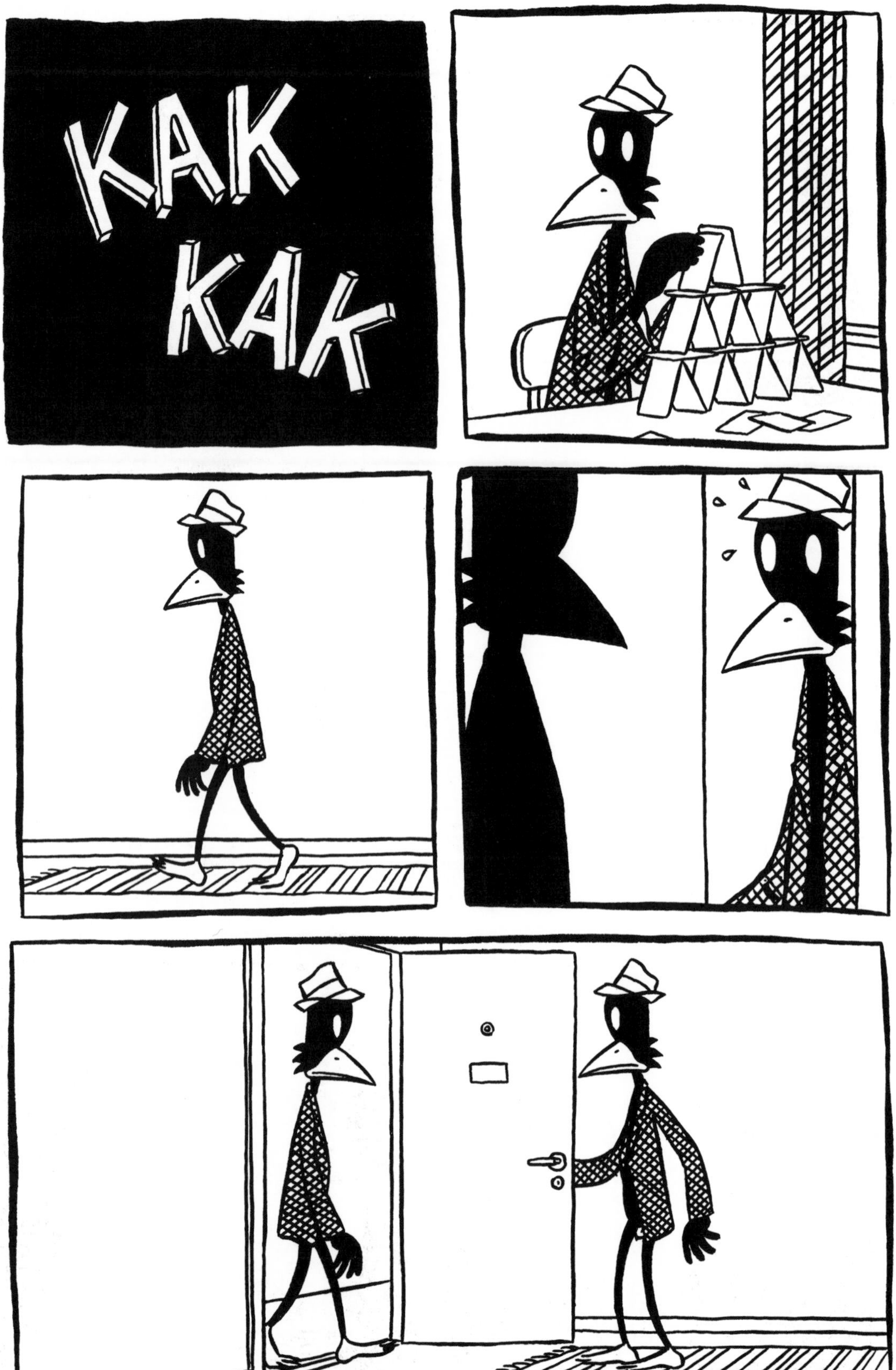
KAK
KAK

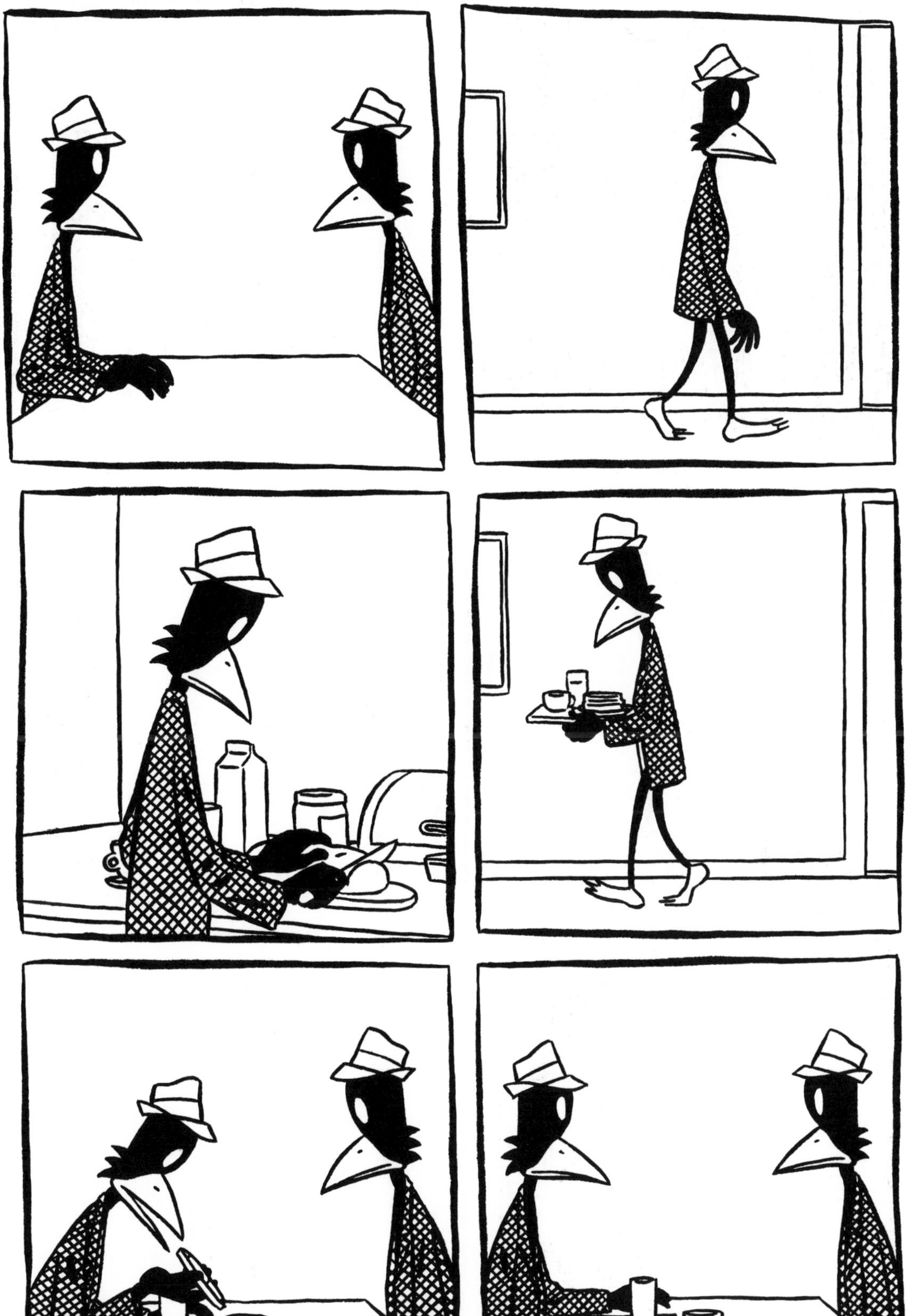

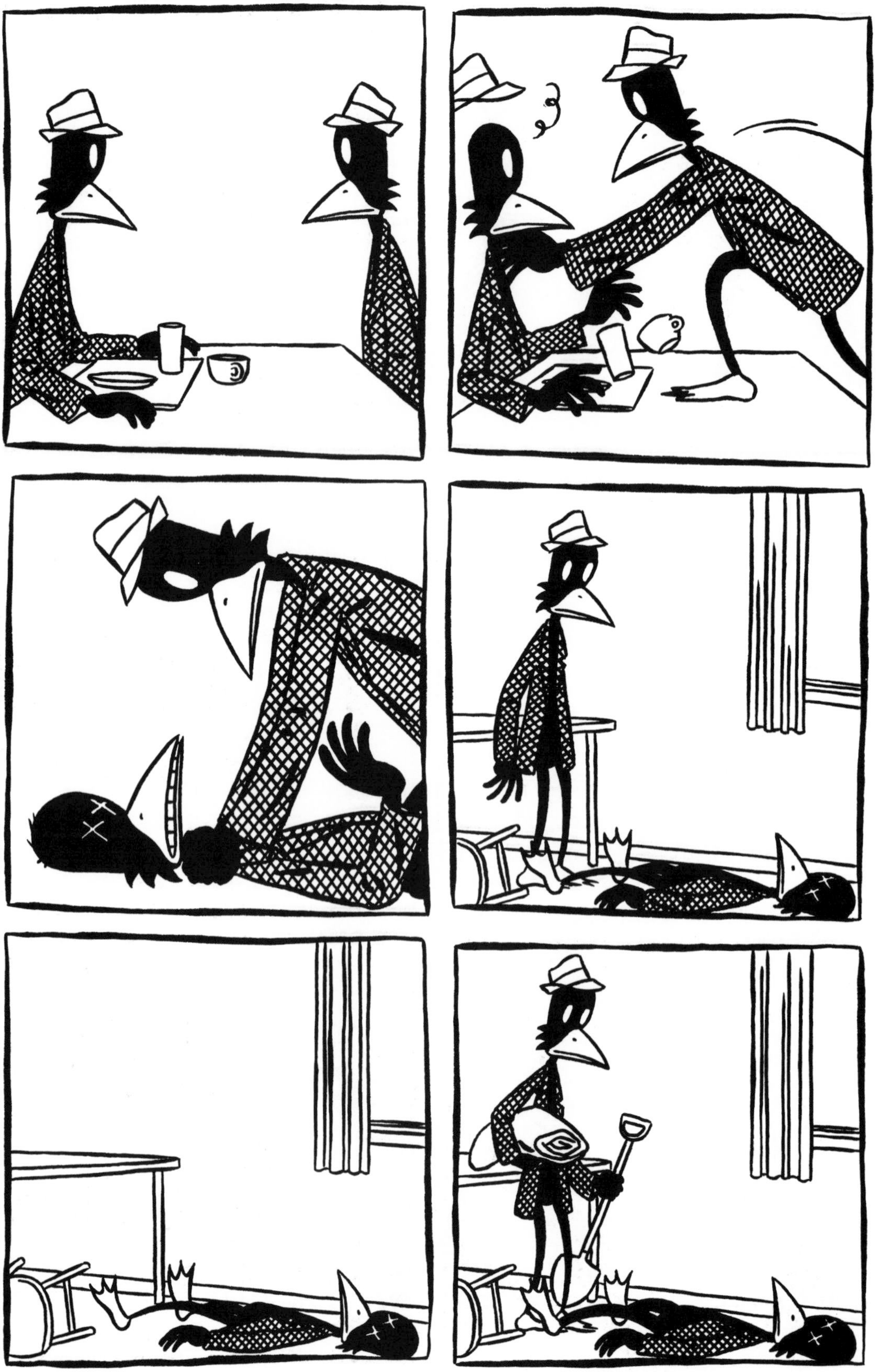

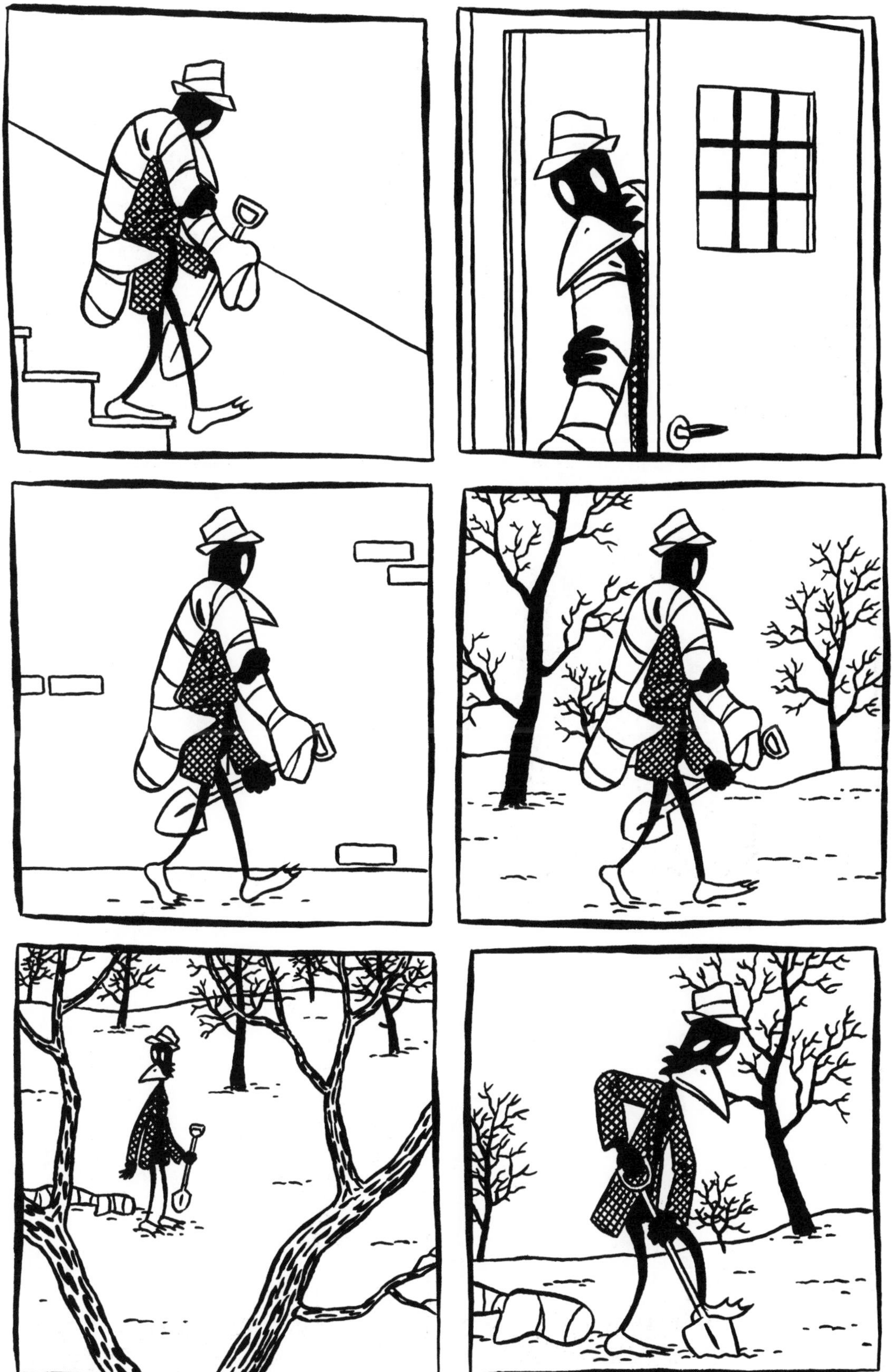

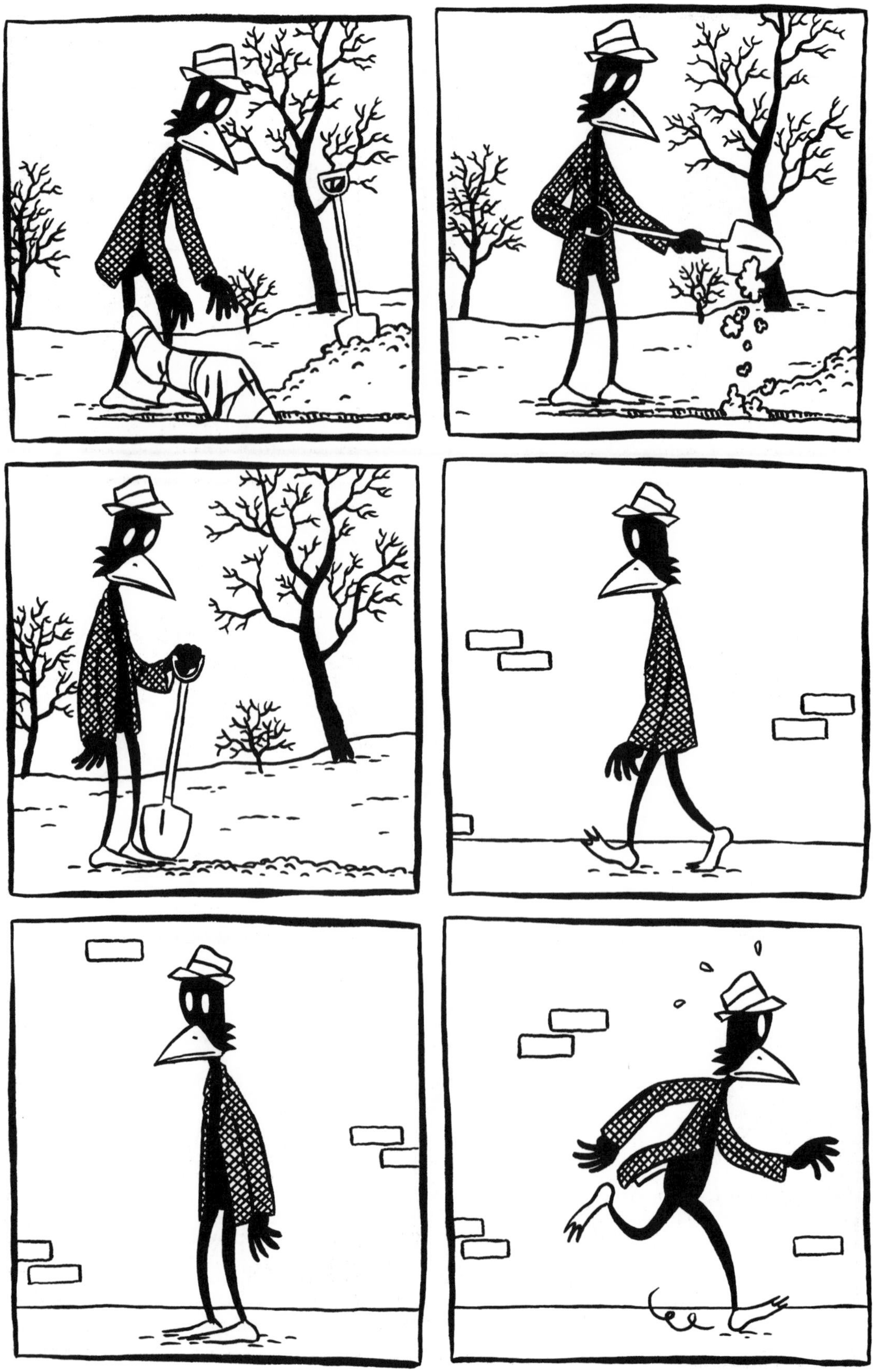

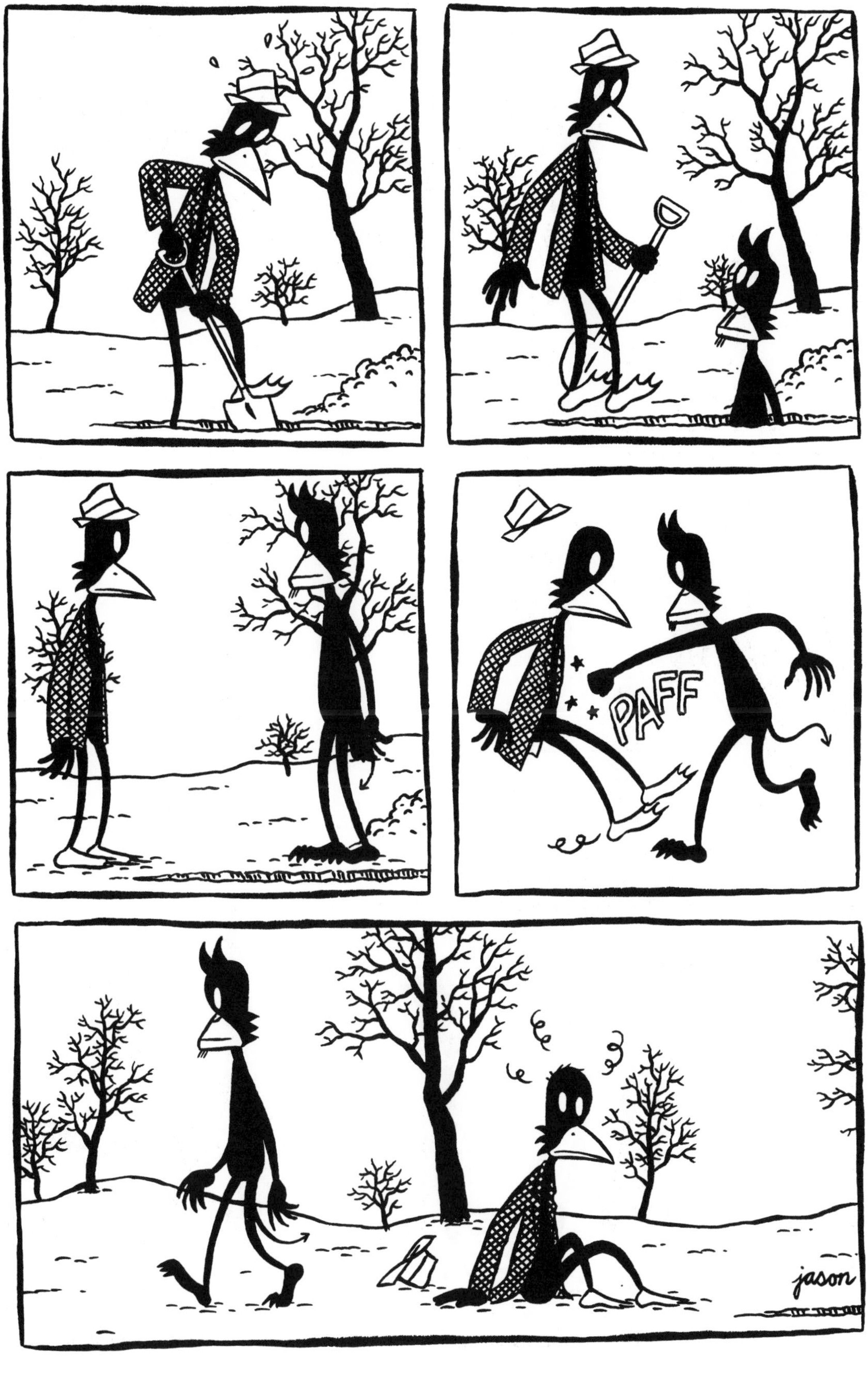
PAFF
jason

9

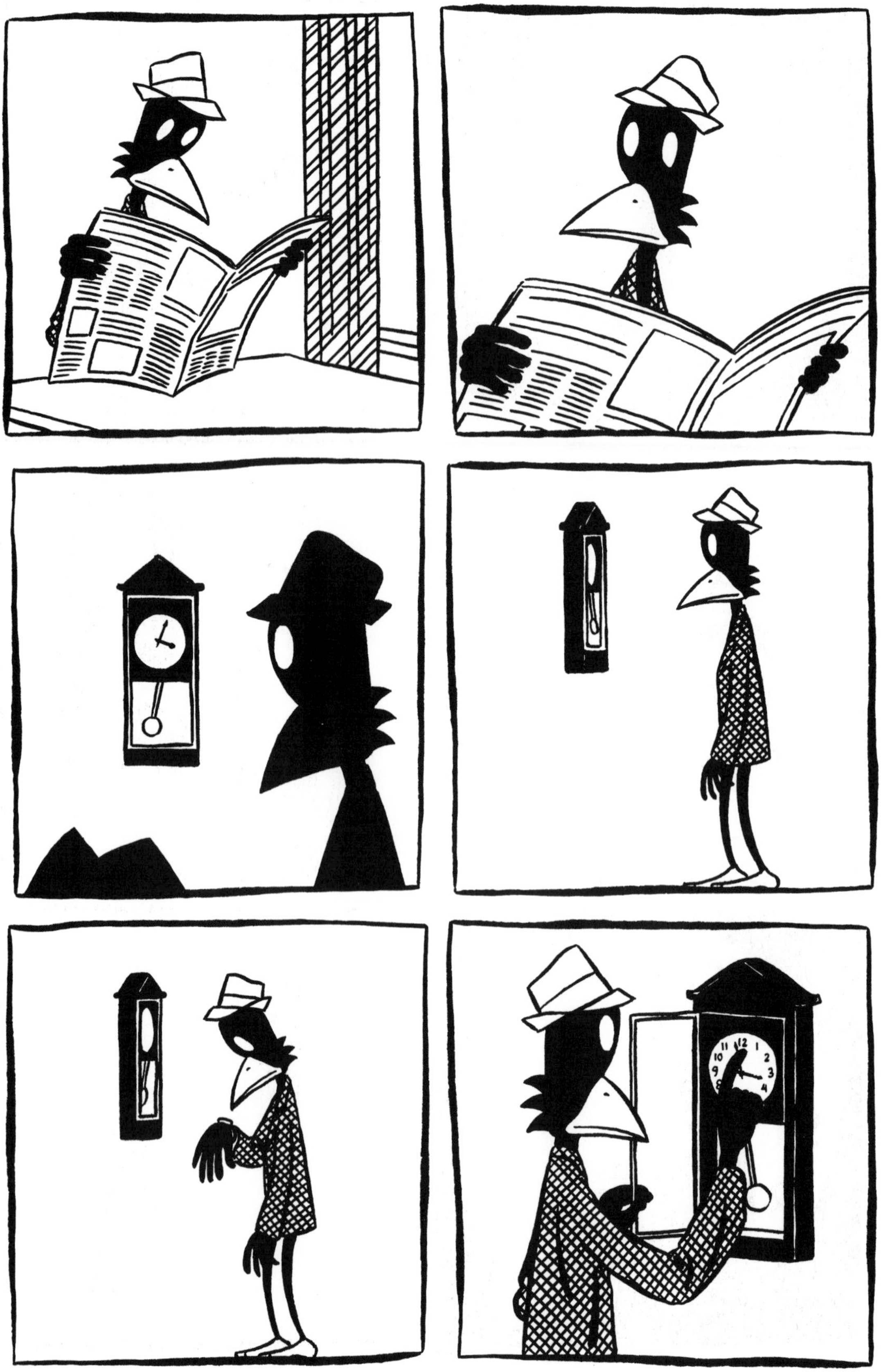

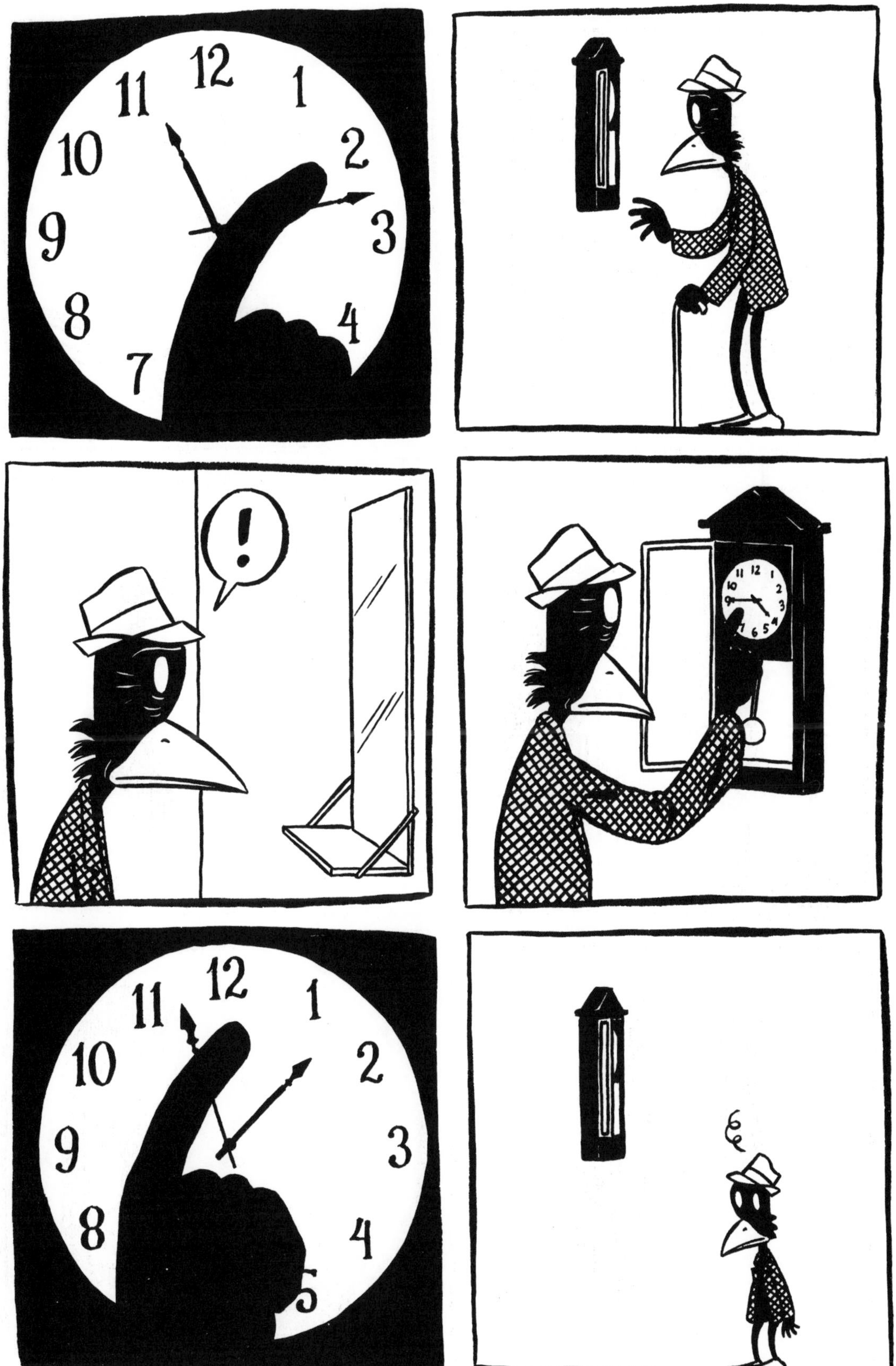
!

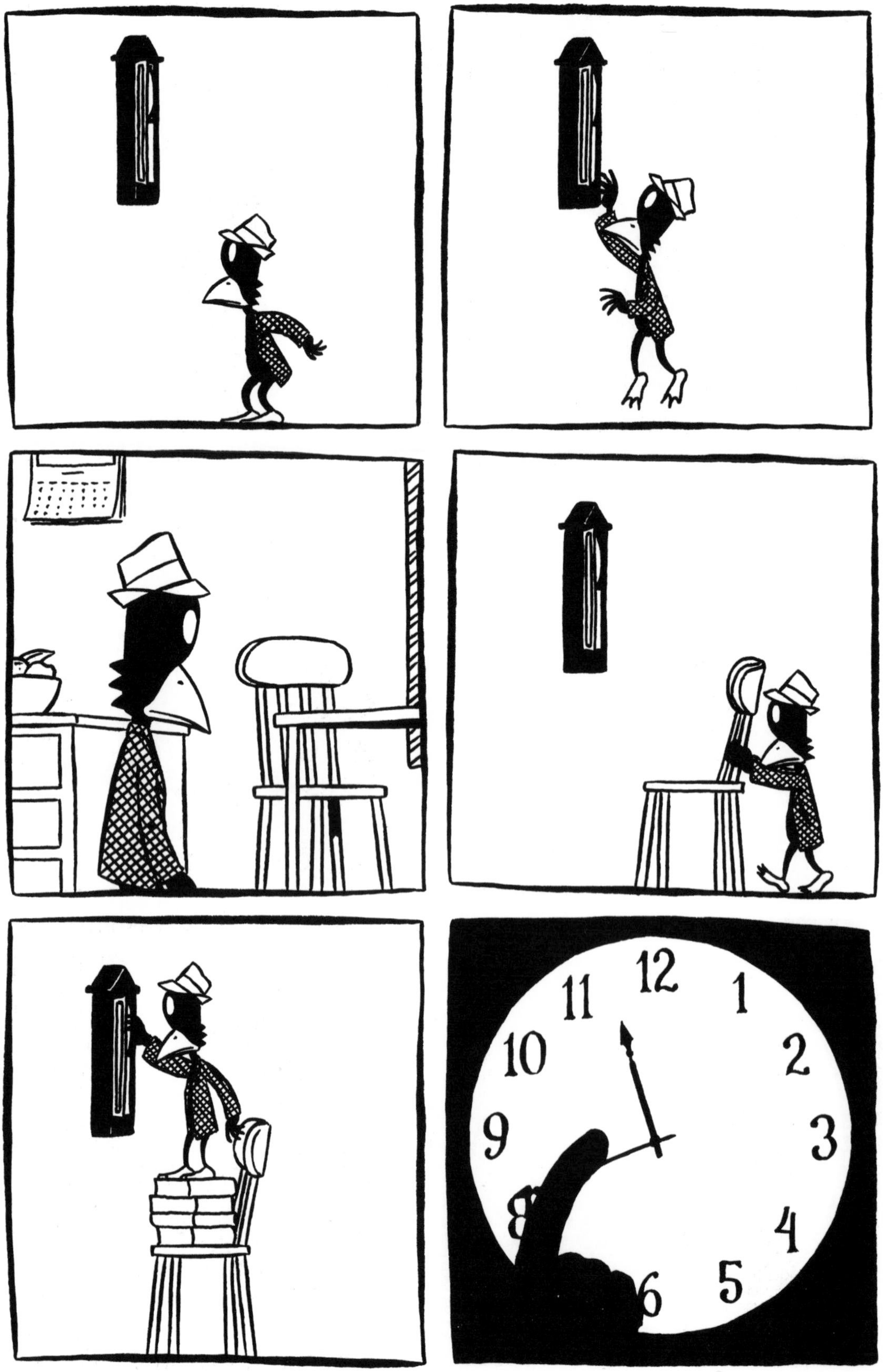
12
1
2
3
4
5
6
8
9
10
11

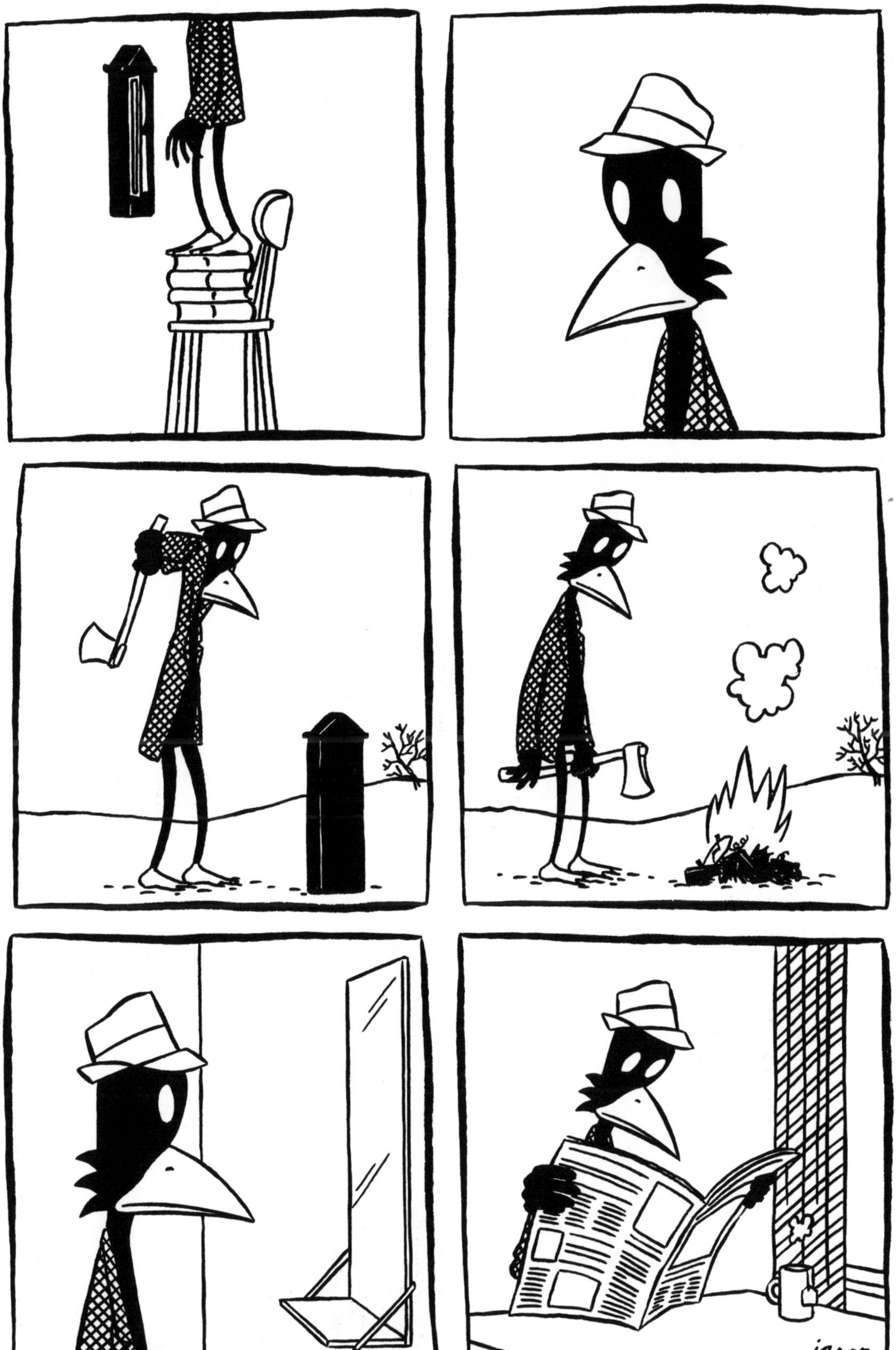
jason

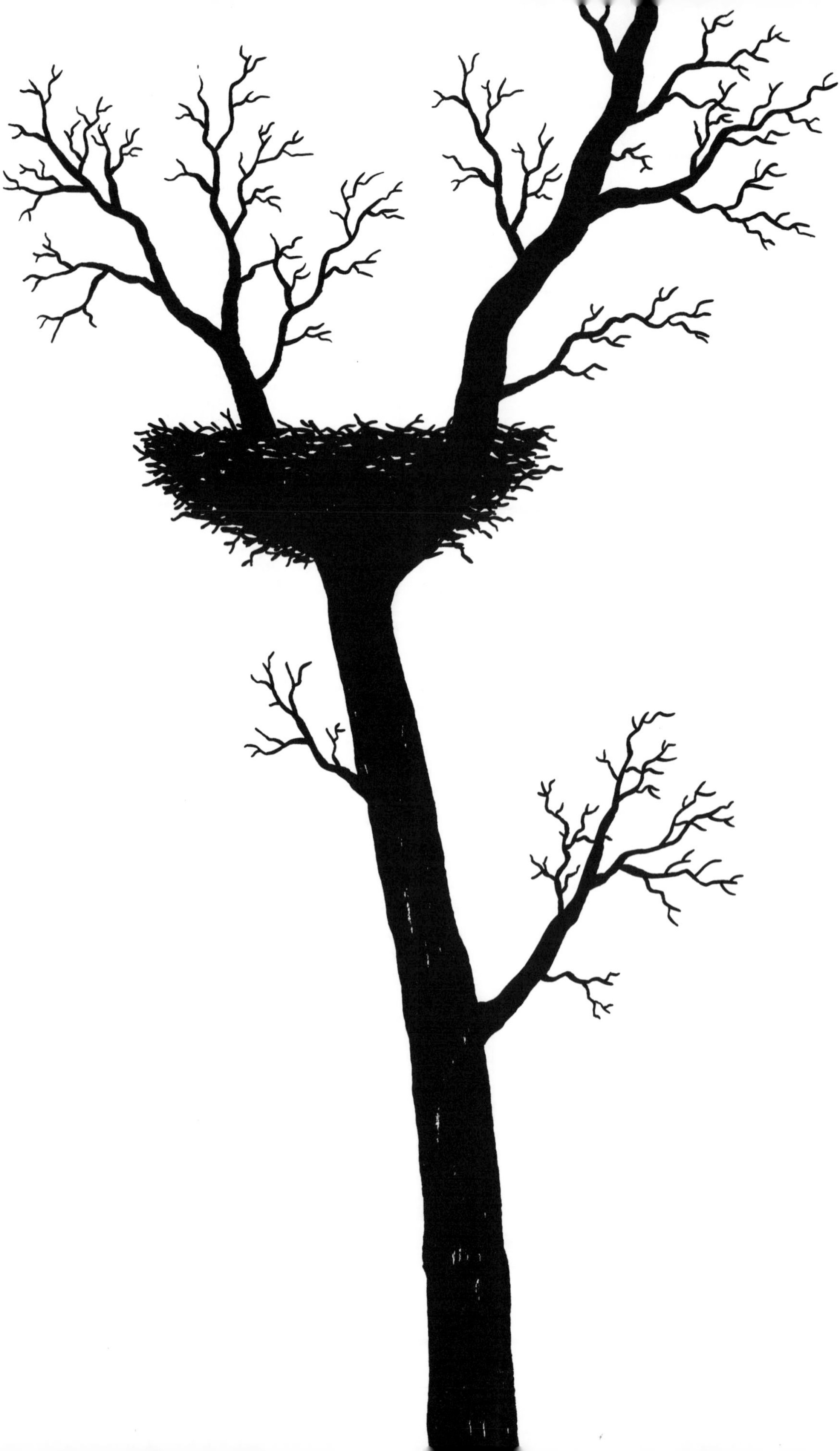

10

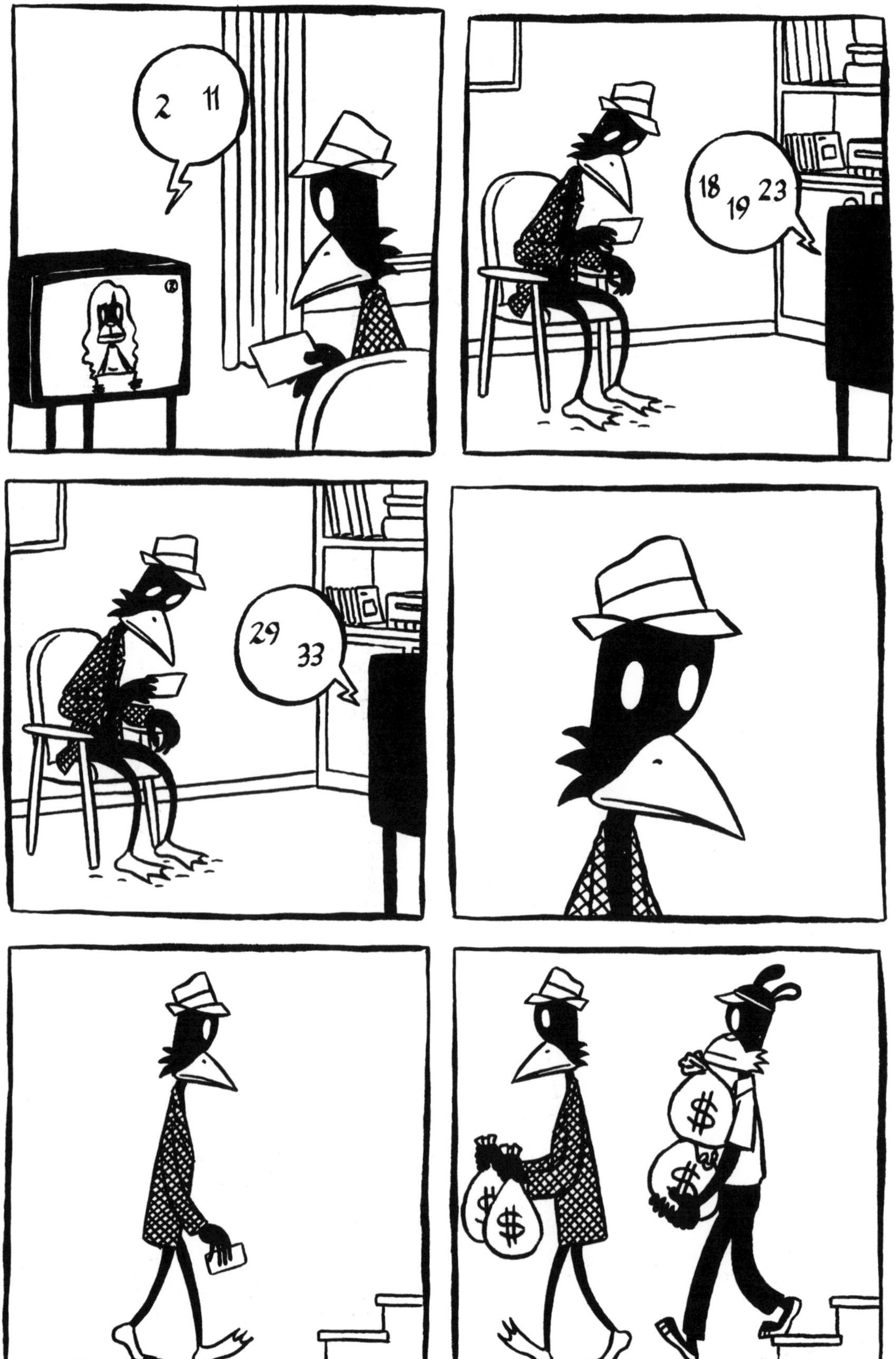
2 11
18 19 23
29 33

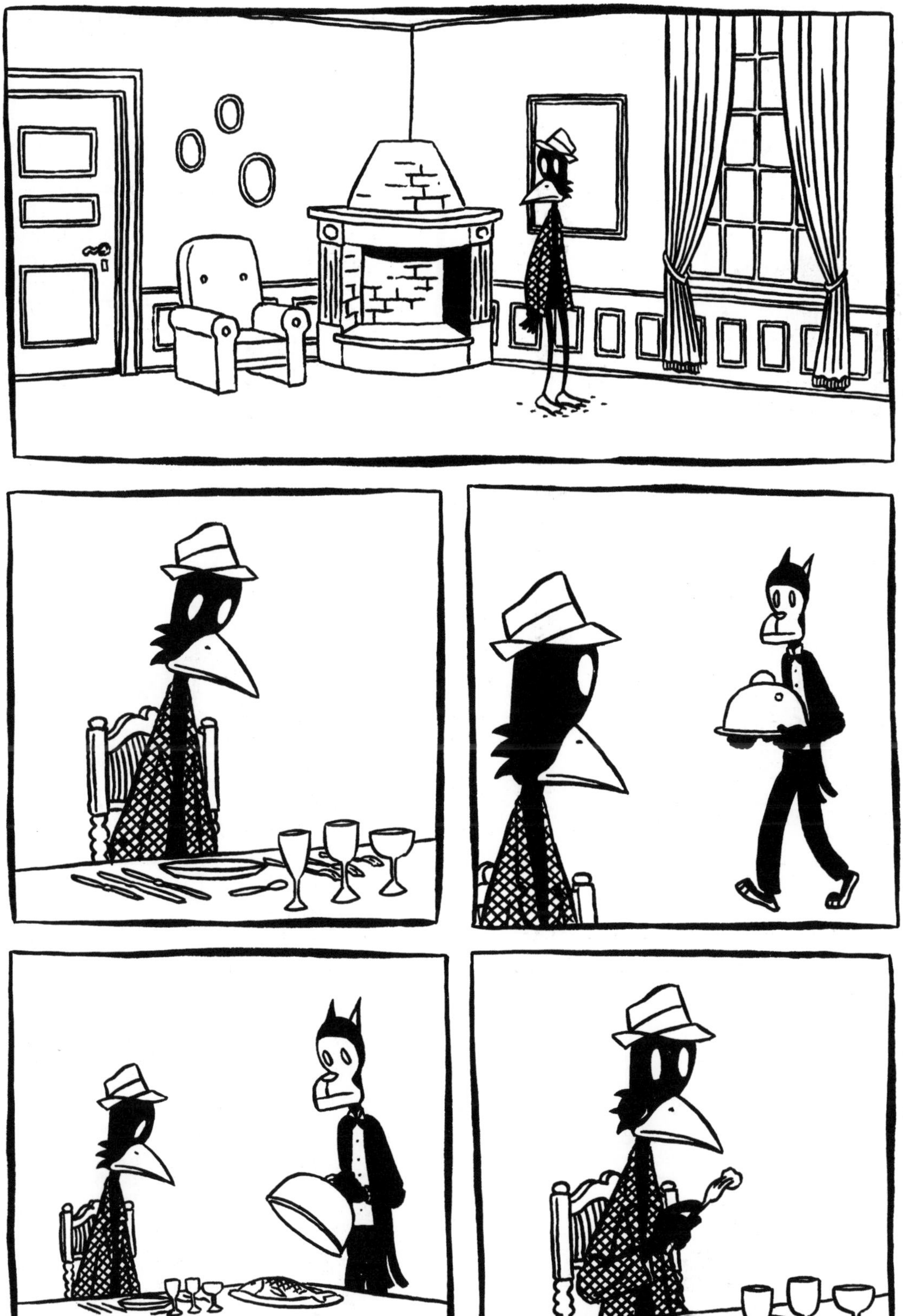

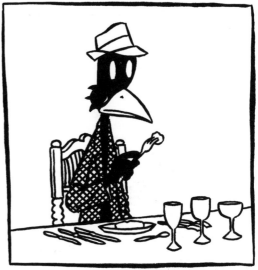

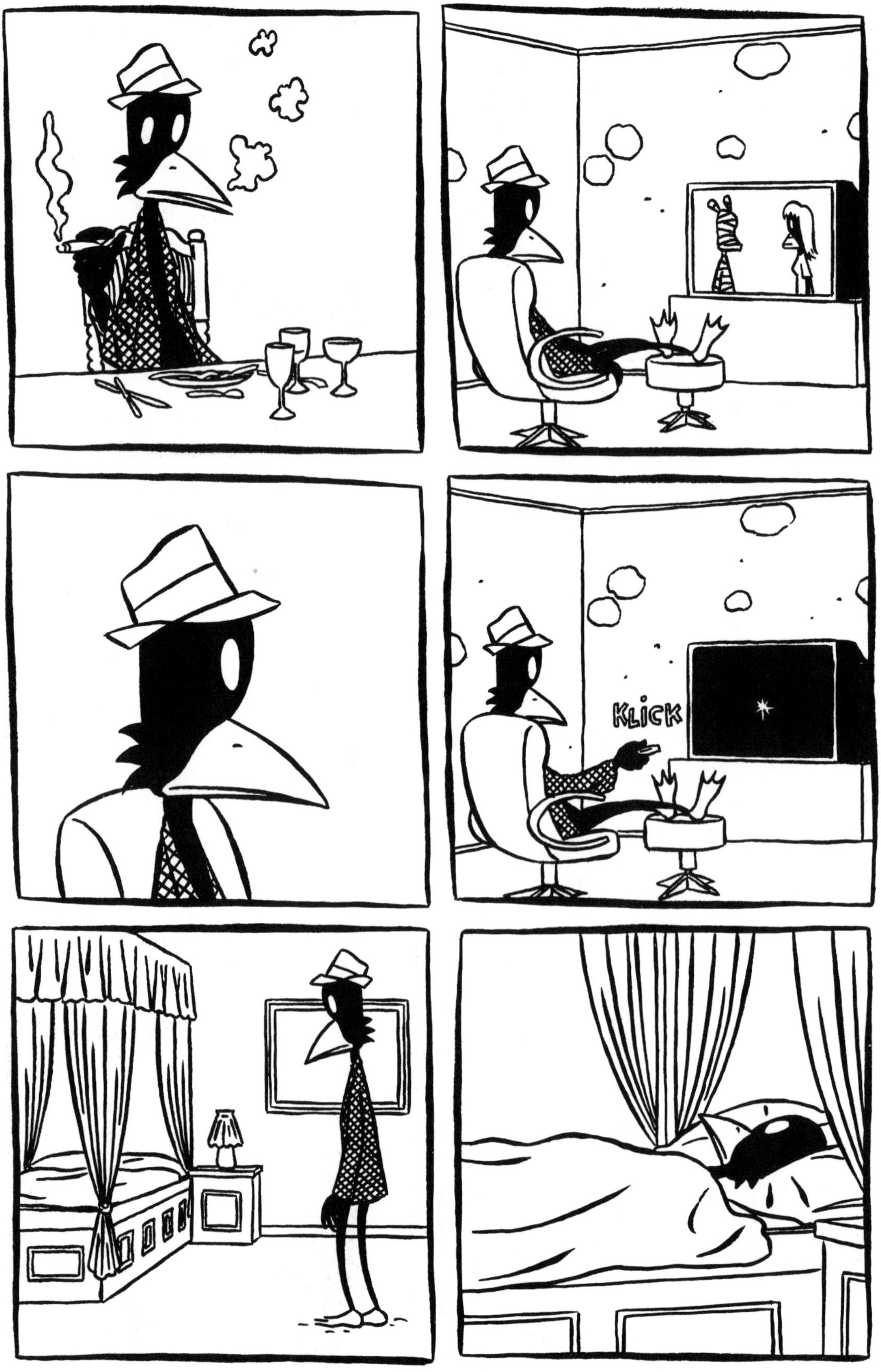
KLICK

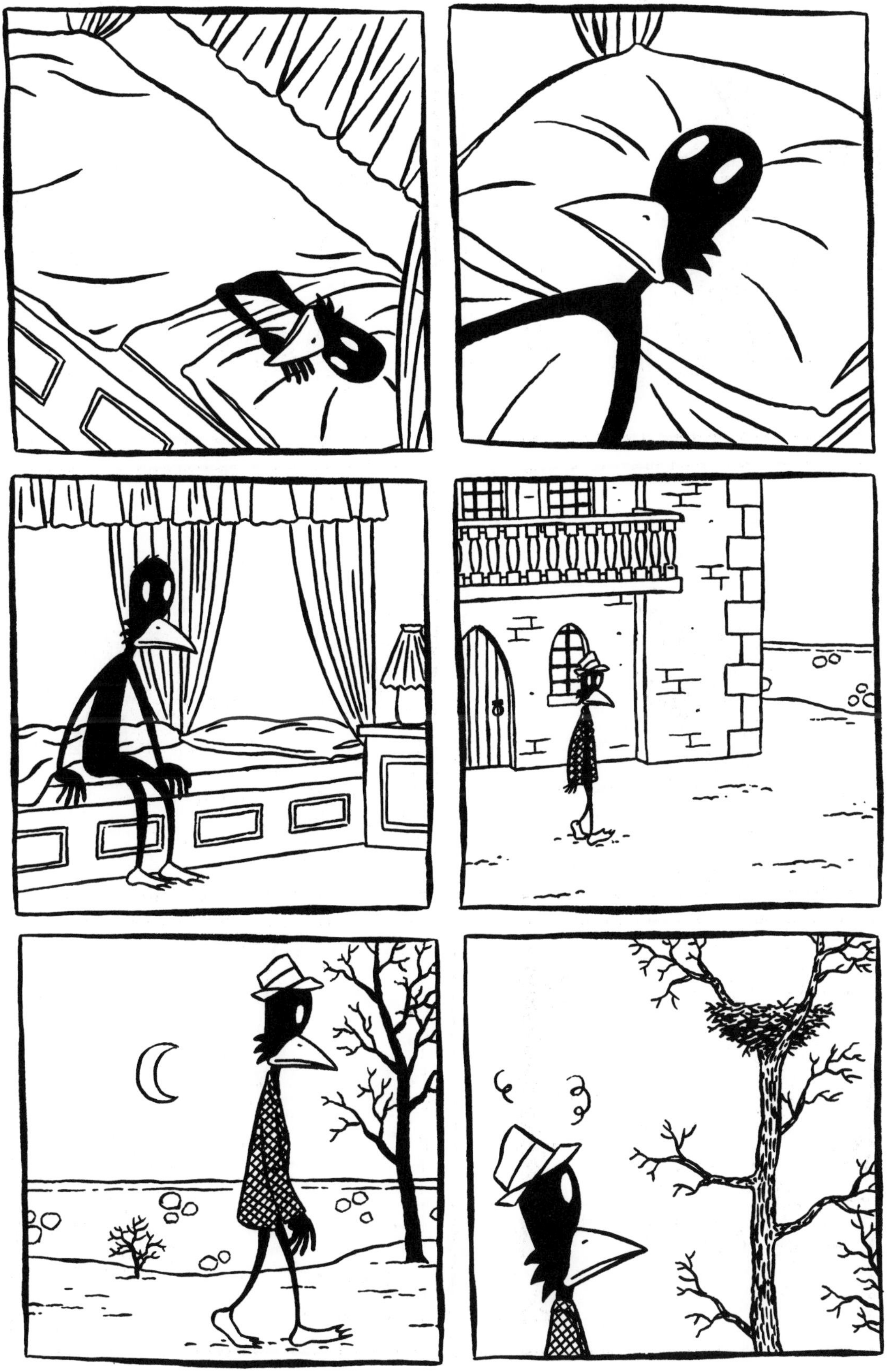

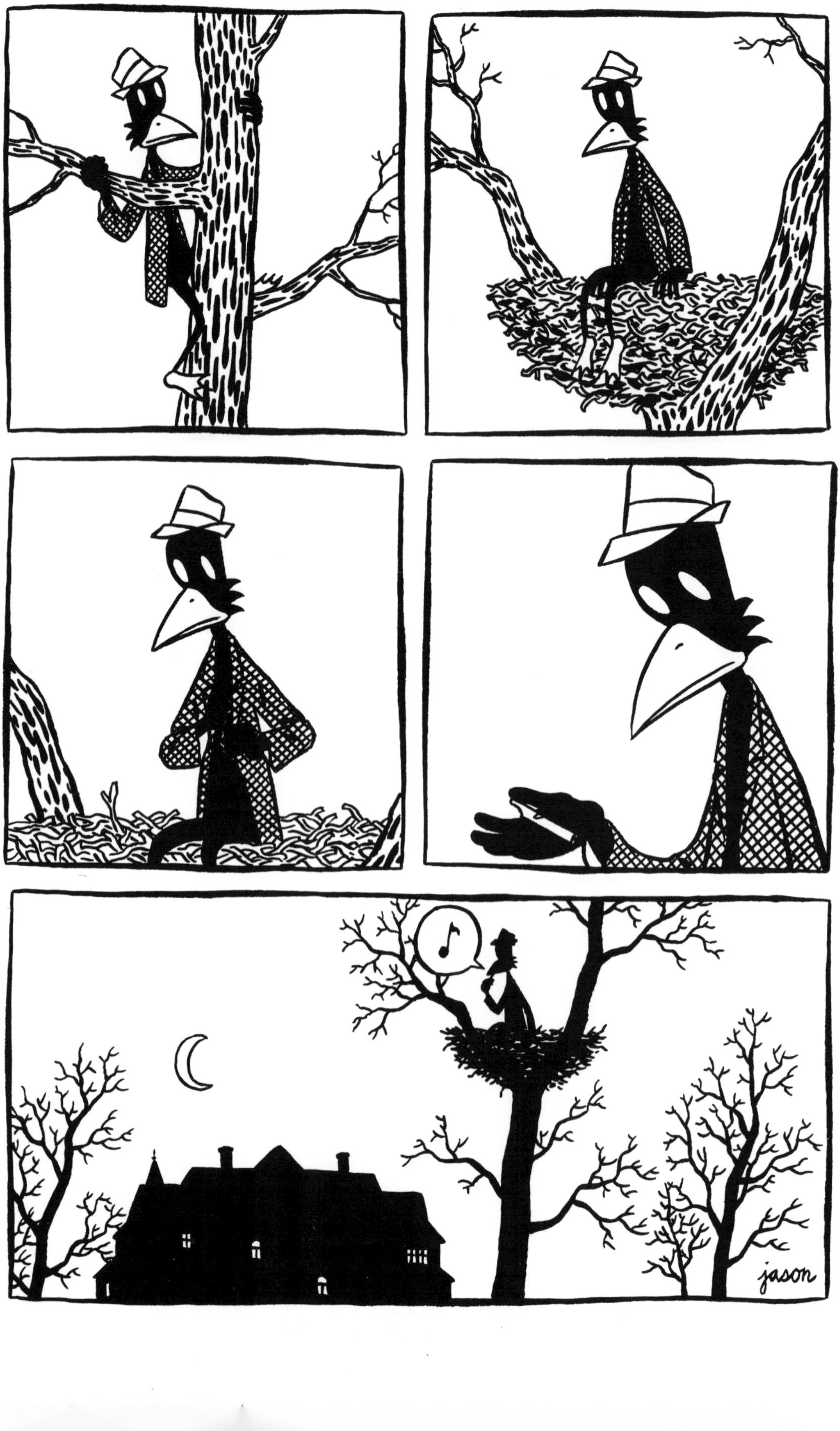
jason

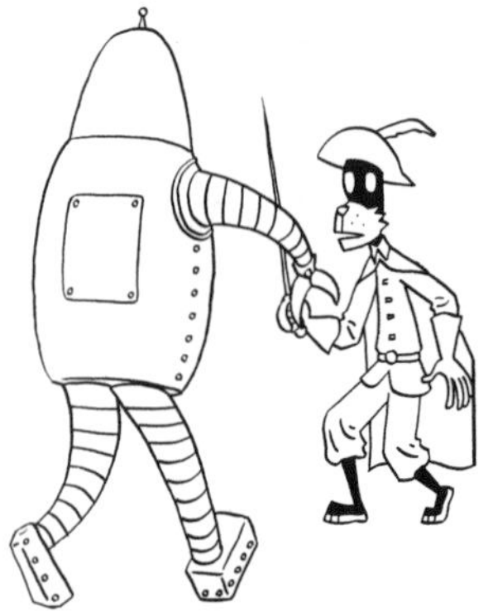

More Jason from Fantagraphics Books...

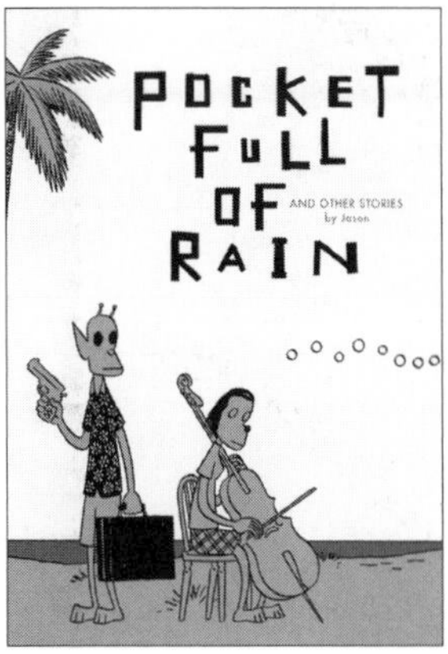
POCKET FULL OF RAIN

Pocket Full of Rain
BLACK AND WHITE WITH COLOR SECTION
144 PAGES / $19.99

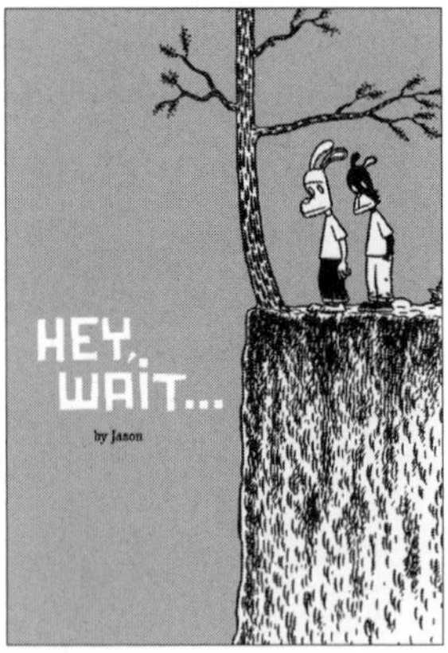
HEY, WAIT...
by Jason

Hey, Wait...
BLACK AND WHITE
68 PAGES / $12.95

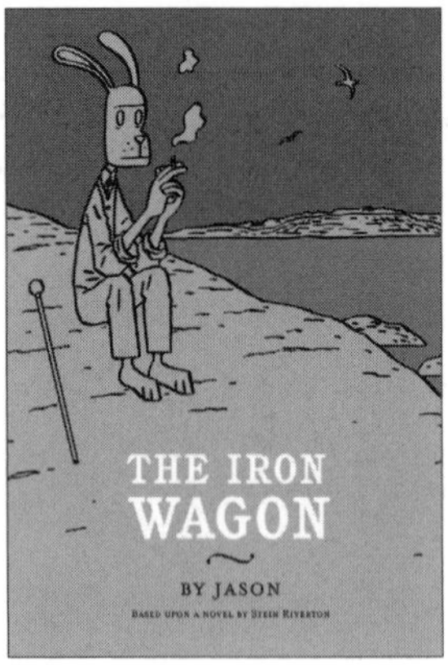
THE IRON WAGON
BY JASON

Iron Wagon
TWO-COLOR
80 PAGES / $14.99
(REPRINTING SPRING 2009)

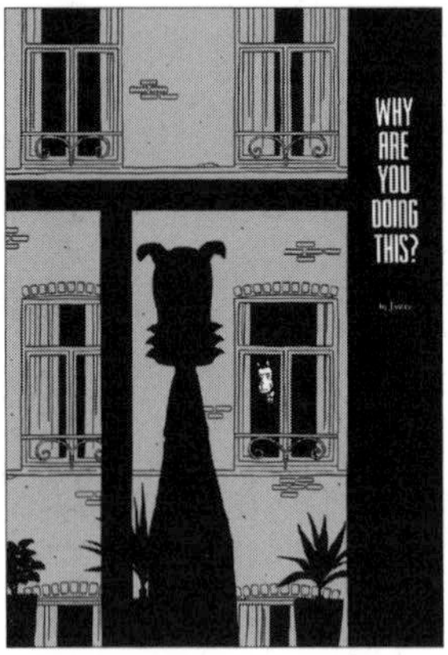
WHY ARE YOU DOING THIS?

Why Are You Doing This?
FULL-COLOR
48 PAGES / $12.95

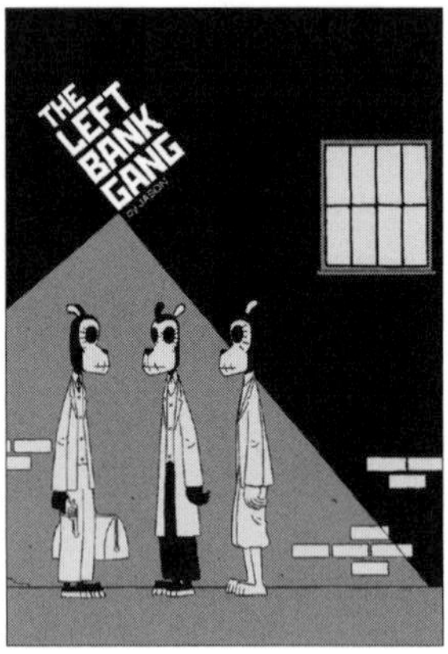
THE LEFT BANK GANG

The Left Bank Gang
FULL-COLOR
48 PAGES / $12.95

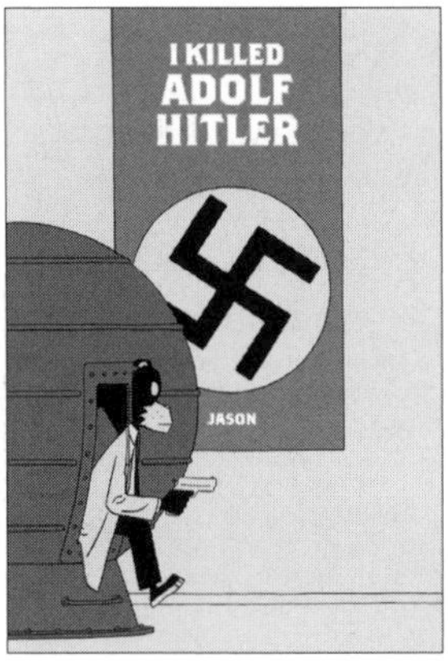
I KILLED ADOLF HITLER
JASON

I Killed Adolf Hitler
FULL-COLOR
48 PAGES / $12.95

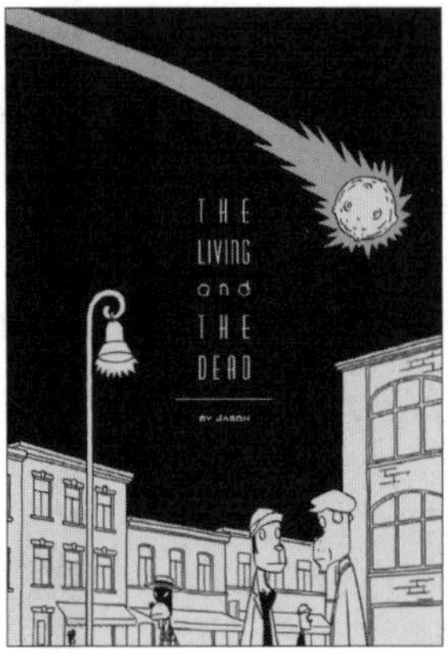
THE LIVING and THE DEAD
BY JASON

The Living and the Dead
BLACK AND WHITE
48 PAGES / $9.95

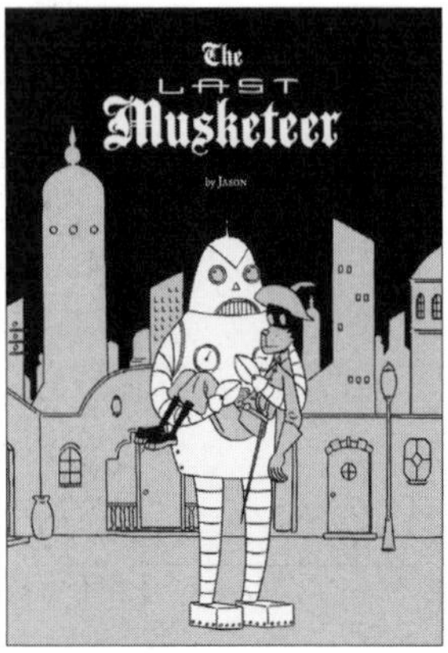
The LAST Musketeer

The Last Musketeer
FULL-COLOR
48 PAGES / $12.95